THE SCIENCE
OF ARCHAEOLOGY ?

The Science of Archaeology ?

RICHARD S. MACNEISH

Robert S. Peabody Foundation

Duxbury Press

North Scituate   Massachusetts

Duxbury Press
A Division of Wadsworth Publishing Company, Inc.

The Science of Archaeology? was edited and prepared for composition by
Beverly Miller. Interior design was provided by Dorothy Booth. The cover
was designed by Ann Washer.

Library of Congress Cataloging in Publication Data

MacNeish, Richard Stockton.
    The science of archaeology?

    1. MacNeish, Richard Stockton. 2. Archaeologists—United States—
Biography. 3. Archaeology. 1. Title.
CC115.M23A37   930'.1'0924 [B]   77–26805
ISBN 0–87872–153–3

Printed in the United States of America

1 2 3 4 5 6 7 8 9 — 82 81 80 79 78

To the guidance and memory of
Alfred V. (Doc) Kidder

CONTENTS

4

ON BEING AN ARCHAEOLOGIST——80

5

ON GROWING UP: FROM ARCHAEOLOGIST TO SOCIAL SCIENTIST——124

6

ON TRYING TO BE A SCIENTIST——171

Contents

PREFACE

QUESTIONS I HAVE OFTEN BEEN ASKED ARE: JUST WHAT IS ARCHAE-ology? What good is it? or, What do you and other archaeologists really do? In this book I will attempt to answer these questions in terms of my own personal experiences and opinions.

To consider the first question, I, as many other archaeologists, used to define archaeology as the reconstruction of the way of life of ancient peoples and the arrangement of these extinct cultures into a historical sequence. Some archaeologists may have defined it in slightly different ways, but most stayed fairly close to this theme and some still do. However, I and a number of my younger colleagues (often called the New Archaeologists) are beginning to define our field rather differently and more in terms of what we hope it will become rather than what it is. Thus, I now define archaeology as the *science* of past cultures. Therefore, one of the major purposes of our study, as for any science, is to formulate in general terms the conditions under which (historical or cultural) systemic events of various kinds occurred and to have these gen-eralized statements or laws about determining conditions or causes be of such a nature that they are able to explain all other cor-responding happenings (other cultural-historical sequences or se-quences of similar events). In other words, I am ultimately search-ing my archaeological data for laws or generalizations about cultural change or processes. Further, I believe that future archae-ological endeavors will utilize systems theory in the search for these generalizations.

Perhaps, one of my colleagues's statement that in terms of development of a science of archaeology "we are in our pre-Aris-totelian state" is correct. If so, we are a long way from fulfilling the goal of a science, but when we do we will be able to answer quickly and fully the second question: What good is archaeology? For the moment and for the sake of speculation, laws of cultural change may be of use not only in explaining the past, but more important, in predicting the future or at least indicating the steps in cultural change we might take in the future. Whether we will

attain these ends before we blow ourselves off the face of the earth
because of our lack of knowledge of laws of human behavior or
cultural change, I certainly do not know. However, even if archaeology does not achieve the lofty status of science, the fact is that
archaeological investigations do add to our general fund of knowledge which in and of itself is certainly "good." In addition, this
knowledge will not only give us some historical information, but
will also give an appreciation of history and past cultural, as well
as esthetic, accomplishments.

On the other hand, for me and many others, archaeological
research will always help satisfy our curiosity about what came before and what led up to such and such a happening. From a personal point of view, and closely connected with satisfying my in-
nate curiosity, has been the thrill of discovery of art and artifact
and the fact that these objects have remained unknown to anyone
until my little trowel or paintbrush uncovered them—often after
long periods of searching for these new and thrilling finds. I have
been doing archaeology now for over forty years but the thrill is
still there and I feel that this thrill should happen to anyone and
everyone. Perhaps this is the real "good" of archaeology—personal
satisfaction. In a world of more and more leisure hours, second
careers, early retirements, and boredom connected with necessary
routine work, there is much to be said for doing something interesting and personally satisfying. Let me also point out that archaeology is not only popular now, but gives every indication of becoming more so.

In many ways the writing of this book is a historical accident.
An invitation to give the Whidden lectures at McMaster University in 1974 and later a massive heart attack gave me the opportunity to rethink American archaeology, my archaeology, and to
raise the question: Where are we going? I have again used the title
of my Whidden lectures for this book: *The Science of Archaeology?* The question mark remains because, as I indicated above, I
do not believe we have achieved a science of archaeology, but we
are approaching a stage of growth in archaeology that will actually
qualify archaeology as a science—albeit a social science. This book
then is an attempt to give, in personal terms, a review of American
archaeology as it has been done and where it seems to be going.

The first two chapters describe my personal growth as an archaeologist—fieldman, analyzer/describer, and theoretician. Chap-

ter 2 concludes with my personal history of the development of American archaeology: a development not unlike my own. Chapter 3 specifically outlines the methods and theory that I believe we must approach in order to arrive at a science of archaeology; that is, good data collection, analyses that permit cultural-historical integrations, cultural-historical integrations that account for interaction spheres, and interaction spheres that are comparable without time and space. In other words, analyses that are amenable to deriving hypotheses, to testing those hypotheses, and to arriving at laws of culture change. In chapters 4 and 5 then I show how I applied my method and theory to my work in Tehuacan, Mexico, and Ayachucho, Peru. Finally in chapter 6 I compare the larger areas of Meso-America, the Andes, and the Near East in an initial attempt to test hypotheses and arrive at scientific laws, or generalizations about the origin of agriculture.

Throughout my career I have been influenced by my colleagues and seniors in archaeology. No record of my perception of the science of archaeology would be complete without mentioning these people. In the text I have noted the individuals who most influenced my development chronologically. Because some readers may be interested in further notes on these people, I have also included an alphabetical "Cast of Characters" (p. 241). This list is further cross referenced to the text.

1

On Becoming a Dirt Archaeologist

ARCHAEOLOGICAL INVESTIGATIONS, LIKE OTHER SCIENTIFIC RE-searches, usually begin with data collection. Thus, I shall begin with how I became involved in archaeological data collection, which usually includes survey, excavation, and collection of related ecological data. In chapter 2, I shall continue on this same personal note on the next higher level, analysis and theory, ending these autobiographical materials with a very general history of American archaeology, which developed through the same general stages. This background will prepare you for chapter 3, which includes my basic thoughts about method and theory in American archaeology. The book will conclude with three chapters showing how my basic stages of archaeology have been applied to one archaeological problem: the origins of pristine agriculture (and the related aspect of the domestication of plants). Thus you will see an example of the application of my methods and theory to a specific problem.

MY INTRODUCTION TO ARCHAEOLOGY

My first real connection with archaeology was in the spring of 1930 in an art history class when I was required to make a notebook on an ancient culture not covered in the course. I looked at the list of ancient cultures and put my name next to "Maya" because it started with M like my own name, and then I went off doing more important things (like playing third base and raising my batting average). Suddenly it was the night before the day my notebook was due, and I, as usual, had done nothing. I questioned my father, my aunt, and my sister and looked in the encyclopedia for something about the Maya. Finally my father, in desperation, suggested I look through the copies of *National Geographic* and *Science Newsletter* that were stacked in neat bundles by year in the furnace room. Shortly after I hit the jackpot: a *National Geographic* article, "Chichén Itzá, an Ancient American Mecca," all about the Maya, which I promptly tore out, punched two holes in, and put in a black looseleaf notebook cover (borrowed from my sister).[1]

But when I (and my classmates) handed in the notebook, our teacher, Miss Ives, suggested we do further work on them. So back to the basement I went, this time finding three articles in *Science Newsletter*—two written in 1929 about the great flying hero, Charles Lindbergh, looking for Maya ruins. I came up with what I considered a good title—"A Mayan Miscellany"—typed a title page, and pasted an aerial picture view of a Chichén Itzá temple above the title. It made a pretty good title page, and so once again, I handed it in to Miss Ives, and my thoughts and efforts returned to baseball.

Finally, it was the last week of school, and it was time for prizes to be handed out. As I sat in the back of class daydreaming out the window, I vaguely heard, "And first prize for the best notebook goes to Richard Stockton MacNeish." in school, until this time, I had never finished at the head of the class in anything. Now for the first time in my life, there was something good about school—Maya archaeology.

By a series of accidents my archaeological interest was not to die, for in 1931 there was another article for my notebook in the

National Geographic, "Unearthing American Ancient History." [2] At the same time, my grandfather, to whom I was very close, went to Yucatan selling clocks. He returned with postcards about the Maya and said he had talked to a real archaeologist, named "Doc" Kidder, in Merida, who was then head of the Carnegie Foundation excavations. A year later I wrote to Dr. A. V. Kidder for a job as a waterboy (or doing anything else) with his archaeological expedition in Chichén Itzá. Somewhat to my surprise, I received a kindly reply complimenting me on my interest in archaeology, encouraging me to study hard so I might become an archaeologist, and very gently informing me that they had many local waterboys. However, this letter further sparked my interests, and I kept up my thickening notebooks. In fact, although I remember various track meets and football and baseball games during my secondary school days, the only academic memories I have are of my Maya notebooks and archaeology, which served for term papers, research papers, math and astronomy papers, and class speeches or reports.

Personally those teenage years were frequently unpleasant and painful. My smoldering teenage revolt gradually turned into open rebellion—against family, suburbia, the capitalistic business world, and the whole idea of going to that snobbish college my family had registered me in at birth. I was ready to go to work in my grandfather's clock factory, make a million dollars in ten or twelve years, and then do archaeology. Finally, reason prevailed—mainly my grandfather's.

BEGINNING TO DIG

In the fall of 1936 I went off to Colgate University with my father's promise that I could get on an archaeological expedition the next summer and then decide whether to continue my studies or do my thing my way. At Colgate I met a fellow aspirant archaeologist, Mortimer Howe, who took me off to do my first fieldwork—digging up a pit at the Nichol's Pond Iroquois site in Central New York State. (See figure 1.1, no. 5.) I learned how to slice and cut with a trowel, and find bits of Iroquois pottery, bone, and

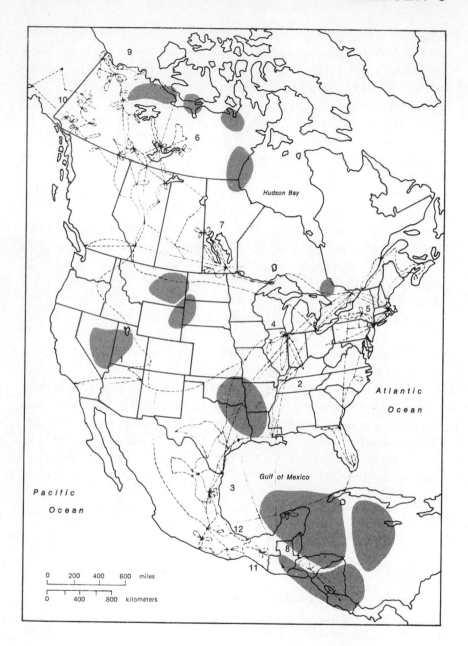

Pacific
    Ocean

Atlantic

    Ocean

Hudson Bay

Gulf of Mexico

0   200   400   600 miles

0   400   800 kilometers

1. Tsegi Canyons, North-			1953
east Arizona	1937		1956
	1938		1958
2. Southern Illinois-		8. Guatemala, Chiapas,	
Kentucky	1939	Honduras	1958
	1940		
	1941	9. Northern Yukon	
	1942	(Coast)	1954
	1944		1955
	1948		1956
			1958
3. Northeast Mexico	1945		
	1946	10. Southwest Yukon	1957
	1948		1959
	1949		1960
	1953		1961
	1954		
	1955	11. Chiapas	1959
4. Central Illinois	1939	12. Tehuacan	1960
	1945		1961
			1962
5. Upper State New			1963
York, Pennsylvania	1936		1964
	1947		1965
	1962		1970
			1973
6. Northwest Territories	1949		1975
	1950		1977
	1951		
	1952	Not on map:	
	1965	13. La Jolla, California	1976
	1966		
	1967	14. Peru	1966
	1973		1969
			1970
7. Manitoba	1950		1971
	1951		1972
	1952		1974

Figure 1.1

MacNeish's wanderings in North America.

flint chips. Then we made exhibits of the sequence of stone tools in Algonkin I, II, and III for Colgate's Lathrap Museum.

The next summer (1937) I was off to Arizona with the Rainbow Bridge-Monument Valley Expedition to do archaeology (and to work out my room and board by doing odd jobs three days a week). One of the first sites I worked on in the Tsegi Canyon of northeast Arizona on a Navajo Indian reservation was a Pueblo I pithouse (figure 1.1, no. 1).[3] It was being dug by Ralph Beals of UCLA, who gave me some inkling of the relationship of archaeology to ethnology and anthropology in general. In addition, I learned how to uncover Pueblo III burials with a paintbrush and spoon. On the weekends I took out Doc Kidder's (by now a god in my limited pantheon) and Guernsey's book and went to visit the sites they had made famous in the Tsegi Canyon area on which much of the Basket Maker-Pueblo sequence was built.[4] My energy was boundless: I dug, I hiked, I climbed cliffs, I learned, I went to dances, I mixed cement by hand, I caught rattlesnakes, I packed mules. Most important, I did and talked archaeology morning, noon, and night—and loved every moment of it.

The next school year at Colgate was a time to get ready to leave to go to the University of Chicago where my peers and advisors in that wonderful world of archaeology in Arizona told me I could really learn archaeology. In the meantime, I went with Mort Howe to dig on the Brewerton site near Syracuse, fix the museum, and help Doc Whitnah teach his classes on the dawn of mankind.

The next summer (1938) I went back to Arizona where I was now a supervisor on the Rainbow Bridge-Monument Valley Expedition. Although I did some work for Watson Smith in a charcoal-filled kiva on Black Mesa and helped dig in other pithouses in Cobra Head Canyon with Ralph Beals, much of the time I worked for George Brainerd of the Carnegie Foundation. I followed Brainerd everywhere, and we talked and did archaeology and I learned and learned and learned: ceramics, surveying, using a light meter to take photographs, cleaning archaeological floors with trowel and shovel in a Basket Maker III shallow pithouse, digging with a spoon, knife, teasing needle, and trowel, and peeling off ash floors with a trowel and paintbrush. Most important, though, I gradually worked out a career plan. First I would learn to dig well and skillfully, then I would become able to analyze archaeological findings, and finally I would become a theoretician.

BEING TAUGHT HOW TO DIG

I transferred to the University of Chicago and did archaeology in Illinois in the summer of 1939. I started with a brief stint at the Kincaid Mound Builder site, which was the place for the summer field school of the University of Chicago, in the black bottoms of the Ohio River in Illinois just across from the town of Paducah, Kentucky, where sternwheelers were still docking (figure 1.1, no. 2).[5] Here were the remains of 2,000 years of Mound Builder and pottery-making Indians. I was taught how to be a shovelman and how to use a mattock in the University of Chicago vertical-slicing technique.

After that I went to dig in a 1500 B.C. village site near Sandoval in central Illinois. We hoped that our excavations would show how these Indians had lived. With workers supplied by WPA a new step in my education as a field worker began. For the first time in my life I was not just a digger but actually supervising three to six WPA men, training them to dig, and recording their and my excavations. I was working for Roger Willis, a master craftsman at digging and a stern tactician. I had to use his specially made WPA shovel and plasterer's trowel skillfully (and keep them both razor sharp). All floors or bottom levels were skinned clean and made level and checked by a carpenter's level; walls were shaved smooth and made vertical and again checked with a level; all loose dirt was immediately swept into a dustpan and removed from the excavation; and all back fill was screened.

Quite correctly, Willis believed that archaeological features such as postmolds, wall trenches, floors, pits, and so forth were difficult to discern in the Midwest, and only by using such careful digging techniques would they be revealed. It was a far cry from the Southwest, where features were obvious and digging needed little real skill.

During the following summers and after graduation, I returned to Kincaid. By 1941, the excavations had become a major

WPA project with about eighty workers, three supervisors, and Roger Willis in charge. Now that I was a supervisor, I set up a training program for my workers to teach them to work as a team and with the skills that Willis had taught me. In fact, my digging standards were stricter than Willis's.

I spent long hours with another supervisor, Norm Emerson, discussing digging and recording techniques. I took notes in the Chicago diary system, and as well kept separate square descriptions. The drawings were done by square and level, as well as on long profile sheets, and separate forms were made for features, photos, and so on. Every week for four months our discussions with each other and with visiting archaeologists from some of the many other WPA projects to the south of us led to further elaborations and improvements of our archaeological techniques and recordings.

Later in the year, Fay-Cooper (Poppa) Cole appointed me supervisor of the project and I ran four digs. I began to learn about setting up a chain of command and training a staff to run this hierarchy. I now had a three-part organization: an administrative group (county supervisor of labor, time keeper, secretary, and coordinator); specialists (a surveyor and his two rodmen, two profile, wall, and floor draftsmen, a photographer, and four specialists in shaving walls and cleaning floors and features); and the digging crew (three or four supervisors who had under them a scribe to take notes and draw, a group of square diggers, including a trowelman boss, cleaner, or shovelman, and a wheelbarrow and/or screenman).

In about a month this system began to run like clockwork. We dug up great archaeological material, and I was going, going, going all the time from one dig to the next, to the specialists, to the administrators. But I had lots of energy, so for my own education we expanded our activities further. As we did this, I decided to use digging techniques I had read about in my classes: MX°7 was to be dug with Doc Kidder's Pecos trenching technique,[6] MX°4 and MX°1A with the balk technique of Sir Mortimer Wheeler,[7] and we would strip the strata of MX°10 and expose the architectural features as Woolley [8] did in the Near East. We also began to dig posthole houses in the WPA manner, leaving each on neat platforms with the excavated postmolds at the edges of these small mesas. While I learned something about more controlled excavations from each of these techniques, in the long run I developed my own system and I used my system or any of the four techniques as the local system warranted. This experience provided lots of different arrows for my bow.

Since there was little to do on the weekends, I would take off to see other WPA digs, as well as talk archaeology with the bosses of the digs—Jim Ford in Louisiana, Chuck Wilder in Guntersville, Bill Haag along the Cumberland River in Kentucky, Jess Jennings and John Cotter in Mississippi, Joe Caldwell in Georgia, Madeline Kneberg and Tom Lewis in Tennessee, Glen Black at the Angel Mounds in Indiana. Although I was junior to these famous archaeologists, I was learning and life was great.

In 1944 and 1945, I dug at the first preceramic site of Illinois (the Faulkner site), learned about digging in mounds at Weaver and Havana in Illinois, and learned historic site archaeology at the Zimmerman site (figure 1.1, no. 4).

LEARNING HOW TO FIND
SITES: SURVEY

Most important was a new aspect of my training as a field man: doing survey. In the fall of 1945, under the auspices of Poppa Cole, I went off to Tamaulipas, Mexico, an area that had been unexplored archaeologically, to attempt to amass evidence of contacts between prehistoric Meso-American cultures and the southeastern U.S. Mound Builders—a much discussed problem of this period. Previously I had done little reconnaissance other than spending a few days in Illinois in 1941 looking for Lewis Focus sites in the hills of Pope and Massac counties.[9] Now it was survey for nine straight months with little equipment, no real intensive previous study of the area, and no settlement pattern hypothesis testing in the field. In fact, the only reason we found two hundred or so sites was lots of energy, good eyesight, and dogged persistence. The most important period of survey was a three-week trip in the spring of 1946 when we found a series of five rockshelters in the waterless Canyon Diablo in the Sierra de Tamaulipas (figure 1.1, no. 3). These were eventually to change my life for it involved me in studies of preceramic corn and early man. Even then I believed the few preceramic tools of my newly defined Diablo complex were thousands of years old—to the complete dismay of all my colleagues who thought they were but a few hundred years old.

During much of the next two years, I tried to raise funds so I could dig these important caves, and I also learned to do analysis (mainly of Iroquois ceramics), to dig in eastern Pennsylvania, and do archaeological salvage in Wolf Creek Dam, Kentucky. Finally, in the summer of 1948 the Viking Fund made me a grant, and I took off that fall for a thrilling, albeit difficult, eight months of digging and exploring in Mexico.

LEARNING HOW TO DIG CAVES: THE LA PERRA TECHNIQUE

First I went to Pánuco in northern Veracruz to see if I could find preceramic remains under sherd deposits like the earliest ones Gordon Ekholm had found in his Period I (from 500 B.C. to 200 B.C.). Although I was not successful, I did find ceramics from a thousand years earlier, and I had the new experience of digging in a deep (twenty-five foot) stratified midden (figure 1.2). I also began to realize that my eastern U.S. habit of digging by thick soil zones or, worse, arbitrary levels, might not allow me to discern specific occupations or reconstruct the way of life of them. This nagging feeling that I should return to the technique of stripping off a specific floor, like George Brainerd had showed me at Swallow Nest Cave in 1938, persisted. Although I dug Nogales Cave in the Sierra de Tamaulipas mainly by arbitrary six-inch levels, gradually during the excavation at Diablo Cave I shifted to soil stripping, and I dug floors X and Y as discrete occupations by trowel as stratigraphic units. Further, I gradually developed a technique of stripping off these actual strata or floors from a vertical profile and digging squares by the alternate square technique so we always could be able to check the stratigraphy. Although much of our back dirt was screened and we lost little, most of the digging was done using WPA shovels, still not the most careful technique.

In the winter of 1949, we dug La Perra Cave with its fine archaeological floors that could be discerned by stripping strata and floors by trowel from a vertical profile and recorded many

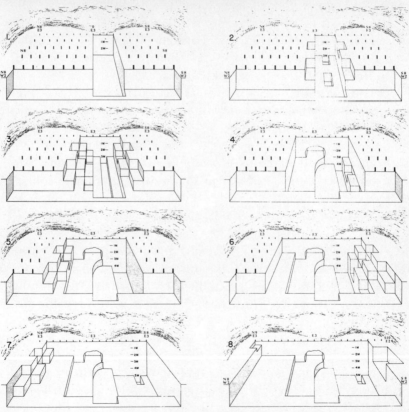

Figure 1.2

The alternate square excavation technique (the La Perra technique) in the south end of Purron Cave and an isometric drawing of the eight stages of the excavation.

11

artifacts and ecofacts in situ. (By ecofact, I mean, relevant archae-ological nonartifactual data or items such as animal and plant remains that were utilized by human beings.) Thus this cave also changed my cave-digging technique.

At my next cave digging (five months in 1953–1954 and three months in 1955) of three caves in southwest Tamaulipas (Romero, Valenzuela, and Ojo de Agua caves), as well as Cuevas Humada and Armadillo in the Sierra de Tamaulipas, we perfected our strata or floor stripping by trowel from a vertical profile. We be-gan to find in these larger excavations concentrations of artifacts or ecofacts on certain portions of the floors. This meant more in situ recording of artifacts, features, and ecofacts, as well as the expansion of the square description type of notes and floor plans, drawings, and feature forms we had developed at Kincaid. These were rich caves, and artifacts and ecofacts just rolled out. Catalog-ing had to be done in the field, and there were quantities of inter-disciplinary materials to be analyzed.

As I did my lab work, measured things with my metric calipers, and did my field drawings on graph paper with inches divided into a decimal system, I began to wonder if it would not be more efficient to map, stake out sites, and do all fieldwork using the metric system. It was, and at my next digging at Santa Marta Cave in Chiapas (1958), I added this metric system improvement (figure 1.1, no. 11).

The biggest improvement came in Tehuacan from 1960 through 1964. Not only did I use these new techniques, but Mike Fowler and Angel Garcia Cook and, to a lesser extent, Kent Flan-nery, Tony Nelken, and Fred Johnson also used them, improved them, and became involved in further improving our strata or occupation vision. We could see strata that were invisible to the uninitiated.

I also began to face up to the problem of determining within reasonable perimeters how long each occupation was, of dis-covering which activity areas were contemporaneous, and what the ranges were of the number of peoples involved in laying down the various deposits. Our mapping of the floors and activity areas, as well as determining what season each had been occupied and how long the foods represented in the ecofacts would last a popu-lation of such and such an estimated size, were brought to bear on this problem. These kinds of data, plus more careful recording of the horizontal in situ position, as well as the use of factor analysis and locational analysis to determine discrete occupations, were techniques we added in my last excavation in the Ayacucho Valley in Peru from 1969 to 1972.

RETHINKING ARCHAEOLOGICAL RECONNAISSANCE

Let us get back to that other aspect of data collection: reconnaissance. In the interim periods between those cave digs from 1949 to 1973, I was a busy archaeologist. (See figure 1.1, nos. 6 and 7.) In 1949 I spent three months surveying mainly the barrenlands of Canada, Northwest Territories. I dug the Bruhm site, the first early man site in Ontario, and surveyed the upper Mackenzie River of Canada in the summer of 1951. Earlier in the year, I had dug the Lockport, Larter, Anderson, and Alexander Point Cree sites north of Winnipeg, Manitoba. In 1952 I dug the Pointed Mountain microblade site at Fort Liard, N.W.T., the stratified sites near Franklin on Great Bear Lake, N.W.T., and the Stott mound and Buffalo Kill near Brandon, Manitoba. I spent 1953 in Manitoba testing the Cemetery Point, Sturgeon Falls, Waulken, Tuokko, Old Fort, and United Church sites. The summer of 1954 saw me back doing survey along the Arctic coast by canoe and whaleboat east and west of the Mackenzie River delta of Canada, and in 1955 and 1956 I dug the best site found in the survey— Engigstciak, on the isolated Yukon Arctic coast—although I also put in a stint of survey around Flin Flon in northern Saskatchewan (figure 1.1, no. 9). I undertook further survey in 1957 in the southwestern Yukon of Canada, as well as in Honduras, and the Zacapa Valley of Guatemala in the winter of 1958 (figure 1.1, no. 8) and survey near Flin Flon, Manitoba, in the spring. During the summer of that year I made a six-hundred-mile reconnaissance down the Firth River of the northern Yukon on foot, hobbling the last hundred miles with a broken ankle. In 1959 a program of excavation began in the southwest Yukon with the Little Arm, Canyon Creek, and Taye Lake sites being tested that year (figure 1.1, no. 10). Gladstone, Moosehide, and Aishihik were dug in 1960 and the Pelly Farm sites in 1961. During the rest of the 1960s, because of major cave digging programs in Mexico and Peru, I pursued few other field activities except surveys in Nova Scotia in 1962, near Fort Liard in the fall of 1963, Guerrero, Mexico, in the winter of 1965, highland Peru in 1966, Fort Liard again in 1967, and Tehuacan, Mexico, in 1970. During this long period of getting more field experience, I spent much of the time in reconnaissance, and this is the period when I learned how to do it.

When I began to organize my thoughts about survey techniques is difficult to pin down exactly. Certainly when I looked for Basket Maker II pithouses in Arizona in 1937 and 1938 or went out into the hills to find Lewis Focus sites, I gave little thought to survey techniques or methodology. I spent that first season in Mexico in Tamaulipas (1945–1946) mainly on reconnaissance. I can't remember thinking very profoundly about what I was doing, but I must have learned how to do something right for I did discover over two hundred new sites. Probably it was during the 1949 cave digging season in the Sierra de Tamaulipas that I began to think about my technique for finding good cave sites, as well as good preceramic sites, in Meso-America. Gradually, however, it occurred to me that the reason I was being so successful was that I was constructing hypotheses about ancient settlement patterns, subsistence systems, and paleoecologies and then testing these hunches in the field by good hard survey work —which meant not only looking where I thought a site might be but also checking areas where our hypotheses indicated that probably there were no sites. For example, I speculated that in the dry Canyon Diablo sites from preceramic food collecting times were probably to be found near water sources—ancient or modern —high enough above them to stay out of the way of flash floods (thus above the high terraces) but not so high that the inhabitants could not get to the water source in a half-hour or less. Survey showed that open sites in this position were most often on the high terraces at potential game crossings, game lures (springs or salt licks), game lookouts, or some other special spot, perhaps where wild foods could be harvested. Often even if there were no bare ground showing artifacts, I did a little digging just to test my hypothesis. About half of the time I found sites.

Even better than the open sites were cave sites in a similar position. Because of the hypothetical seasonally nomadic nature of the ancient inhabitants, caves were likely to be stratified with layers of one occupation on top of previous ones. I also learned to predict which kinds of caves in these strategic positions probably had plant preservation, deep stratigraphy, and abundant artifacts. I had to take into account such factors as the size and shape of the cave and ask whether the back sloped downward in such a manner so that there would be more deposits the deeper one dug; whether the roof was blackened by fire; whether the cave faced away from the direction from which storms came; what kinds of artifacts and how many occurred on the talus slope; whether the cave floor soil was dry and ashy; whether there were stalactites or stalagmites or other evidence of water in the cave. Thus the "MacNeish luck" in finding good caves was, in fact, not luck at all.

These were the kinds of thoughts that I mulled over in my mind in 1949 in Tamaulipas, Mexico. By the time I got to Yellowknife on my next survey assignment in the Northwest Territories of Canada, I was ready to do some stocktaking about archaeological reconnaissance techniques and methods. As I best remember it, my first conscientious start began as I looked out the cracked window of Inghram's Hotel at the boreal forest bathed in the rays of the midnight sun of June and thought that if one could develop successful survey techniques in this godforsaken wilderness, then one could find sites anywhere. However, looking over my notes, I find that I wrote down almost nothing about survey techniques until I taught my first class in methods and theory of archaeology in Calgary in 1965. At that time I outlined the techniques I had developed during the preceding years:

1. Initial background preparation on area to be surveyed.

2. Preliminary hypothesis concerning site location based on background materials and cultural sequential generalizations or considerations.

3. Testing hypotheses in the field, modifying and setting up new hypotheses, testing them, and so on.

4. Field analysis of artifacts from sites to establish preliminary chronology (by seriation—arranging types in chronological order on the basis of overlapping trends) and to determine potential stratified sites or sites with special features.

5. Resurvey for contextual data and special problems, such as to determine activity areas by areal collecting; to estimate popu-

lation by intrasite survey and site dimensions; to determine settlement patterns on the basis of correlation of factors of site environmental location, site permanency, residential structures, special features, arrangement of site, size, and settlement type sites; and to reconstruct the social and behavioral aspects of the occupied sites.

Certainly the first four of these procedures were primarily developed during the 1949 seasons in the Northwest Territories and northernmost Saskatchewan, as well as in the 1950–1951 seasons along the Liard, South Nahanni, Mackenzie, Great Bear, Rat, and Peel rivers and around the west end of Great Bear Lake and Lake Athabasca, as well as others. I read everything possible about the Northwest, particularly on ecological data, discussed the ethnography endlessly with June Helm, hitchhiked rides with bush pilots everywhere, canoed down the Mackenzie two or three times, and talked to and met Indians, trappers, and other local peoples from all over the territory. Further, I began to look at the various ecological regions or areas in terms of a hypothetical archaeological chronology. Nonspecialized hunters of extinct animals were earliest; specialist hunters of extinct and modern fauna were next; Archaic hunters, fishermen, and gatherers came third; and finally were the specialized groups leading to those of the ethnographic record. When I put all this information together with the ecological zones, I developed various hypotheses about their ancient settlement patterns—for example, that the camps of the earliest hunters in the barrenlands east of Yellowknife would be where eskers had been cut by ancient streams, for these eskers were like railroad tressels that wound across the barrenland swamps where the herds of caribou traveled and the fords between sections of eskers were where it was easiest to kill the animals (who were wading rather than running). Often hypotheses about later sites led me to guess that the next ones would be on eskers of high beaches where hunting, fishing, and trapping might have been good, while the most recent sites would be a canoe portage or peninsulas in the bigger lakes where the fishing was ideal.

My first chance to test these hypotheses came when I traveled upstream like a greenhorn with a trapper guide and in eight days discovered twenty-two sites. What is more, I was able to discern a seriation of types that seemed to indicate a sequence of four tentative archaeological cultures or complexes: Artillery Lake, Lock-hart River, Taltheilei, and Whitefish Lake. This sequence, except for the first complex, still stands—albeit with new names and much jargon. The success of this trip continued for the rest of the 9,000 miles of exploration (done on $1,700) of this 1949 season, as well as in the following seasons of 1950 and 1951 in the North-west Territories. To show just how busy we were for the next two seasons of about 20,000 miles of survey, let me quote myself:

> *A brief itinerary will serve to indicate the area covered. In 1949 a brief 12-day canoe trip was made down the Mackenzie from Fort Providence to Norman Wells. Intensive survey, however, did not begin until 1950, when the author went from Edmonton to Peace River, Hay River and on to Fort Simpson. From Fort Simpson a trip with "Dick" Turner was undertaken up the Liard and up the South Nahanni River as far as just north of Deadman's Valley. Then I returned to the Liard River and went upstream to Fort Liard. At Fort Liard short trips were made to sites nearby. After returning to Fort Simpson the survey continued down to Fort Norman where the season ended. In 1951 the survey started at Fort Norman with a trip up the Great Bear River and along the western shores of Great Bear Lake. Next, I went back to Fort Norman and gradually worked my way down the Mackenzie River, stopping at all forts, villages, or likely looking sites down to the mouth of Peel River near Aklavik. After a brief stop-over at the mouth of the Peel and at Fort McPherson, the survey went up Peel River for 90 miles and back. Then a brief side trip from Fort McPherson over McDougall (Rat) Pass to Bell River and back was undertaken. As it was getting late in the season, I returned to Norman Wells and made a brief trip up the Canol Road for 80 miles.*[10]

And then I went back when landslides closed the road. Needless to say, since such exploration trips were often poorly planned and always underfinanced, adventures were numerous. That Rat River trip stands out in my memory, for it started by my wading ashore in shoulder deep, frigid water at Loon Lake; then I spent four days slopping along in the Muskeg and Rat rivers with a guide who had only seen the route frozen in winter, had a confrontation with a grizzly, which I killed at fifty feet near the "mad trapper's cabin," and finally made a white-water river trip on a raft made by tying logs together with strips of the flannel sheets of my bed-roll. However, these initial attempts of systematic survey were a great success, for our number of Northwest Territories sites went from three to sixty-two, a 2,000 percent increase.

I spent 1953 and 1954 digging, although I did find some 242 new southeast Manitoba sites in 1953 in new environments where I tested some new hypotheses about ancient site locational prefer-ences. In 1954, I made an intensive survey in widely separated culture areas: southern Tamaulipas and the Yukon Arctic coast, as well as the adjacent deltaic region of the Mackenzie River. By this time, I had added a new aspect to my reconnaissance tech-niques, which might be called *settlement pattern studies.* (I was largely influenced by the writings of Gordon Willey about his ini-tial endeavors in the Valley of Peru.) Now for the first time I be-gan to devise site survey on five- by eight-inch cards, which re-corded a site number done in uniform site designation system using grid coordinates, site geographical location, artifacts found, and a few comments about number and kind of structures on each. With caves, guesstimates were made about possible refuse depths. Our total sites for Tamaulipas rose to 344, and on the Canadian coast we added another 30, but, more important, we could now successfully find sites of many periods of a long time span, as well as tremendous stratified sites with long sequences.

As important as the spectacular sites I found was a steady improvement in my recording of data, as well as the kind of settlement pattern-related problem attacked. Our forms for the 1956 survey around Flin Flon, Manitoba, and Saskatchewan, for example, included a section for site size in square meters. During the 1957 season I covered about 50,000 miles and began to put on the form detailed information about the environment and paleo-ecology of sites found. Also, in these survey seasons, as well as the ones that followed in Honduras and Guatemala in 1958, the six-hundred mile hike down the Firth River in the summer in 1958, Chiapas and Oaxaca in 1959, and Tehuacan in 1960, I improved this general system of recording. I made more and more attempts to derive information from reconnaissance data about population size of sites, population trends, seasonality of sites, function of sites, and demography.

Most of my ideal survey techniques and methods were in

operation by the time I began my Tehuacan work in 1961. Much of this actual surveying was done in 1961 and 1962. We resurveyed for settlement pattern reasons and made fine Brunton compass maps of some sites in 1964. This survey was extended in 1970 and 1972 and again between 1974 and 1976. As of 1977 about seven hundred sites had been found representing about 1,500 occupations over a 10,000- to 20,000-year period. Further, the materials from more than half the sites have been analyzed and have been classified as to their cultural phase and time period. We have evidence of a population growth from about 20 ± 10 people to over $100,000 \pm 20,000$ and evolutions of some fifty settlement pattern types based upon conclusions of such variables as site ecozone locations, seasonality, activity areas, site permanency, residential structure, specialized features and structures, their arrangement, site, and habitation type. My survey techniques and methods have moved a long way. My survey work for a week at Fort Liard in 1965, which netted about fifty sites, and in highland Peru in 1966 and in Ayacucho, where we discovered some 500 sites, added little to the methods we had already developed.

There is still considerable room for improvements in both reconnaissance methods and techniques. Certainly this survey method of testing hypotheses and site location often does locate the best site in the area quickly and cheaply and is, I think, far superior to the full coverage or statistical random sampling method of the New Archaeologist, which has been used recently in some parts of the Valley of Mexico region. This latter technique not only does not find many good new sites for excavation, few early Formative sites, but no preceramic sites whatsoever.

THE INTERDISCIPLINARY APPROACH

The final part of my education in data collection concerned learning about the interdisciplinary approach. Like my developments in archaeological survey, a crucial turning point in my learning about this approach was the 1949 season in the Canyon Diablo of Tamaulipas. I had faithfully preserved, cataloged, and noted the nonartifactual archaeological materials I had dug up in the season from 1937 to 1948, such as bone, stone, charcoal, and even soils. However, I had never really thought much about what was going to be done with them—other than that they were to be sent to some expert. In the Diablo Cave, however, I had what seemed to be the first early man remains of Mexico, and I had two sets of experts come in. Each came up with diametrically opposed opinions. One wrote, "From the evidence now available, I can see no means of arriving at a dependable popular dating in terms of centuries or millenniums of any of the Canyon Diablo terraces." The other felt the final stages of the soils with the next-to-earliest Lerma artifacts "might be just after the time of the terrace—8,000 to 12,000 years ago," and the earlier Diablo artifacts might be older than that.

Initially I was somewhat upset by these differing opinions. By the time I arrived in Canada and was ready to finish the analysis and write up these Canyon Diablo materials, I realized that the only way to resolve this dilemma was to restudy the basic soils of the terraces that the experts interpreted so differently, as well as to get the bone identified to see if it came from animals of the Pleistocene and find out if the associated carbon would give a radiocarbon date of Pleistocene times.

Like many other archaeologists working with the multidisciplinary approach, I found out at this time that knowing what you wanted to do and getting it done were two different things. I sent off my early soil samples in two directions. One was to see if the pollen in it might be of Pleistocene times. Two years later the specialist wrote back saying that he could find no pollen in these soils. I sent the other sample off for soil grain analysis. Three years later the results came, tending to confirm the 8,000- to 12,000-year-old theory, but those involved were quick to state they knew nothing of the Pleistocene geology of Mexico and did not really know whether their analyses were applicable. Not until 1952 were the associated bones (except one) identified. The one bone the specialists were not sure of was a tooth of a beaver in the terrace deposits. Equally frustrating was the study of the carbon samples, for one of the specialists did not send on all of the original ones in 1950 to the next person.

In spite of these multidisciplinary difficulties, the analysis of plant materials (corncobs dug up in 1949 in the Canyon Diablo) was to lead to more rewarding developments. At the end of the 1949 season I had turned over my plant remains and carbon samples to Helmut de Terra for the newly organized Viking Fund Laboratory in Mexico City. He promised to send the corncobs to Paul C. Mangelsdorf, the famous Harvard professor, who was then classifying corn for the Rockefeller Foundation Agriculture Research project. De Terra also had me pack twenty-four bottles of carbon from my various levels for a young Chicago physicist, Willard Libby, who had just worked out a new dating technique.

The next couple of years in Ottawa were busy ones. I not only did my duty for the National Museum of Canada, but I found time to get my Panuco report written and to contact the experts about the Canyon Diablo materials, but *que lastima!* the botanical materials still were in Mexico. One bottle of carbon that I had given to Helmut de Terra had been sent to Libby, who with his new carbon 14 technique had dated it 658 years ago ± 150. This sure as hell was wrong for the oldest corn. So I wrote to Libby asking about the provenience of the specimens, and sure enough, de Terra had sent him the bottle from the top deposits associated with late Los Angeles ceramics and had sent none of the earlier bottles. Libby said he would be glad to date the others free of charge if I could get them to him.

There was only one way to solve these problems, so in 1951 I went to Mexico City at my own expense. José Luis Lorenzo helped me, and the botanical specimens were not hard to find; they were sitting in the same spot in a corner of the Viking Fund lab, in the same boxes, just as I had left them—but with three years' dust. José soon found the boxes of bottles elsewhere, and they were intact except for one compartment labeled "Late—not important," which was empty, and, of course, the one sent to Libby. Next there was the task of getting a permit to export these materials, but this was no problem, for Dr. Eduardo Noguera, who was head of Monumentos Prehispanicos of the Instituto, was, like myself, a friend of James "Himy" Griffin—and in Mexico there is the time-worn adage that any friend of his is a friend of mine. Thus, our specimens left Mexico with the best possible legal exportation permit. Getting the specimens back for redistribution to the correct experts was not very difficult. Although there was one comical moment when the customs man in Miami, with good bureaucratic sampling techniques, gingerly picked out a large well-formed, 4,000-year-old human fecal specimen—interdisciplinary studies hung in the balance!

Finally, by the time I left for the field in Canada in May of
1951, all the specimens had been redistributed to the correct experts. I worked away digging in the north and got back to Ed-
monton at the end of September when I picked up my mail. There
was a telegram from Chicago. It said, "Your corn has a radiocarbon date of 4,445 years ago ± 280." I let out an expletive not
normally heard in the austere halls of the Canadian banking world
and continued ripping open letters before the embarrassed eyes
of the clerks and tellers until I got to another one—this time from
Cambridge, Massachusetts—that contained the statement, "Yours
is the most primitive corn yet found in Mexico. When can you
come to Cambridge?" I grabbed all the letters and walked across
the street to the telegraph office and sent the words of Libby's
telegram to Mangelsdorf, sent Mangelsdorf's message about corn
to Libby, and sent the texts of both letters to the director of the
National Museum with a request for permission to go to Cambridge.

The first morning I was in Dr. Mangelsdorf's office at the
Botanical Museum, Mangelsdorf and I set out to put the corn
specimens in chronological and stratigraphic order, for "these pine
cones" had been badly jumbled by United States Customs. Peggy
and Walton Galinat cleared off a table, and I began sorting out
the cobs by square and level. Just about the time that I was placing the last few specimens, Paul asked, "Do you know anything
about botany?"

My honest answer was, "No, not much." After all, archaeologists in U.S. institutions spend much of their time learning
phonemics, personality and culture, esoteric kinship systems,
strange customs of primitive peoples, and so forth and do not have
time for fields like botany, zoology, pollen analysis, soils, and
geology—all disciplines they will have to use.

Mangelsdorf's next statement was, "Well, you have put the
cobs into a precise evolutionary sequence." During the rest of the
morning and afternoon, Mangelsdorf examined the specimens,
asking me about them and explaining to me what they meant. A
number of times he said that we ought to find some more like
these, but I figured he was just kidding. He wasn't. He was particularly serious about my going back to Tamaulipas to get more
corn and about our starting a long-term archaeological-botanical
program. Mangelsdorf wanted to find out when, where, and how

corn was domesticated. All we knew then was that it happened in some valley between Chile and the St. Lawrence River of Canada (corn's modern distribution) and probably it had been grown before 4,500 years ago (the date of the La Perra corn). What was corn's wild ancestor? What developments had taken place (genetically) with domestication? How long did genetic development take? How and why was this plant, as well as others, domesticated? These questions and many more comprised the "corn problem," and men had been speculating about the answers for four centuries. Now our cobs from the Tamaulipas cave had begun to give some concrete answers to these queries. What we needed were more caves with older cobs.

I told Mangelsdorf that I was sure there were more caves with corn in Tamaulipas, but it might take two or three years (and a lot of money, say $20,000) to find them. He insisted that money was no problem and that I should start planning.

Early the next morning I began to outline another Tamaulipas corn-hunting project application for funds. One of the most significant items of the application concerned provisions for cooperating with experts. Unlike previous projects where we had found specialized materials and then looked for experts, this time we were going to look for nonartifactual archaeologic materials as a scientific team. The experts were to be a forethought rather than an afterthought.

In 1954 we finally began this corn-hunting expedition in southwest Tamaulipas, where three caves in the Canyon Infiernillo yielded enormous quantities of ecofacts in stratified layers, along with artifacts. Initially we separated the artifacts from the ecofacts in our improvised lab. We had shelves of boxes full of plant and animal bones classified as to square and level. Then we began to notice that there were concentrations of remains on floors—*activity areas*—so we began our separation in the field. Specimens in specific floors became preserved in various manners—bones into plastic bags, plants and feces into tin foil, and pollen, soil, and carbon specimens into bottles of various sizes and shapes. At the end of the season, Paul Mangelsdorf visited us at the site as an official visitor of the Rockefeller Foundation so he could see the corn we had dug up.

For the next two weeks he studied both the corn, preserved in tin-foil wrappings from many squares and levels, and teosinte and tripsacum grass specimens (relatives of corn). The corn, teosinte, and tripsacum were separated out and recataloged, as were all the other remains of domesticated plants: beans, squashes, pumpkin gourds, and amaranth. We sent the cucurbit remains to the Missouri Botanical Gardens and the U.S. Department of Agriculture and the beans to a student for scientific study and classification. The rest of the plant remains—some 200,000—represented more of a problem. There were twenty cubic meters of them, which were not easily transported. We finally decided that Mangelsdorf would separate out a type specimen of each plant specimen for later identification by one of his students, and I could do the counts of the rest of the type specimens from the various squares and levels in the next season. With that done, Mangelsdorf left for Mexico with the type specimens, got the legal permission, and returned to the United States to start his studies. After fulfilling other research commitments, I returned to Tamaulipas for artifact analysis and work toward accomplishing the multidisciplinary studies.

We separated out the bones and shipped them off to zoologists. Then a textile expert, Irmgard Johnson, sought us out and came to Tamaulipas to analyze the fine collection of ancient woven fabrics and string. (Increasingly in my brush with interdisciplinary studies, this sort of thing happens: experts find you to initiate studies rather than your finding them.) Finally, after seemingly endless hours of counting our botanical types as to their square, level, and occupational floors and classifying our multitude of artifacts, we packed them in neat cubic-meter boxes with specialized compartments for plants and the artifacts in beautifully made wooden cabinets, put them on a truck, drove to Mexico City, and unloaded everything in a well-organized manner at the Department of Prehistory. Once having arranged them so they would be available to future scholars and a credit to Mexico's national pride, we received official permission for taking out not only a type collection of artifacts but sample boxes of plant remains and the large collection of feces that I thought might be relevant to the study of ancient diets. Unfortunately, all of the material I shipped off—the valuable plant remains and artifacts, including a tremendous collection of ancient woven mats and twelve mummies—disappeared on their journey.

This, however, was not the real disaster of the 1954–1955 seasons, for not only did we not find the early ancestral corn we sought, but also the final reports never got written for the simple reason that our multidisciplinary studies never were completed or coordinated. For the next couple of years, I pondered why this endeavor with specialists from other fields did not work. Gradually, my thoughts on the problem began to jell; and at the National Research Council conference by the Committee on Archaeological Identification in Chicago in 1952, where I found most other archaeologists were having similar troubles, I put my thoughts down on paper.

1. First and foremost, I had a great deal of trouble finding, and wasted a good deal of time looking for, just the right scientists to undertake the various kinds of identification. Therefore, I would recommend that somewhere there be a list of what scientists are available in various areas and in various disciplines, so that one would know where to send the actual materials. If such a list seems impracticable, then at least there should be a committee that could steer archaeologists to the correct specialists.

2. Very often I found that the archaeologist's approach to the specialist was very wrong. First of all, not enough data about materials were sent to the specialist. Second, the archaeologists often did not indicate just exactly why they wanted these materials identified. Third, archaeologists did not seem to realize that the specialists often were interested in the identifications for very different reasons, and no effort was made to present material so that its identification could be useful to the specialist. Finally, I feel that archaeologists should make a conscious effort to give their material to the specialist in such a way that the specialist can publish on it, either alone or in conjunction with the archaeologist.

3. As my studies went along, I began to realize that identifications were best done by individuals who were real specialists. This point, I believe, needs some emphasis and should be taken into consideration when one is planning a project.

4. I believe, also, that some attempt should be made to have the specialist visit the archaeological excavations when they are in progress and also have a chance to see the area in which the work is being done.

5. I have the feeling that after the identifications are all

completed and the field work all done, there should be some
sort of conference by the various specialists and the archae-
ologists to discuss the Paleo-ecological problems of the par-
ticular area. The archaeologists, with their finer means of
dating, could contribute to studies of the botanists, zoologists,
and geologists. Of course the reverse would be true also.

In conclusion, I believe that if archaeologists going to the
field would take into consideration these five points, there
would be considerably fewer problems in identifications, and
perhaps the final reports might be a good deal better than
they are.[11]

USING THE INTERDISCIPLINARY METHOD

At this conference, I met Fred Johnson, an archaeologist
whose work on the Boylston Street Fishweir in the 1940s really saw
the beginning on interdisciplinary endeavors.[12] Our initial contact
on interdisciplinary studies came to fruition a few years later when
I undertook the Tehuacan researches in 1961. At this time, Johnson and I wrote a whole host of interdisciplinary scientists into
our initial grant proposal. We contacted all of these scientists and
defined our problem of determining the changes in the exploitation of the ancient environments (subsistence patterns, domestication, agriculture), as well as determining the changes in the ecosystem itself. We followed my five-point program, and the findings
came out in five volumes—less than five years after the project
began.[13] We also rather neatly scheduled the scientists so they followed each other but rarely overlapped and really never inter-
fered or competed with our digging program.

Chronologically, the first specialist was Monika Bopp, who
came to Tehuacan in the spring of 1961 to collect pollen from the
profiles of our excavations. Two years later, another pollen expert
arrived. The purpose of the pollen studies was to determine the
agricultural changes, give us clues as to chronology of the strata
of the various sites, and determine the changes of vegetation
through time. Because of poor pollen preservation in our earlier
levels, these worthy objectives were not attained.

C. Earle Smith, then with the U.S. Department of Agriculture, Crops Research Division, came to Tehuacan in the summer of 1961 to make a botanical survey of the valley and the surrounding mountains. He continued the survey in August 1962, and in 1963 he identified the vegetal remains from the archaeological sites. His subsequent analysis of these materials gave us pertinent information on the flora of the valley and about the ancient subsistence patterns.

Closely allied to the study of the ancient subsistence was the analysis of the archaeological cucurbits, undertaken in the spring of 1962 by Hugh C. Cutler, then executive director of the Missouri Botanical Gardens, and Thomas W. Whitaker, a retired senior research geneticist of the U.S. Department of Agriculture; the study of beans, made in the fall of 1962 by Lawrence Kaplan, now with the University of Massachusetts in Boston; and the studies of corn, undertaken by Paul C. Mangelsdorf and Walton O. Galinat, both then of Harvard University. To obtain more precise information about diet, the late Eric O. Callen of Macdonald College of McGill University undertook a study of the prehistoric feces preserved in the dry rockshelters.

Supplementing these studies on subsistence and environment were the zoological researches. Kent V. Flannery, now with the University of Michigan, arrived in the summer of 1962 to make a faunal survey of the Tehuacan Valley. In 1963 he analyzed the numerous animal remains that had been uncovered in excavation. This information, both zoological and botanical, gave us a full picture of the diet and also indications of the actual seasons of the cave occupations.

Data derived from the botanical and zoological studies furnished us with hints about chronology in the Tehuacan region. The most significant endeavors in this line were in the capable hands of Frederick Johnson of the R. S. Peabody Foundation. Not only did he teach the archaeologists in 1962 and 1963 how to collect carbon carefully, but he collected the majority of the carbon specimens himself, organized the information about them, and then selected the specimens for radiocarbon determinations. Finally it became his lot to interpret the material dated.

Other specialized information came from a variety of sources. There were geological studies of the Tehuacan Valley and the rest of the region, investigations of prehistoric and modern irrigation systems, and a study of the morphologic features of the human skeletal remains taken from the excavations. Most of these studies took place in 1964 and continued after the field project closed. In addition, information was collected concerning the ethnohistory and ethnography of the Tehuacan Valley. Needless to say, there were endless discussions of various problems of interpretation, and, of course, our specialists corresponded with each other. Still later, a series of conferences on various subjects was held with those involved so our data could be correlated and readied for publication.

These original studies stimulated others to do projects in the Tehuacan Valley that are relevant to the original endeavors. In fact, interdisciplinary studies often have a snowballing effect. In 1969 C. Vita-Finzi of the University of London came to Tehuacan to undertake geophysical and soil studies, and in 1970 George J. Gummerman, then of Prescott College, and Jim Neely, then of the University of Texas, undertook a test of color infrared photography of the Tehuacan Valley for NASA. Further studies in the latter realm are planned, so interdisciplinary studies continue and there is still much to do.

Basically, however, the techniques and methods of the interdisciplinary approach I developed for Tehuacan have not been significantly added to in my later investigations in Ayacucho, Peru. Nevertheless, the approach could and should be much improved in years to come, particularly the realm of interpretation and descriptions of the results of such endeavors.

REFERENCES

1. SYLVANUS GRISWOLD MORLEY, "Chichén Itzá, an Ancient American Mecca," *National Geographic Magazine* (January 1925).
2. SYLVANUS GRISWOLD MORLEY, "Unearthing America's Ancient History," *National Geographic Magazine* (December 1931).
3. A. V. KIDDER, *An Introduction to the Study of Southwestern Archaeology*, R. S. Peabody Papers of the Southwest Expedition, vol. 1 (New Haven: Yale University Press, 1924).
4. SAMUEL JAMES GUERNSEY and ALFRED VINCENT KIDDER, *Basket-Maker Caves of Northeastern Arizona*, Papers of the Peabody Museum, vol. VIII, no. 2 (Cambridge, Mass., 1921).

5. FAY-COOPER COLE, ROBERT BELL, JOHN BENNETT, JOSEPH CALD-
   WELL, NORMAN EMERSON, RICHARD MACNEISH, KENNETH ORR,
   and ROGER WILLIS, *Kincaid, a Prehistoric Illinois Metropolis*
   (Chicago: University of Chicago Press, 1951).
6. KIDDER, *Introduction.*
7. MORTIMER WHEELER, *Archaeology from the Earth* (Oxford,
   Clarendon Press, 1954).
8. P. R. HALL and C. L. WOOLLEY, *Excavation at Ur* (London, 1925).
9. FAY-COOPER COLE et al., *Kincaid.*
10. RICHARD S. MACNEISH, "Archaeological Reconnaissance in the
    Mackenzie River Drainage," *Annual Report of the National
    Museum for the Fiscal Year 1951–52,* Bulletin No. 128 (Ottawa,
    1953).
11. RICHARD S. MACNEISH, "The Independent Investigator," in *Iden-
    tification of Non-artifactual Archaeological Materials,* ed. Walter
    W. Taylor, National Academy of Sciences-National Research
    Council Publication 563 (Washington, D.C., 1957).
12. FREDERICK JOHNSON et al., *The Boylston Street Fishweir,* Papers
    of the R. S. Peabody Foundation for Archaeology (Andover, Mass.,
    1942).
13. DOUGLAS S. BYERS, *Environment and Subsistence: The Prehistory
    of the Tehuacan Valley,* vol. 1 (Austin: University of Texas Press,
    1967).

2

On Growing Up in and with American Archaeology

LET US NOW MOVE ON TO THE NEXT STAGES OF MY BECOMING an archaeologist: analysis and theory. Since my personal development closely parallels the general trends in New World archaeology and since both are now much interested in theory, I have closed this chapter with a brief sketch of my personal view of the trends in New World archaeology. This will prepare the reader for the next chapter, where I outline the methods and theory of American archaeology.

DATA ANALYSIS AND DESCRIPTION

Classification, Typology, and Description

The second major development in my becoming an archaeologist was learning how to do data analysis and descriptive interpretation—in the jargon of the trade, being a lab person. My first fieldwork in Arizona brought me in contact with people using pottery types. I listened to discussions on pottery types,[1] memorized all the Tsegi Basket Maker III, Pueblo I, II, and III pottery types in Hargrave and Colton's handbook,[2] guided Anna Shepard,[3] collected clay and wood for her pottery making at Cobra Head Canyon, collected dirt and potsherds out of the Tsegi Canyon banks for John Hack's geological studies, and arranged arrowheads in chronological order for Colgate Museum. But in reality, all this kind of typological analysis was a mystery to me. In fact, I was becoming more confused by all the new terms—the McKern system with its patterns, phases, aspects, and foci versus the Gladwin system with its roots and branches, trait lists and how a trait was different from a type; the folk-urban continuum or social structure as indicated by the material culture content; the functional interrelationships of military and hunting activities as indicated by the bones, points, palisades around house clusters and houses often being burned at Kincaid, and so forth (figure 1.1, no. 2).

I was also faced with the task of writing up my thesis on the Lewis Focus and in charge of the Kincaid lab work for the final reports.[4] Now I really had to learn something about data analysis, classification, and typology. My Lewis Focus thesis was mainly descriptions of the sites and materials I had dug up and placement of the materials in their chronological positions. I enjoyed doing the maps and cross-sections and describing the site excavation and features, but suddenly I realized that not only were the projectile points and chipped stone artifacts different from each other, but each one had a whole set of complicated attributes, which I had to describe in terms of groups—types. This I did by duplicating what Cole and Duell had done in *Rediscovering Illinois* for Fulton County, Illinois—typology at its worst.[5] My pottery descriptions were little better for the types were divided only on the basis of surface features, such as smooth, cord-marked, brushed, and so forth.

There was one good result of this study; I met Jimmy Griffin. When I first saw him, he was leaning over my lab table covered with my Lewis potsherds and lecturing a group of students about them. As he finished, he looked up at me across the table with a twinkle in his eye and said, "Right?" and implied they were of the Middle Woodland Period, 500 B.C. to 300 A.D., like Hopewell. My response was, "Dr. Griffin, I don't think you know what you're

talking about, and certainly your temporal assignment is wrong."
He exploded, and during the next three hours we argued as he in-
spected the rest of the lab. It was an unfair fight, for he had knowledge of millions of potsherds, as well as years of experience, and
all I really knew were a few Lewis sherds, so I fought a rearguard
action, in the best Scottish manner, retreating from the onslaught
before overwhelming odds while taking horrendous losses but
never surrendering. Finally, he was at the door to his room and I
weakly said, "Well, damnit, one of these days I'll dig up some
Lewis potsherds on top of Hopewell ones," and he grinned, asked
my name, and told me to come up and see him at his repository of
potsherds at the University of Michigan. It was not only the beginning of a great friendship, but also I had now started to learn
about ceramic analysis because I would be communicating with
Jimmy.

　　This initial argument about how ceramics indicated chronological relationships also was very relevant to my major endeavors
in doing the Kincaid report, because basically one of the main
problems was a chronological one as well as a descriptive one. In
essence my two assistants and I took the field notes, drawings,
notes, and artifacts for each of the sites, analyzed the data, and
wrote up the excavation of each site and its stratigraphy in terms
of their major foci and sequential floors of the final Middle Mississippi occupation. It was a long and arduous task, but it caused
me no trouble since I had carefully dug MX°7, which had the last
three ceramic foci in stratigraphic order, and I had also excavated
the Faulkner site with the first preceramic remains of Illinois under the earliest ceramics. All other stratigraphy of other sites was
then tied into this basic chronological framework.

　　I learned more about establishing a chronology when I was
talked into a study of the trade sherds at Kincaid. This attempt to
align the foci in chronological order by cross-dating to other sequences in the eastern United States not only confirmed the Kincaid sequence and established historic relationships with other
areas but indicated that there was a sequence within the Kincaid
focus of the Tennessee-Cumberland aspect of the middle phase of
Mississippi pattern. Neatly confirming this latter indication were
the basic dendrochronology (tree-ring dating) dates. I not only
learned how to do this dating system from Florence Hawley
and Bob Bell, but I also collected all twelve of the dated char-

coal specimens (as well as three hundred or four hundred others that could not be dated). More edifying than my studies about the Mississippi chronology was a study done by Ken Orr correlating the various Mississippi occupations at Kincaid, thereby indicating its expansion over time. This analysis of about a hundred Mississippi attributes—such as type of vessel handles, hoods on water bottles, and salt pans—showed trends through time in the stratified Mississippi levels. But more important, his analysis showed, by use of the statistical formula chi-square, that the temporarily and spatially significant attributes (later called *modes*) were not due to chance but probably to conscious human selection. Here was a technique I was to use in the future over and over again in order to get trends that would allow for correlating the layers of a stratified site with those of other sites in a chronological order, stratified or not.

I was moving toward understanding ceramic typology but still not doing it well in 1945 when I analyzed the lithic remains from the Faulkner site, the first preceramic site ever found in Illinois. My study showed me how useless the McKern classification system was for obtaining chronology or chronological relationships.[6] It also showed that even with poor lithic typology, Archaic relationship could be established and a site could be placed in its relative chronological position. But similarly, the trait lists the McKern system required did not tell you whether your site was an ancestor, a descendant, or merely a sibling. In spite of this I estimated by these comparisons that Faulkner, because of its artifact similarities with Black Sand (then thought to be of the time of Christ) and its points like Folsom (geologically dated at 18,000 years ago), was probably 6,000 to 9,000 years old, a guess 4,000 to 7,000 years nearer to the time than any opinions of my colleagues.

Besides these major duties, before I left for Mexico in 1945, I also had time to work on maps and documents on the historic Illinois village with Sally Tucker, and I even went out and found a couple of them, which we planned to dig. Around this same time, I was also doing salvage archaeology on the stratified Havana mound group, about to be destroyed by the Illinois Hydro-Electrical Co., for the Illinois State Museum, and I was also digging on weekends at the stratified Weaver site (figure 1.1, no. 4). I found the first Hopewell longhouse and the first recognizable stratigraphy of Hopewell remains, and I discovered that the Ogden-

Fette focus was not one focus, but three, and that pottery types 2a, 3, and 3a, rather than showing sequence, hid it. Dr. John Mac-Gregor, who had hired me to salvage the Havana mounds, decided he would analyze the pottery using the Southwest technique and methods of analysis instead of telling me to do it. After he had marked off a table in terms of my levels or strata, he began to break the pottery so that he could examine the nonplastic inclusions fixed in the sherds, as well as the clay itself. He divided the sherds into a series of paste groups, some of which were different from one layer to the next (that is, they had temporal significance and were time-marker modes). Then he did the same thing for pottery hardness, color, thickness, surface finish on the inner and outer side of the sherds, the numerous kinds of decoration, and the rim profile that indicated the shape the pots had once had. He had examined almost thousands of ceramic features (*attributes*) and had found that about three hundred or four hundred were good time markers.

One day when I went to Springfield, I found instead of hundreds of little piles of sherds neat boxes laid out by levels with names of types on them. MacGregor explained to me that these types were composed of clusters of sherds having in common various groups of ceramic attributes or features that marked off the time periods in unique ways. For instance, one type was found only in the lowest level; the attributes of these sherds were large-shell limestone temper, plain surfaces, and crescentic and dentate stamp decoration. Further, when rims occurred in the early levels, they were always wedge-shaped and bottoms, when they occurred, were flat. In other words, here was a cluster of modes along with nonsignificant attributes (like color and thickness) that had a unique early temporal distribution. After MacGregor had separated the sherds in numerous groups on many attributes and found out what groups of attributes had temporal significance (modes), he had then shoved the little groups back into big groups (types) that had the same or very similar temporal distribution. It marked off my Havana layers beautifully, and the useless type 2a that hid temporal trends was now classified into about thirty real types that showed cultural change well. Needless to say, I went back and treated my stratified sherds from Weaver, as well as those from nearby Clear Lake site that had stratigraphy, in the same manner.

By the time I left for the first Tamaulipas expedition, I had some sensitive Middle Woodland pottery chrono-types, and on the basis of the trends of the distribution of types of the interdigitated levels of the three sites, I had the first sequence of Illinois Hopewell in terms of foci, periods, and cultures. In essence, my establishment of types and periods in all work after this period was done in similar manner.

In Tamaulipas, my typology was based upon projectile point types. I learned how to classify them and determine their attributes, and I also learned about other lithic types—gouges, scraper planes, and the like. Thus, my work in eastern Tamaulipas resulted in my establishing artifact types and setting a tentative chronology of culture complexes for that area (figure 1.1, no. 3).

Now that my basic training in establishing chronology was over, the next stage of my endeavors in this line started with my work with Iroquois pottery types (figure 1.1, no. 5). It began as my 1946 Tamaulipas work came to an end when Jimmy Griffin offered me a fellowship to come to the University of Michigan to work on his Delaware project. Griffin and I were both interested in ceramics (and I wanted to learn more from him on the subject). Because I had worked on Iroquois sites ten years before and since the historic Delaware had pottery much like the Iroquois, it seemed logical that my part of the Delaware project would be to undertake the ceramic typology. On a less formal basis, there also was Jimmy's general uneasiness about the collection of data and classifications in northeastern archaeology in the so-called Mississippian period.[7] Further, he had rather definite ideas about culture and continuity in the eastern Woodlands that just did not mesh with the prevailing idea about Iroquois migrations into the northeast.[8] He wanted to explode this poorly documented speculation that felt that the Iroquois developed their distinctive culture somewhere else and then suddenly made an invasion from this unknown region, leaving no sites along the route and then took over the northeast. He felt that I was just the sort of trouble-maker to do the job. I agreed with him. So in the fall of 1946, I migrated (unlike the Iroquois) to the Museum of Anthropology in Ann Arbor, fired with enthusiasm, to become, I hoped, a dynamic dynamiter.

Things were great. I had a desk in the ceramic repository full of potsherds from all over the eastern United States, and three great night-stalking colleagues of roughly my age. In Griffin's office, next to mine, books on the Iroquois and related fields were piled up, and most of the time when I went in to borrow one, Griffin and I became involved in an archaeological argument, usually loud and vociferous, that often lasted a couple of weeks and was far superior to any formal academic course I ever took.

By midwinter 1947, I had read every available book or article on the Iroquois, seen every relevant potsherd, argued with all my colleagues on the subject of everything Iroquois, and had a long list of Iroquois collections in private and public hands.

My analysis was based upon (1) the assumption that each Iroquois tribe had distinguishable and distinctive ceramic complexes, which had had distinctive developments, and (2) the strategy of the direct historic approach; I would start with ceramic complexes of known tribes and work back into the prehistoric. Thus, the first set of data was to be the sherds from sites identified as belonging to specific tribes. The second set of data was material from prehistoric Iroquois sites that we could link with the tribally identified historic sherd complexes. Eventually we found out that these materials linked with still earlier Owasco and Point Peninsula remains, which was our third set of data.

Our techniques for building a chronology were not the best. There was little or no stratigraphy of Iroquois or Owasco components, tree-ring dating (which I often recommend) had (and has) not been attempted, and the method of radiocarbon determinations was not yet known. The first two dating techniques are still not utilized in Iroquois archaeology, and the third lacks reliability because most components are relatively recent and carbon 14 errors are great. Thus then, as now, chronology was based upon trends of ceramic attributes or modes or mode clusters called *types* that could be connected with dated historic sites.

My mode clusters of Iroquois utilized the correlation of three kinds of ceramic attributes: forms (125), decorative motifs (241), and manners of decoration (5). The naive techniques I used for typology have been described elsewhere and certainly are not worthy of being restated here. Obviously I was not using all the possible ceramic attributes nor was I applying statistical formulas to determine if the ones I used were, in fact, the most significant or sensitive to temporal change, that is, the best modes. Nevertheless, in the Iroquois and pre-Iroquois studies, I used about 500 motifs, 250 forms, and a dozen decorative techniques, which I clustered into about 100 types. These types were based on the examination of about 500 site collections with approximately a half-million sherds, but only about 60 of these components (12 pre-Iroquoian) with about 20,000 rim or necksherds (5,000 being pre-Iroquoian) were utilized in my initial study.

After a couple of years of study, in spite of the horrible way, archaeologically speaking, in which most of the data with which I had to work had been dug and documented originally, the inadequacy of the size of sherd samples used in my study, and the naiveté of my ceramic analysis, I had done just what Griffin wanted me to do. We destroyed the migration myth of the Iroquois, showed that there was culture and continuity in the Iroquois area and that it was not Mississippian, and built a new theoretical structure: the in situ hypothesis of Iroquois prehistory. In essence my reconstruction still stands, and students continue to augment it.

In 1948 I moved on into other fields of doing typology and building chronologies. I spent the 1948–1949 seasons back in Tamaulipas, Mexico, and established ceramic and nonceramic types for the Sierra de Tamaulipas (figure 1.1, no. 3). I also dug a Panuco site in the Huasteca using the techniques of ceramic typology I had learned from MacGregor, I expanded the six-period sequence of Gordon Ekholm backward by three phases, about a millennium—from roughly 200 B.C to 1200 B.C.—and my comparative studies realigned it to ceramic phases of Mexico in a more realistic manner.[9] In writing the report, I learned from Ekholm how to classify clay figurines in the new manner—using mode and mode-attribute clusters—which was superior to the Hay-Vailliant type of classification. Ironically enough Kidder, himself, wrote the foreword to this monograph.

By this time both Jim Ford and Alex Krieger were strongly influencing my typological studies and building of chronologies. In fact, in the summer of 1949 by a typology of lithic materials,[10] I built up by seriation [11] a tentative sequence of four complexes for the barrenlands of the Northwest Territories.[12] From 1950 to 1952 I used typology with limited excavated materials and established a 9,000-year sequence for the Fort Liard area of northern Canada [13] and a three-period sequence for materials I dug up on the west of Great Bear Lake (figure 1.1, no. 6).[14] In another pioneering effort, in southeast Manitoba on the basis of stratified materials, I built a 6,000-year sequence that remains unchanged (figure 1.1, no. 7).[15]

My next endeavor was a description of chronological studies in 1954 and 1955 in Mexico and on the Yukon Arctic coast (figure 1.1, no. 9). Although the methods and techniques I used in both areas were about the same, there were some minor differences in the material being classified. First of all, the Firth River sequences may have started some 20,000 to 40,000 years ago, thus involving a whole range of relationships to Siberia and Asia, and second, later Eskimoid cultural manifestations utilized a host of bones and ivory tools that I had previously not had experience in typing.[16] In the Sierra Madre of southwest Tamaulipas, where we found a 9,000-year sequence, I had new things to type: wooden tools, knots, string, mats, baskets, and textiles.[17]

It was not until the Tehuacan expedition that my techniques of chronological-oriented analysis were changed significantly.[18] From about twenty-five beautifully stratified sites, as well as surface sites, about 500,000 ceramics, 200,000 pieces of debitage, and 15,000 nonceramic artifacts of a wide variety of mediums were uncovered.[19] I had a well-organized laboratory and a student trained to run it, and further, during the last part of work, my friend, Jim Ford, who was working over the mountain on the coast of Veracruz, was available to argue with me about typology, diffusion, temporal relationships, and so forth. Thus, using the best tenets of typology and systems for establishing chronology and relationships that I had been using for many years, in record time we set up our types, established our 12,000-year cultural sequences (then the only complete one in the New World), and indicated ancient temporal and spatial relationships.

Standardizing Typology and Description

I had begun to feel all was not right, however. At a session on lithic typology at the Americanist Congress of 1962, I pleaded for a more standardized set of definitions of attributes to be codified into some sort of a major handbook and suggested that perhaps modes could be determined more uniformly by statistical formulae programmed for computers. In the afternoon session Alex Krieger, who had attempted to codify attribute definitions, echoed my sentiments and suggested that a center for nomenclature and taxonomy be set up similar to the one used for the Linnaean classification in the biological sciences.

Paul Weir, then director of the American School for Anthropological Research of Santa Fe, later offered the facility of the school for such a center, as well as funds for a meeting, and Krieger and I expanded our plans for the conference and the center. We had one meeting with a number of others, set up some uniform definitions for lithics, and started to codify projectile point attributes for IBM cards so that further statistical research could be done for deriving modes. We all left the conference feeling fairly pleased with ourselves and all with assigned duties to record our projectile points in the prescribed IBM card manner.

Eventually I did fill out some of the cards for Tehuacan projectile points, and a staff member suggested that I expand the system to include all lithic attributes. But our reports of lithic typology in Tehuacan utilizing the older system were going so well that we never progressed very far with this new method. However, it still seemed like a good idea, and when I started a brief teaching stint at Calgary in a year-long methods and theory seminar for the top graduate students, I had them define the attributes of all kinds of lithic materials, code them on IBM cards, and have the computer separate them into classes on the basis of similarities. This work helped to standardize lithic terminology and organize it so anybody could record the lithic attributes.

The Ayacucho program then presented the opportunity for expanding this system.[20] In the first two seasons, I classified (using the old system) a tremendous amount of lithic materials skillfully dug from a series of beautifully stratified ancient sites. Then a graduate student with computer expertise joined the expedition to get field experience. By the time the third season rolled around, we had decided to try out the new system for lithic typology. We had excellent materials, the student had free computer time available at the University of New Mexico, and we had lots of cheap but willing Peruvian social anthropology student labor to record the attributes on IBM oriented forms.

We first made a set of basic instruction card definitions for lithic material (noting the dorsal and ventral surface, tip or distal end, right and left edge, and so on) and put together booklets of attribute definitions to be placed on the cards. Columns 1 to 23 of the cards were concerned with metrics, columns 26 to about 124 concerned features of manufacturing techniques (chipping features) attributes, and the rest of the columns were concerned with morphological forms. For instance, column 124 concerned the general outline of artifacts (line 0 was indeterminate, line 1 preshaped, line 2 ovoid, line 3 lenticular, line 4 round, line 5 squarish, line 6 rectanguloid, line 7 triangular, line 8 teardrop shaped, and line 9 stemmed or basically notched). These instructions, definitions, and printed sheets for filling out the attributes were then printed in Spanish, and from ten to twenty Ayacucho University students took each chipped artifact one at a time and recorded its defined attributes on the correct form sheet, which also gave the area, site, depth, and horizontal provenience, as well as a portion for a drawing of the artifact.

By September 1971, 5,000 or 6,000 of our approximately 20,000 lithic artifacts had been so recorded on our field sheets. These data were then transferred to IBM cards and fed into the computer, which was programmed to do cluster analysis. Within two years, we had dendritic graphs of the various attribute cluster groups, and the types had been plotted on tables that showed the stratified occupational zones of the various excavated sites. For cluster groups (now recognized as types because of the chronological as well as morphological uniqueness) that were particularly similar, we undertook chi-square analysis to determine whether they should be lumped or kept separate because of their temporal distributions. Another aspect of the study was to have the computer give percentages of each attribute for each type (uniform type description), and we checked the zone and type chronological alignment by factor analysis, which gave us indications as to what our cultural phases were in terms of clusters of types factored out as being of discrete temporal periods.

Similar studies are now being undertaken with the lithic debitage (chips, flakes, and cores) by Carl Phagan and Ruth Ann Knudson, both archaeologists who are skilled chippers of flint. Eventually we will print all these data showing not only Peruvian lithic artifact types, but also the definition of attributes, technique, and method as well.

Archaeological chronology studies in the future may become organized and stabilized as to their technique and methods and perhaps even housed in some sort of international centers. I wish I could say the same about the other aspects of descriptive analysis, which concern the analysis and descriptions of cultural contexts (studies that describe the ancient ways of life of the people whose remains are dug up). My own development in this line has been rather different from that of chronological studies, although, of course, they went together in part.

Analyzing Cultural Contexts

In the early 1930s and 1940s I was only peripherally interested in cultural contexts. Some ethnologists and social anthropologists indicated that we might be able to interpret how the various kinds of artifacts were made and used by comparing them with those of modern living primitive people. Often I had ethnologically oriented discussions with June Helm, John Murra, and Joe Caldwell about the use and functions of artifacts, and I speculated about whether my Middle Mississippi people might have had a way of life like those of Redfield's folk society. I was impressed by Walter Taylor's *Study of Archaeology* in 1948, which charged that we were not using all of the information we dug up to reconstruct ancient lifeways.[21] Then during my 1948 Iroquois pottery studies, I was impressed by findings that had appeared in excavated Iroquois longhouses (figure 1.1, no. 5). Refuse pits containing burned corn, beans, and bones indicated what the subsistence practices of the people had been. The worked bone that appeared near fireplaces on the house floors meant that this was where butchering had been done, and piles of chips elsewhere might indicate where they had done flint knapping. The longhouses themselves suggested that the inhabitants had clans, and the effigy pipes might mean medicine societies, fortification, warlike behavior, and so forth.

My first real interest in reconstructing ancient lifeways did not come until my 1949 digging of La Perra Cave with its well-preserved bones, plant remains, feces, and associated artifacts (figure 1.1, no. 3). Here obviously were good data for determining the ancient subsistence of these peoples. The bones of animals with certain quantities of meat could be translated into liters of food from meat, the wild plant remains into liters of these foods, and the corncobs could be transferred into numbers of kernels that made amounts of liters of food from agriculture. The material provided a basis for reconstructing proportions of ancient subsistence at various periods—which percentage was meat, which was from wild plants, and which was from agriculture. Further, the cut and burned bones, the burned corncobs, the associated grinding stones, and the pottery with burned food adhering to it hinted at how the inhabitants had prepared their ancient food. By comparing the projectile points associated with animal bones, the baskets with plant remains, and the digging sticks with corncobs with the practices and foods of modern living primitive people in the Southwest and Great Basin, we could suggest ancient subsistence activities—hunting, seed collecting, and agriculture.

The 1954 digging in southwest Tamaulipas in various caves where we found even more plant remains further stimulated me to reconstruct ancient subsistence patterns of the many stratified floors representing a sequence of periods and cultures. We found over 3,000 human feces on these floors. Eric Callen, a scientist from Canada, dissected them to determine undigested food particles and also to reconstruct ancient diets and food preparation practices.

Other practices of these ancient inhabitants were reconstructed by comparing the archaeological artifacts and ecofacts with those of living primitive peoples, with the assumption that they were used and made in an analogous manner. Arrowpoints meant hunting, baskets meant basket weaving, flint tools meant knapping, and so on. This was pretty naive use of *ethnographic analogy*. However, other material we dug up in the rich Romero Cave in the winter of 1954 began to cast doubts on my method of using ethnographic analogy for describing these ancient cultural contexts. We had neat floors with lots of material, some of it concentrated in certain areas on the floor. The materials in these areas (later called *activity areas*) were obviously related and involved with the same activity. For example, 2 pebble hammers, 1 antler flaker, 6 cores, 3 used-up cores, 70 chips, 120 flakes, 2 point blanks (Abasolo points), 2 complete points, and 3 complete Tortugas points were uncovered in the southeast part of layer 4 of one of the caves. Obviously, flint knapping had occurred here, but exactly what kind I could not determine from the ethnographic record. Also, I had lots of wooden artifacts or partially made wooden artifacts that were only rarely described in the ethnographic monographs; but even the few published studies about them said little or nothing about actual manufacturing tech-

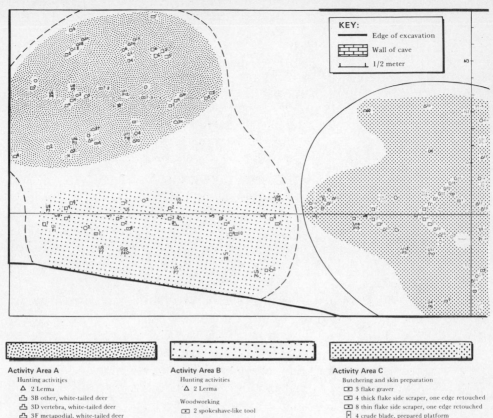

Activity Area A

Hunting activities
- △ 2 Lerma

Trapping
- 3B other, white-tailed deer
- 3D vertebra, white-tailed deer
- 3F metapodial, white-tailed deer
- 3N radius, white-tailed deer
- 3P scapula, white-tailed deer
- 3T antler, white-tailed deer

Trapping
- 6H humerus, cottontail

Butchering and/or skin preparation
- 4 thick flake side scraper, one edge retouched
- 5 thick flake side scraper, two edges retouched
- 6 thick flake side scraper, one edge utilized
- 7 thick flake side scraper, two edges utilized
- 2 crude, keeled end scraper
- 3 crude, ovoid, plano-convex end scraper
- 4 crude, long, flat-flake end scraper
- 3 flake chopper
- 6 ellipsoidal chopper
- 4 crude blade, prepared platform
- ☆ 1 worked antler or bone

Flint knapping
- ◇ 18 muller or hammerstone
- 4 blocky-core chopper
- 5 domed scraper-plane or core
- 6 flat-topped scraper-plane or core
- ○ cores
- U number of flakes without platforms per square
- P number of flakes with platforms per square

Activity Area B

Hunting activities
- △ 2 Lerma

Woodworking
- 2 spokeshave-like tool

Skin preparation and/or butchering
- ? end scraper fragment
- 2 crude, keeled end scraper
- 3 crude, ovoid, plano-convex end scraper
- 4 crude, long, flat-flake end scraper
- ? side scraper fragment
- 8 thin flake side scraper, one edge utilized
- 10 thin flake side scraper, one edge retouched
- 3 crude blade, unprepared platform
- 2 slab chopper

Flint knapping
- ○ cores
- U number of flakes without platforms per square
- P number of flakes with platforms per square

Activity Area C

Butchering and skin preparation
- 3 flake graver
- 4 thick flake side scraper, one edge retouched
- 8 thin flake side scraper, one edge retouched
- 4 crude blade, prepared platform
- 2 crude, keeled end scraper
- 3 crude, ovoid, plano-convex end scraper
- 4 crude, long, flat-flake end scraper
- 3B other, white-tailed deer
- 3C rib, white-tailed deer
- 3E phalanx, white-tailed deer
- 3F metapodial, white-tailed deer
- 3H astragalus, white-tailed deer
- 6D femur, cottontail
- 6F ulna, cottontail
- 6G radius, cottontail

Plant collecting and preparation
- ◇ 4 cylindrical pestle
- ◇ 19 metate fragment
- 2 setaria cf. macrostachya
- 4 grass quids
- 20 prosopis juliflora seeds (mesquite)
- 55 agave spp. leaves
- 38 opuntia spp. leaves (prickly pear)
- 39 opuntia spp. seeds (prickly pear)

Flint knapping
- ○ cores
- U number of flakes without platforms per squar
- P number of flakes with platforms per square

Winter microband occupation 7 — — — — — — — — —

Spring microband occupation 8 ————————————

Figure 2.1

*Activity areas of Zone XXIII of Coxcatlan Cave (Tc50),
with a key to their artifacts and ecofacts.*

nique and use. This was even truer of the hundreds of knots, pieces of string, baskets, beautifully decorated mats, and textiles we had found. Fortunately Irmgard Johnson of the National Museum of Anthropology of Mexico explained to me how many of the kinds of string or yarn were made, as well as whether the various textiles were made on a loom; she could even tell what kind of loom had been used. She occasionally used ethnographic data in her explanations, but more often than not, she actually made the string or yarn and showed that when it was made in certain ways, telltale marks were left indicating that it could have been made only in that manner. Thus, with my other artifacts, such as baskets, mats, and wooden tools, I began to try to make and use them and record the use or wear marks that resulted. I was beginning to do *experimental analogy archaeology.*

This is when I began to realize that ethnographic analogy did not give proof of how a tool was made or used but only gave a hypothesis about how it might have been used that had to be checked by experimental analogy or archaeological association. For instance, one bone tool shaped exactly like an awl used by the Shoshone tribe came from an activity area filled with baskets and basket fragments; what is more, it had back and forth polish on it, not round and round polish as did awls for piercing leather. Ethnographic analogy gave the hypothesis that this was an awl, but experimental analogy—the back and forth polish we got when we used it for weaving, as well as its association with baskets— determined that it was probably a weaving tool. Thus by the time of the Tehuacan expedition of 1960, we were beginning to be more sophisticated in our reconstructions, and we knew that ethnographic analogy gave hypotheses, not proof. It suggested a new approach, which we used when we began to study the tremendous amount of data from ancient Tehuacan cave floors.

We attempted to reconstruct the way of life on 200 to 300 ancient floors with a thousand or so activity areas, as well as give floor plots of each for others to use for their interpretations in the future. As we moved our estimation from liters of food to kilograms to calories by looking at nutrition charts and we used artifacts as well as food to estimate various kinds of subsistence per season per ecozone per culture, our subsistence reconstructions improved. We were able to reconstruct textile-making activities as well as many other technological activities and even determine the seasonality of floors. We made guesses about ancient populations and length of occupations, and we undertook fairly sophisticated attempts to reconstruct chipping activities. But our description of pottery use and manufacture, as well as the reconstructions of many other technological activities, were very poor, although they were better than our attempts to reconstruct ancient social organization or information. We still had much to learn.

Our methods improved slightly with our analysis of the Ayacucho materials. We used photomicroscopic observation of use-wear on artifacts in the technique S. Semenov invented in Russia. This was done for us by Carl Phagan, then a graduate student who chipped flint and had done studies of flint knapping activities.[22] Bone studies and subsistence analysis should be much improved in our future studies. We are still fumbling along, perfecting techniques as well as improving methodology, and our field—as well as I—have a long way to go.

All data collection, analysis to determine chronology, and study of cultural contexts leads mainly to reconstructing ancient cultural history. Basically this is telling *how* things happened, and further analysis of these cultural-historical integrations—cultural sequences—should lead to determining *why* things happened. Once we begin to ask this question we have entered the realm of theory.

ARCHAEOLOGICAL THEORY

Theory, according to *Webster,* is the establishment "of apparent relationships or underlying principles of certain observed phenomena which has been verified to some degree," doing or attempting to do "science," if you will. Determining exactly when I started on such an arduous road is very difficult. Certainly my father's attempt to teach me mathematics and show me his work in spherical geometry, as well as my mother's interest in chemistry, must have affected me at an early age. While I remember nothing that happened in my secondary school years concerned with science, two teachers stand out in my mind in my early college years at Colgate. One was "Hy" Hylander, who taught biology and general science with a sort of enthusiasm that was contagious. The other was "Doc" Adams, a great teacher, who taught logic and the philosophy of science. In fact, he introduced me to two books, Mill's *Method of Logic* and Cohen and Nagel's *Scientific Method,* which I read in various places for pleasure.

The big advances in my thinking came when I studied at the University of Chicago in the 1930s when it was a center of intellectual ferment. The undergraduate social science courses with Dr. Paul Douglas in political science, Dr. Louie Wirth in sociology, Dr. "Ollie" Olson in paleontology, Dr. W. Krogman in physical anthropology, Dr. H. Cole in history, Dr. Andrade in linguistics, and others were memorable. In my senior year the Radcliffe-Brown functionalist anthropology propaganda began with courses by Fred Eggan, Lloyd Warner, and Sol Tax giving the folk society course for Robert Redfield. Now I was beginning to learn the jargon of social science, if not the methodology. The course I remember best was the methods one taught by Robert Redfield. It often was compared with the Inquisition, for students had to write three papers on the works of various famous social anthropologists. This work required our reading four or five monographs of each. We each were to be discussants on three other papers, and we were to read our three written papers in class, only to be criticized by the discussants and, worse, by Redfield, who had had experience as a cross-examining trial lawyer. My first paper was on Ruth Benedict, and I chose to defend her pattern of culture. What they did to me in the criticism period could best be described as slow drawing and quartering. The next paper was on the works of Emile Durkheim, and I did a little better, in large part because I had read more, had carefully checked the logic of my paper, and was more enthusiastic about the comparative methods.[23] Redfield agreed with me that Durkheim's hypothetical dichotomies of his division of labor were related to his own folk and urban concepts. In my final paper and its defense, I even drew a compliment from Redfield to the effect that it was pretty good, particularly for an archaeologist. This paper, on Julian Steward, emphasized his great monograph, *Basin-Plateau Aboriginal Sociopolitical Groups.*[24] Steward was actually talking about something that could be called a science of archaeology: cultural systems of functionally interrelated parts, an ecological approach, hypotheses based upon deductive analysis of sequential systems, and testing of these hypotheses by the comparative method to derive generalizations. If I had a theoretical base in the 1940s, it came from Julian Steward's ideas. These ideas were modified by two other friends with whom I often talked theory, Leslie White and Jim Ford—hard-core evolutionists or neo-Marxist (or cultural) materialists.

I wrote down some of my thoughts on method and theory in my monograph of the Sierra de Tamaulipas, and in the final section of that book, I attempted to derive hypotheses about cultural change by analysis of that sequence and suggested testing it by the comparative method.[25] From many standpoints, my advances in theory were limited in the 1950s; perhaps I was just too busy to think or reflect on science.

In the 1960s, I started to move toward an interest in systems theory, especially when I realized that in the 12,000-year-long Tehuacan sequence, no single cause—materialistic or otherwise—was going to explain all cultural change at all times.

The penultimate stage in my development in theory occurred when I went to Ayacucho to do further investigations on the origin of agriculture. Basically the object of this project was to obtain comparative data to test hypotheses based upon the Tehuacan cultural data from a new standpoint and to analyze archaeological phases (now thought of as a cultural system) to determine why and what made them change. By 1972, I was ready to examine my equally long Peruvian sequence to see if these data were comparable and to test my Tehuacan-derived hypothesis. I began to set down my hypothesis about why agriculture originated and to test my analytical conclusions with comparative data.

Then in 1973 McMaster University appointed me Whidden Lecturer and offered to publish my speeches on theory. The result was an earlier volume entitled "The Science of Archaeology?" Since then I have suffered heart trouble and heart surgery. I spent part of my recovery period reconsidering theoretical matters, and the result is this second book. Even now I am working on theory concerning energy flow systems in Tehuacan. I hope that each effort will get better and better, and perhaps one of these days, I can remove the question mark from the title of this book.

THE GREENING OF AMERICAN ARCHAEOLOGY

My own personal development as an archaeologist somewhat parallels what has happened to the field of New World archaeology as a whole over the last century and a half. Thus, it seems appropriate to consider briefly the development of New World archaeology during that period before jumping into a full consideration of theory and method.

The Period of Discovery: Data Collection

The first question is, When did New World archaeology begin? Unfortunately, the answer is just as cloudy as the answer at present of when man came to the New World. Certainly the early explorers asked where the Indians came from and who had built the ancient archaeological monuments in the New World. These were the problems of this first period of American archaeology, the *period of discovery* (or, if I name it in terms of life stages, the *period of the conception of archaeology*). When the period began is difficult to determine for it is probable that some sailor of Leif Ericson or Columbus or the early Spanish conquistadores dug in ancient graves or monuments to find answers to the above questions. If so, they were the true founders of American archaeology, but as of now, I see only one legitimate claimant for our fatherhood with documents to prove it: Thomas Jefferson. He reported on his 1784 excavations of mounds in Virginia to determine the nature of these mounds, if they had been built by Indians, and if so, when they or others had built them. His report, published by the American Philosophical Society in 1799, is a paragon of meticulous reporting based on careful digging, as well as thoughtful note taking and with well-reasoned conclusions. Jefferson compared the mound skeletons he found with those of known Indians and estimated the antiquity of the mound by counting the rings on the trees that were growing on top of the mound.

Others who did digging or used archaeological data to answer these problems of this period, which lasted until about the Civil War, plus or minus ten years, include Ephram George Squier and Edwin Hamilton Davis, who dug and mapped mounds in the 1840s; Dr. Montroville W. Dickeson of Natchez, Mississippi, who in 1846 dug up an early human pelvis; Caleb Atwater who in 1820 reported mounds in Ohio; Albert Koch with his 1830 fossil digging in Missouri; and Paul Lund's 1830 work in Lagoa Santa Caves in Brazil.

The Evolutionary Period: Data Interpretation

The end of this period and the beginning of the next coincided with the rise of Darwin and the theory of organic evolution, with its obvious implication concerning the possibility of cultural evolution. In both hemispheres this event marked a turning point in archaeology and the rise of a new period that could be called the *evolutionary period* (or the *period of the early infancy of archaeology*).

The questions asked at this time were of an evolutionary nature and revolved around the problem of whether man had evolved in the Americas as he had in the Old World. Was there a Paleolithic period? Was it followed by a Neolithic and then civilized periods as it was in the Old World? Often this latter question was ill defined, and there became a sort of sequel: Who were the Mound Builders? Were they part of the evolution of the American Indian? Both problems were attacked with considerable vigor, and the first great period of American digging ensued. At this time, roughly from the Civil War to the turn of the century, exploration characteristic of the previous stage continued. There were the great discoveries of Frederick Catherwood and John L. Stephens in the Maya area, John Powell's explorations in the American West, Gustau Nordenskiold, William Prescott, and Hubert Bancroft's well-documented discoveries in Mexico and South America, the Whetherills' excavations at Mesa Verde, and many others. Unfortunately, many of these were not so well dug or documented.

Often the literature of the time vibrates with opposing views about American Indian evolution. Two opposing forces began to appear—the government experts, who believed that there was no New World Paleolithic or very old Indian remains, and the experts and professors in the private museums, foundations, colleges, and universities, who believed that there was early New World evidence. John Powell and Cyrus Thomas led the government troops early on, and William H. Holmes and Ales Hrdlicka carried on in the later period. In opposition to them were a host of profes-

sors and archaeologists, among them George Peabody, Frederick
Putnam, and Othniel Charles Marsh of Harvard, Charles Peabody
of Andover, Ernest Volk of New Jersey. Throughout these two periods, the government forces were not only vociferous but vicious.
They usually carried the day until the final victory of the Folsom
site in 1926 when forces for early man in the New World not only
won the war but opened the way for earlier and earlier New
World remains to become accepted, until today when the forces
(including me) for the concept of man coming into the New
World some 70,000 years ago, plus or minus 30,000, are steadily
validating their claims.

Although the Paleolithic problem was not resolved during
this period, the other problem—concerning the Mound Builders—
was. From many standpoints, two mound diggers, Warren K.
Moorehead and Robert Singleton Peabody, who often backed him,
were leaders in getting evidence that Mound Builders were American Indians and that they were of various types and periods,
mainly in the two to eight centuries before the discovery of America (by Columbus or Leif Ericson). A host of others—Clarence
Moore, Stephen Peet, William Nickerson, William M. Beau-
champ, Henry Schoolcraft, Cyrus Thomas, and Henry Henshaw—
also were involved in mound digging, often with methods that
left much to be desired and which were to be vilified by the New
Archaeologists of the next couple of periods. However, they did
bring a solution to what was then a major problem of archaeology:
they preserved in large quantities irreplaceable artifacts that
otherwise might have been lost or looted. In fact, if these mounds
had stayed until today when looting is so rife, probably only a
small percentage would now be preserved.

The Reactionary Period: Better Data Collection

The *reactionary period* (or *traumatized infancy period*) had
its good and its bad points. Certainly Franz Boas and his followers
attacked the evolutionary theorists with considerable force and not
only almost completely stopped speculation in this line but almost
stopped any consideration of theory (other than historical) by
archaeologists. Second, American prehistoric archaeology was
clearly made a field of anthropology and cut off in a decisive manner from classical archaeology and from much of Old World ar-

chaeology (which with good reason had remained an independent field from anthropology). Since American archaeologists were now studying American Indians, along with the New World ethnologists and social anthropologists, this melding of interests initially had considerable value. Now, however, because of the bias of ethnology and social anthropology against archaeological investigations, as well as other theoretical considerations and their lack of producing any new or useful ethnographic analogous materials, plus the fact that many anthropologists use archaeology for administration and/or political purposes, this originally happy marriage has long since foundered. But in spite of this one unfortunate direction, the Boasian approach with its insistence on rigorous data collection and the scientific collection of archaeological information for the reconstruction of sequences of ethnic ways of life had great virtue. It led to great projects with fine chronological data, such as those done by Alfred Kidder, Nels Nelson, Leslie Spier and others in the Southwest, Julio Tello and Max Uhle in Peru, George and Suzanna Vaillant in the Valley of Mexico, Kaj Birket-Smith, Thorkel Matthieson and Diamond Jenness and others with the Eskimo. Data collection and archaeological field techniques were much improved, and a great emphasis was placed on building solid archaeological chronologies. The paradigms of archaeology were the same as those of ethnology—histories of ethnic groups—and theory could wait until we had collected "sufficient" data.

The Descriptive Period:
Analysis and Description

The archaeologist could not go on playing without purpose in the dirt forever. One of these days he had to put together all the things he had dug up and think about what it meant. Thus began the *descriptive* (or *synthesizing*) *period* from roughly 1931 to 1962 (to put it in life stages, the *primary school childhood period*).

The amount of digging moved ahead at a logarithmic rate, an increase made possible by the WPA, the coordinator of Inter-American Affairs (the Viru Valley project), salvage archaeology, and eventually archaeology in departments of anthropology, which had greatly expanded because of American's post–World

War II foreign affairs interest in other places, people, and, therefore, periods. In no time at all, attempts were made to synthesize
this great and rapidly accumulating mass of new archaeological
data, and books and articles doing just that began to appear.[26]

There was a need for a theoretical basis, however. As more
and more analyses of archaeological materials were made and as
more and more anthropology departments diversified, the Boasian
approach centering on the reconstruction of ethnographic peoples
appeared to be very sterile to many archaeologists. American archaeologists were also being influenced by such Marxists or cultural materialists as V. Gordon Childe [27] and Grahame Clark; [28]
others listened to Leslie White's neoevolutionist talk about energy
and culture; [29] some of us heard another approach to systems
theory from the functionalists like Alfred Radcliffe-Brown; [30]
some like Clyde Kluckholm [31] and Walt Taylor protested the lack
of theory in our archaeological approaches; others like Al Spaulding just protested about most of what we were doing.[32] Archaeologists were not only talking to anthropologists but, more significantly, by the 1960s they were beginning to talk back to them,
particularly to the ethnologists, whose data they had outgrown,
and to the social anthropologists, who talked of closed cultural or
social systems, not the ones that at times had tendencies to become
the kind of open systems archaeologists were interested in.

Revolutionary Period: Theory

Thus, the *revolutionary period* (or *revolting adolescence*) set
in. We are still in this stage, which I find difficult to describe,
largely because we are still in it. Some, especially those who call
themselves the New Archaeologists, feel that they can define this
new trend, which they consider began with the writings of Lew
Binford in the early 1960s. One of his disciples, Mark Leone, has
perhaps most lucidly written about this New Archaeology in *Contemporary Archaeology,* in which he identifies its three characteristics: an adherence to Leslie White's theories on cultural evolution, a concern with ecology or at least cultural ecology, and the
advent of systems theory with a use of computerized statistics.[33]

I do not disagree that such trends are occurring in this new
period, but I feel that Leone has not gone far enough. His statement is limited. Although a few may be interested in the theories

of Leslie White, I believe that there is now a major interest in social or cultural theory, and the hypotheses archaeologists are interested in testing with the comparative method come not just from cultural materialism and neo- or paleo-Marxism but also from functionalism, cultural ecology, history, economics, geography, demography, biological ecology, and so forth.

Leone's second characteristic, which concerns an interest in ecology, also represents only part of what, I believe, is really happening. What has developed, perhaps out of the studies of cultural ecology of Julian Steward, as well as the concern of the functionalists like Radcliffe-Brown with social and natural systems, plus the development of sophisticated systemic biological and physical ecological systems, has been a sincere interest by archaeologists in systems theory and cybernetics. This means reconstructing or constructing from the archaeological record not only models of ancient cultural systems but conceiving the sufficient (triggering) or necessary (prerequisite) causes of systemic changes in terms of crises in the flow of elements or types of feedbacks in cultural systems that may become at times open (unstable) systems.

The third general characteristic, which concerns the use of computers, represents only the surface of the iceberg. The important development is that archaeology has become deeply involved with many other disciplines—not just statistics and computers. This relationship has been almost as varied as the personalities of the archaeologists concerned. Certainly the old multidisciplinary approach with groups working in many fields doing research in the same area continues, and, of course, the Boasian approach exists where the five so-called fields of anthropology—physical anthropology, archaeology, ethnology, linguistics, and social anthropology—do research together on an area, region, or people. These types of studies often are attempted by an anthropology department more for administrative reasons than scientific ones.

Most important has been the development of an interdisciplinary approach, which is based upon three assumptions. One is that a number of different fields attacking the same problem will more likely produce better solutions than but a single approach.

The second is that the interdisciplinary approach will be interstimulating and have a sort of "hybrid vigor" effect. Often the two or more fields attacking a similar problem use rather different techniques and methods that often are unknown to each of the groups involved, and further, this close working together may lead to each using the other's methods or techniques to modify their own or both to develop new methods and techniques because of the interstimulating experience.

A third assumption seems to be that the barriers between many of the disciplines and fields are rather arbitrary. Thus, archaeology becomes another part of the general social sciences and may become intimately associated with many other fields, such as botany, geology, and vertebrate paleontology. While we still may have a major concern with culture, like anthropology, once we have said this or repeated the litany, "archaeology is anthropology or it is nothing" (perhaps to get grants or opportune advancements in institutions dominated by social anthropologists), it is time to move on and face reality. Archaeology has a kind of uniqueness, for it almost alone is trying to become a science of past culture or the material results thereof, but its interrelationships are numerous and diverse. Thus, although it is interdependent with many other disciplines, it is also independent, and now seems to be the time to cut its umbilical cord to anthropology.

Having touched upon the theoretical assumptions of the interdisciplinary approach, let me say a word as to its methodology or strategy, which is unique and distinguishes this approach from others. Basic to the whole approach has been the explicit defining of a specific problem so that it is relevant to archaeology and to other fields. This does not mean the archaeologists necessarily initiate such definitions, and certainly, in my own case, the problem of the origin of corn agriculture was defined by Paul Mangelsdorf, an economic botanist and geneticist. However, once this initial step has been taken, then real cooperation must begin. This means the education of each in the fields of the other as to what techniques, methods, and assumptions they are laboring under and with. In my own experience, this has meant taking scientists from other disciplines and showing them our field or excavation techniques or methods, how we record the data, how we analyze archaeological data to draw conclusions from or interpretations of the data concerning our mutual problems. Then it is our turn to learn about their work, so we let them do their kind of data collecting with their assumptions, methods, and techniques, which in

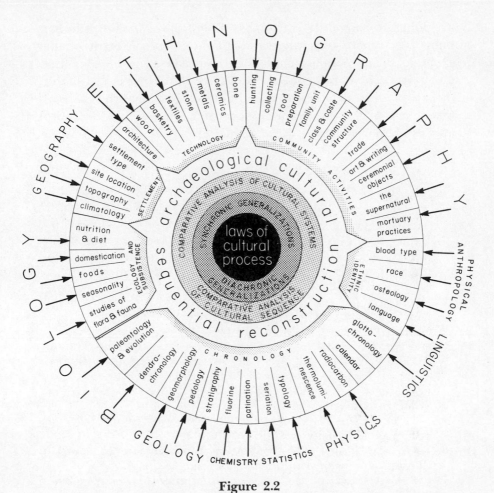

Figure 2.2

The interdisciplinary approach to archaeological problems.

turn we learn about. Once we accomplished this basic learning, we could turn to attacking our defined problem with data derived from their or our methods and techniques and sometimes with data collected based upon new methods developed from the inter-stimulation we gave each other.

This is my concept of the interdisciplinary approach, and in a later part of this volume, I hope to explain it further by examples. The interdisciplinary approach and the recognition that archaeology connects to many other fields is a hallmark of the latest period in New World archaeology when so many archaeologists

are doing so many different things. Where this is leading I do not
know exactly, but certainly the result should be different conclusions, goals, and perhaps methodology—maybe a science of archaeology. If so, then archaeology's next stage should be called *matur-
ity*. I think this stage is still a long way off, but nevertheless let us
take a step in that direction and consider some of the theoretical
aspects of archaeology.

REFERENCES

1. RALPH L. BEALS, GEORGE W. BRAINERD, and WATSON SMITH, *Archaeological Studies in Northeast Arizona,* University of Califor- nia Publications in American Archaeology and Ethnology, vol. 44 (Berkeley: University of California Press, 1945).
2. HAROLD S. COLTON and LYNDON L. HARGRAVE, *Handbook of Northern Arizona Pottery Wares,* Museum of Northern Arizona, bulletin 11 (Flagstaff, Ariz.: Northern Arizona Society of Science and Art, 1937).
3. ALFRED V. KIDDER and ANNA O. SHEPARD, *The Pottery of Pecos* (New Haven: Yale University Press, 1936).
4. FAY-COOPER COLE and THORNE DEUEL, *Rediscovering Illinois* (Chicago: University of Chicago Press, 1937).
5. FAY-COOPER COLE et al., *Kincaid: A Prehistoric Illinois Metropolis* (Chicago: University of Chicago Press, 1937).
6. R. S. MACNEISH, "The Pre-Pottery Faulkner Site of Southern Illinois," *American Antiquity,* vol. 13, no. 3 (1948).
7. J. B. GRIFFIN, *Cultural Change and Continuity in Eastern United States Archaeology,* Papers for the Peabody Foundation for Archae- ology, vol. 3 (Andover, Mass., 1946).
8. R. S. MACNEISH, *Iroquois Pottery Types,* bulletin 124 (Ottawa: National Museum of Canada, 1952).
9. GORDON EKHOLM, *Excavations at Tampico and Panuco in the Huasteca, Mexico,* Anthropological Papers of the American Mu- seum of Natural History, vol. 38, pt. 5 (New York, 1944).
10. A. D. KRIEGER, "The Typological Concept," *American Antiquity* 9 (1944): 271–288.
11. J. FORD, *A Quantitative Method for Deriving Cultural Chronology,* Technical Manual no. 1, Pan American Union (Washington, D.C., 1962).
12. R. S. MACNEISH, "An Archaeological Reconnaissance in the Northwest Territories," *Annual Report of the National Museum of Canada for the Fiscal Year 1949–50* (Ottawa, 1951).
13. R. S. MACNEISH, "The Pointed Mountain Site Near Fort Liard,

Northwest Territories, Canada," *American Antiquity,* vol. 19, no. 3 (1954).

14. R. S. MacNEISH, "Two Archaeological Sites on Great Bear Lake, Northwest Territories, Canada," *Annual Report of the National Museum of Canada for the Fiscal Year 1953–54,* bulletin 136 (Ottawa, 1955).

15. R. S. MacNEISH, *An Introduction to the Archaeology of Southeastern Manitoba,* National Museum of Canada, bulletin 157 (Ottawa, 1958).

16. R. S. MacNEISH, "The Engigstciak Site on the Yukon Arctic Coast," *Anthropological Papers of the University of Alaska,* vol. 4, no. 2 (Fairbanks, 1956).

17. L. KAPLAN and R. S. MacNEISH, "Prehistoric Bean Remains from Caves in the Ocampo Region, Mexico," *Harvard University Botanical Museum Leaflets,* 19, no. 2 (1960).

18. R. S. MacNEISH, A. NELKEN-TFRNER, and I. JOHNSON, *The Prehistory of the Tehuacan Valley,* vol. 2: *The Non-Ceramic Artifacts* (Austin: University of Texas Press, 1967).

19. R. S. MacNEISH, F. PETERSON, and K. FLANNERY, *The Prehistory of the Tehuacan Valley,* vol. 3: *Ceramics* (Austin: University of Texas Press, 1970).

20. R. S. MacNEISH, A. NELKEN-TERNER, R. VIERRA, and C. PHAGAN, *The Non-Ceramic Artifacts,* in *The Prehistory of the Ayacucho Valley, Peru,* forthcoming.

21. WALTER W. TAYLOR, *A Study of Archaeology,* American Anthropological Association Memoirs, no. 69 (Washington, D.C., 1948).

22. S. A. SEMENOV, *Prehistoric Technology* (London: Cory, Adams and MacKAY, 1964).

23. EMILE DURKHEIM, *The Elementary Forms of the Religious Life* (London: Allen and Unwin, 1915).

24. JULIAN STEWARD, *Basin-Plateau Aboriginal Sociopolitical Groups,* Smithsonian Institution Bureau of American Ethnology, bulletin 120 (Washington, D.C., 1938).

25. R. S. MacNEISH, "Preliminary Archaeological Investigations in the Sierra de Tamaulipas," *Transactions of the American Philosophical Society,* vol. 48, part 6 (1958).

26. COLE and DEUEL, *Rediscovering Illinois;* J. FORD and G. WILLEY, "Interpretation of the Prehistory of the Eastern United States," *American Anthropologist,* n.s. 43, no. 3 (1941); WILLIAM D. STRONG, *Introduction to Nebraska Archaeology* (Washington, D.C.: Smithsonian Institution, 1935) ; JOHN R. SWANTON, *Essays in Historical Anthropology of North America,* Smithsonian Miscellaneous Collections, vol. 100 (Washington, D.C.: Smithsonian Institution, 1940); A. V. KIDDER, *An Introduction to the Study of Southwestern Archaeology,* R. S. Peabody Papers of the Southwest Expedition, vol. 1 (New Haven: Yale University Press, 1924); GEORGE C. VAILLANT, *Aztecs of Mexico* (Garden City, N.Y.: Doubleday, 1926);

R. S. MacNeish, "A Speculative Framework of Northern North American Prehistory as of April 1959," *Anthropologica*, n.s. 1 (1959).

27. V. G. Childe, *What Happened in History* (Baltimore: Penguin, 1954).

28. John Grahame D. Clark, *Excavations at Star Carr: An Early Mesolithic Site at Seamer Near Scarborough, Yorkshire* (Cambridge: Cambridge University Press, 1954).

29. Leslie White, "Energy and the Evolution of Culture," *American Anthropologist,* n.s. 45, no. 3 (1943).

30. A. Radcliffe-Brown, *Structure and Function in Primitive Society* (New York: Oxford University Press, 1952).

31. Clyde Kluckholm, *The Conceptual Structure in Middle American Studies in the Maya and Their Neighbors* (New York: D. Appleton-Century Co., 1940).

32. A. Spaulding, "The Dimensions of Archaeology," in G. E. Dole and R. S. Carneiro, eds., *Essays in the Science of Culture* (New York: Thomas Y. Crowell, 1960).

33. Mark Leone, ed., *Contemporary Archaeology* (Carbondale: Southern Illinois University Press, 1972).

3

On the Hopes of American Archaeology

THE SCIENCE OF ARCHAEOLOGY?

Science and Causation

A Definition of Science   Within the past few decades, a number of disciplines have become sciences; that is, they have discovered and formulated in general terms the conditions under which events of various kinds occur, the generalized statements of such determining conditions serving as explanations of all or most corresponding happenings. Obviously the methods of each of these disciplines will be somewhat different, for the events and the conditions they study are of a rather different nature.

The events that concern archaeology are past human activities, which we can discover through studying products of these activities, such as arts, artifacts, or modifications of nature that are the result of human behavior. It is assumed that such entities are

59

not only reflections of ancient activities but that these activities as manifested in the arts, artifacts, or other features were part of a more encompassing system, which might be called a *cultural system*. Furthermore, this system existed within and was interrelated to an even more general system, the *ecosystem*—that complex of components of the environment or natural elements of the universe that are related to each other in a more or less stable manner.

At present, archaeology is trying to become the science of past cultures, a complex of traditional beliefs and conventional understandings that determines patterned behavior and activities. Because we cannot observe at first hand the past patterned behavior, we must instead look at the art, artifacts, and other manmade and used features that materially reflect the past cultures.

Causes and Conditions of Change   Ideally we hope to discover and formulate in general terms the conditions under which one cultural system changes into another one (an *event*). One kind of condition that can bring about this event is a change (or changes) in one or more of the interrelated cultural subsystems that changes the other related subsystems sufficiently to establish a new cultural system. Conditions that trigger or stimulate the event are often referred to as *sufficient conditions* (or *sufficient causes*). In archaeologically observed change, there can often be another set of conditions that allows for these triggerings of sufficient conditions to occur, which by themselves would not cause one cultural system to change into another. Such prerequisite conditions, when they are present, are often called *necessary conditions* (or *necessary causes*).

In addition to our being able to formulate in general terms the sufficient and necessary conditions (as manifested in the archaeological record) that lead to changes of state, developments, or evolution of one cultural system to another, we must devise a "generalized statement of such determining conditions [that] 'must serve' as explanations of the corresponding happenings." [1] This means that archaeology must not only be able to make general statements about why certain sufficient conditions, and perhaps also necessary conditions, have brought about changes in the cultural systems, but it must be able to test these general statements against other independent developments that have gone through the same or a very similar process caused by the same or a very similar set of conditions.

Generalization   Here there is a problem for archaeology: the very nature of the data—past human activity and the results thereof—makes efforts to be scientific take a rather different form from that of the well-established hard sciences. Although we may be able to collect our data in an exact manner like other sciences do (although in fact we usually do not) and analyze these organized data in a manner so as to derive hypotheses to explain why things occurred (which we rarely attempt), we cannot set up experiments —corresponding happenings under controlled conditions—to test the validity of these hypotheses. Our data are dead, and we cannot recreate them to see if the same process would operate in the same manner as it did before. Thus, even the best scientific generalizations about laws of past human activities that we can hope to attain must be of a more probabilistic nature than mathematical equations formulated in the so-called pure sciences. Obviously our methods of deriving generalizations must be very different.

Systemics

Systems in General   Since I consider culture to be a system, it is necessary before going any further to explain what I mean by a *system*. I accept Odum's definition of it as "a complex of elements or components related to some others in a more or less stable way at any one time."[2] This definition emphasizes the stability aspect of the interrelations of the elements, but it also implies that there may be a crucial point when the relationships between the entities in that network become so unstable that the system or the structure of the system may change into a new system or structure, where the elements will become related in still another causal network with a new kind of stability. Thus, some systems may be closed, and relationships within them may be stable. Others may be open; their entities are often in an unstable relationship that may lead to a restructuring of the system. I believe that cultural systems belong to this latter type. Further, although any ecosystem may be either an open or closed system without man's influence, it becomes an open system when it interacts with a cultural system. Since a cultural system is an open system, a significant change in one or more of the subsystems may change its relationship to all other subsystems, resulting in the formation of a new cultural system.

Cultural Systems   Culture as a system has a series of interrelated subsystems within it on at least three general levels of adaptation or interaction. On the most basic level is a series of subsystems concerned with the adaptation of populations or their activities to their ecosystem (*technosubsistence system*). In this group is the subsistence subsystem, the technological subsystem, the settlement pattern subsystem, the exchange subsystem, and others. While these subsystems or elements are related to the elements of the ecosystem in a complex causal network of interaction involving energy flow, or input or output, they are interacting with each other as well as to other subsystems at other levels of adaptation within the cultural systems. They would be extremely closely linked with the series of subsystems concerned with the adaptation or interrelation of individuals or groups of individuals to each other, the *social system*. Within this group are the family and kinship, economic, political, rank, and class subsystems, which again have a causal network of behavioral relationships with each other, as well as with the elements or subsystems of the ecosystem, the environmental adapted subsystems, and the final level of subsystems of the cultural systems. This final group—often called the *ideological system* or *system of values*—relates man or man's activities to the cosmos. The various sets of traditional beliefs and groups of conventional understandings are examples of subsystems of this domain and are interrelated informationally to each other, as well as to all the other subsystems. Thus, a cultural system is composed of a network of interrelated subsystems that are in turn related to a causal network of elements of the ecosystem.

Archaeological Generalizations   The only method I see at present for deriving archaeological generalizations is through comparison, a kind of hypothesis testing. One of the ways the hypothesis to be tested may be derived is by analyzing a sequence of reconstructed cultural systems. One would thus attempt to determine the conditions that caused one cultural system to change through time into a subsequent state (or states) within some well-defined spatial unit, often perhaps a particular kind of ecosystem. Then the statement of the conditions under which this cultural system changed into another in that particular area could be compared with all other analyzed independent developments of similar sequences of cultural systems, without regard to time and with space being independent. If all, or a preponderant majority, of these sequences with their causative conditions turn out to be extremely similar in terms of statistical probabilities to that from which the initial hypothesis was derived, then we can conclude that the hypothesis has been confirmed. At this point the hypothesis becomes a generalized statement of the conditions under which certain events occurred and may serve as an explanation of all previous corresponding happenings. In other words, the hypothesis has become a scientific law or generalization about human behavior or cultural activities.

The Basic Data for Archaeological Science

Cultural-Historical Integration   Although occasional lip-service has been paid to making generalizations and to this kind of prerequisite comparative method and the necessary preceding kinds of analysis of sequential systems, few archaeologists have seriously attempted to use any of the preceding methods. What seems to have happened is that they have not been able to make the transition to this higher level of scientific method from a lower level, which includes primarily collection, organization, and description of data and interpretation of that data at the level of cultural-historical integration.[3] This lack of use seems to stem in large part from the fact that the cultural-historical integrations that have been attempted have not been presented in such a manner so that one can determine exactly what the chronology was of each fully interpreted cultural system in any relatively independent area. Nor can one easily determine the sequence of the various subsystems that may have been causative factors within each of these cultural systems or other related larger systems in these reconstructions or constructions of past ways of life. In other words, cultural-historical integrations are often not amenable to precausal interpretations.

This problem of forming cultural-historical integrations or, to put it another way, "the reconstruction of the life of people in the past and the arrangement of this life into a historical development," is a many-headed monster.[4] First, there is the problem of the aims of archaeology defined as history or prehistory. The purpose of history is the arrangement or reconstruction of human activities into a chronicle of cultural events during literate times, and that of prehistory is the arrangement of human activities into a chronicle of cultural events during preliterate times. In most cases, neither prehistory nor history need have any interest in going on to the higher levels of "sciencing," in generating the explanatory statements that are definitionally requisite to archaeology. Both disciplines are basically descriptive, even where they consider the conditions or explanations of specific or unique events. This often means that the integrative units of time and space for describing formal cultural and ecological content are slightly different in emphasis from those archaeology uses in moving on to the higher levels of sciencing.

For going on to sciencing, the ideal cultural-historical integration or reconstruction would be one that includes sequences of the fullest possible reconstructed systems within an interaction sphere that also includes sequences of activities or cultural subsystems within and through each of the larger cultural systems. The term *stage* for the various parts of the fullest reconstructed cultural system in a sequence can be used here; it is an excellent device for synthesizing a history or chronicle of events of many areas. But it is very static, tends to cloak the types of stimulating cultural interactions of rather different contemporaneous cultural systems that may be basic in causing changes in one or both of the systems, and is internally inconsistent with the strategy of making archaeology a science. *Cultural phase*—a cultural system and the sequences of genetically related phases or cultural systems—seems to be better for our needs.

Interaction Spheres   I also prefer to use the concept of the *interaction sphere* rather than the cultural area for the spatial integrative unit.[5] By interaction sphere, I mean the behaviorally delimited spatial unit within which an interstimulating set of interactions has taken place between (or among) cultural systems so that the cultural systems themselves have become significantly changed. This concept, which has none of the rigidity of the cul-

tural area concept with its implied cultural-environmental correlations, seems much more useful to studies seeking cultural
causality.

Horizons and Traditions   In terms of temporal integrative
units, the concepts of both tradition and horizon can be made
consistent with the sort of ideal cultural-historical integrations
that would be amenable to scientific studies. The necessary sequence of activities or cultural subsystems can be considered as
traditions, defined as "temporal continuity represented by persis-
tent configurations in single technologies or other systems of
related forms." [6]

With a little redefining, the integrating concept of horizon
can be fairly useful. *Horizon* has been called "a primarily spatial
continuity represented by cultural traits and assemblages whose
nature and mode of occurrence permit the assumption of a broad
and rapid spread. The archaeological units linked by a horizon
are thus assumed to be approximately contemporaneous." [7] I
would adapt the definition to make it more amenable to higher
studies by calling it *a period in which approximately contemporaneous cultural systems are related in an interaction sphere.*

Cultural Phases   Thus, the units that seem important on the
cultural-historical integrative level are sequences of phases (regional chronologies), interaction spheres, horizons, and traditions.
They would be derived from and consistent with a series of integrative units on a slightly lower level of abstraction. The most
important of this level is the *cultural phase*—a cultural system
composed of a series of cultural subsystems represented by clusters
of specific kinds of artifacts representing activities that occurred
at a number of components (occupations) in a region (that space
covered by a phase) in a specific time period (preferably defined
in years) when a specific assemblage of (chrono) types was in use.

Cultural Occupations and Activities   These units are derived
from and should be consistent with ones of a still lower level of
abstraction. The most important one at this level would be the
component: associated activities (often represented by artifact
clusters in a series of activity areas) that occur at one spot (an oc-

Table 3.1

Levels of Abstraction of Units or Terms

	Content	*Space*	*Time*
Sequence of cultural systems	Sequence of phases	Interaction sphere	Sequences of tradition and horizons as well as sequences of cultural subsystems
Cultural system	Phase	Region of the phase	Assemblages of types for a period
Cultural sub-system in a subsystem	Component	At a locality or site	Types—modes-attributes clusters existing for certain times
Human activities for a specific purpose (cultural subsystem)	Artifact clusters	Activity areas	Assemblages of artifacts with specific attributes of one moment
Human activity	Artifacts	In situ position	Attributes resulting from use or manufacture at a single moment

cupation in a specific site or locality) and, for heuristic purposes, may be considered a single moment in time. At such moments in time there would be specific types in existence. Types are defined as *attribute-mode clusters that have significant temporal and spatial distributions.* Thus, on this level our classificatory units would be components, localities, occupations of specific times (calendrical dates or seasons of the year), and types. Of course, on the lowest level of abstraction would be the artifacts (and ecofacts) found in an in situ position or in an activity area with other artifacts representing human activity; such artifacts would have attributes representing use or human design at a single moment. Table 3.1 shows the basic hierarchy from the artifacts to cultural phases in terms of various levels of abstraction.

Thus units and even types of study exist on various ideal levels of abstraction. Now let us consider them from an operational standpoint by starting with the finding of an artifact and working our way up to making generalizations or laws about human activities—a science of archaeology.

THE STRATEGY OF ARCHAEOLOGY

Data Collection

Archaeological Reconnaissance   The earliest procedure in arriving at generalizations is *data collection,* and it begins with archaeological reconnaissance. Although successful archaeological survey is often talked of as being the result of lots of energy, pure luck, and inspiration—and I've been accused of using all of them —it actually should involve the use of knowledge about patterned behavior, definite tactics, and hypothesis testing. A hypothesis (or hypotheses)—based on knowledge derived from ethnology, general ecological knowledge, previous archaeological findings, or the finding of the first artifacts—should be set up about where in the ecosystem a certain group (or groups) with certain artifacts representing certain subsistences or adaptive preferences lived. This hypothesis must be tested in the field by examining such environmental zones to see if the same complexes of artifacts occur in these spots. If the hypothesis proves valid, then many sites of this type may be discovered rapidly; if not, then the hypothesis must be modified and again field-tested. The ultimate goal is to find sites that will give a stratified chronology of artifact complexes, as well as enough archaeological contextual information, so that the cultural systems of each time level can be constructed. The better the survey, the easier will be the excavation and field research.

Excavation   This preliminary data collection leads to intensive data collection, much of which comes from excavation. Excavation, done with the most careful techniques possible and accompanied by the best recording known, has two purposes in mind: chronological and contextual observations. The old, reliable technique for establishing a chronology was digging stratified sites, preferably by peeling off superimposed occupation layers. Now there are many other techniques for obtaining relative, chronometric, or absolute dates of specific occupations by interdisciplinary studies, so that these kinds of data may be collected for any occupation stratum, whether in a stratified site or not. The collection of contextual data from occupational layers requires equally careful excavation techniques with particular attention to the locational position of each artifact and ecofact. This information must be supplemented by environmental data collected by the interdisciplinary approach.

Interdisciplinary Data Collection   The preliminary collection of ecological data may often start with surveys in zoology, botany, soils, geology, climatology, and related fields to define the present-day ecosystem and/or ecosystems or microenvironments within which contextual archaeological excavations are occurring.

Description and Preliminary Analysis

Laboratory analysis and description usually are thought of as following the data collection phase, but some sort of work of this nature during the data collection period can greatly enhance the excavation. Preliminary analysis, during data collection or excavation can reveal the lacunae in the chronology and contextual field and thus could indicate where one should collect more data to get a fuller picture.

In spite of the amount of laboratory work done during the data collection phase, the important analysis usually comes during the phase following data collection; like data collection, it is divided into a chronological and contextual approach.

Defining the Chronology   Although the interdisciplinary studies may give fine chronometric and temporal dimensions to the chronology, the basic description of the chronology must be done in terms of the artifact sequence. This means that the artifact and/or its attributes must be considered potential time markers, for the following reasons:

>   1. *Culture is a continuum of interrelated concepts, ideas, and beliefs, through time and space. In other words, any group of people living at a particular time and in a specific place have received a set of concepts, ideas, and beliefs from their predecessors and ancestors. What is more, their culture or cultural system (or that of their ancestors) may have been influenced by the culture of peoples surrounding them. Further, the culture of this particular group at this time and place will be passed on to future generations.*
>   2. *Culture is constantly changing, owing to a variety of*

cultural mechanisms, or to put it another way, a cultural system is an open system. This change may show considerable variation, both as to the particular aspects of the culture which may change and in regard to the speed of change.

3. Culture both patterns and gives consistency to customary behavior. In other words, culture is a system that has an internal order. At any one moment in time, a culture will have a certain core of ideas and beliefs about what is "the right way" to make a pot or a tool, and this "right way" will appear to the maker as consistent with the other aspects of his culture and environment.

4. Artifacts are reflections of culture or activities or the "frozen energy" of the cultural system. As such, they are part of the cultural continuum, are constantly changing, and reflect the internal order of a culture.[8]

In terms of these assumptions, let us consider the method by which artifacts can be studied so that they become recognized types or time markers. All artifacts have at least form and dimension. They are made by different techniques and constructed from different materials. The multiple variations of the interrelated aspects of an artifact are considered to be the artifact's attributes, which are reflections of activities done within the framework or structure of a cultural system. To determine and record the attributes of artifacts is one of the first descriptive tasks of the archaeologist. This must be done by observation, actual handling of the material, and perhaps a variety of statistical techniques.

Once the attributes have been determined for a series of artifacts, comparisons may be undertaken by observation or by using statistical techniques to discover the modes, special attributes that have significance in time and space.[9] When a series of artifacts from one occupation is compared with those from other occupations of a different time period or with those from a different place, some of their features (attributes) may be found to be the same; others may differ. Once the significant artifactual changes are determined, a major portion of the preliminary study has been accomplished. In concentrating on the abstracted mode, however, we have focused on only a small temporally sensitive portion of the whole artifact, and it becomes difficult to discern the overall artifactual changes. We also cannot see the culturally compulsive internal order to which the artifact and its various attributes belong.

Further comparisons, therefore, must be made with artifacts from other sites or occupations of either different time periods or different places to determine groups of artifacts that possess a series of modes clustered together. These groups of artifacts with attribute-mode clusters—a series of interrelated features having significance in time and space—are called *artifact types*. They are tools for establishing chronology and are abstracted by the archaeologist from the continuum of culturally patterned ideas and concepts utilized by the ancient toolmakers. If the types serve as well-defined time and/or space markers, they are valid types for that purpose, and it does not really matter whether the ancient peoples would recognize them as distinctive entities.

Besides serving as time markers to segment a length of cultural sequence, the artifact types are useful in determining the chronological relationships among a number of different sites. The types from any one excavation with a series of superimposed levels of different time periods, of course, show cultural change and trends. When the artifact types from two or more excavations, each with a series of superimposed occupations, are compared, the various occupations can then be aligned in chronological order in terms of the overall trends established by the artifact types. Further, when types from a single occupation, or even from a surface collection, are compared with the artifact types derived from multioccupied sites, these single-period components can be placed in their relative chronological position on the basis of similarity or difference. This relative dating of sites or components within one region by artifact trends tests, supplements, and confirms other methods of relative and absolute dating.

The use of artifact types need not be confined to determining relationships within one area or region. Comparing types of different areas may indicate relationships that can become the basis for aligning the cultural sequence with other sequences, determining changing interaction spheres, or even fixing the territorial limits of those spheres.

At present in New World archaeology, there are considerable differences of opinion about the techniques that should be used in typological studies and the description of types. This difference lies mainly between those of the older school who "eyeball" (personally handle, measure, and study) the artifact, and those adherents of New Archaeology who use a variety of statistical and computer techniques to measure and analyze the artifact.[10] In my own experience, I have mainly used the older techniques with some success and have little success with the computer techniques so far developed. This, however, does not mean that modes and types will not be better determined in a more standardized manner in the future by using the computer, and techniques such as factor analysis, cluster analysis, chi-square programming, etc. Further, there is no reason why the computer print-out may not serve as the type description and all typologies placed in a single computer memory bank with an international organization putting out reports on classification nomenclature as the botanists do with the Linnaean classification of plants. At present, we are a long way from taking this step in archaeological scientific technique, but it will happen. Be that as it may, the general assumption and methodology of typology as mentioned previously will not change fundamentally and the establishment of a chronology of types will continue to be a necessity that must follow data collection.

Defining Cultural Contexts   Generally the study of chronology comes slightly before the study of cultural contexts and is not so complicated. The purpose of studying cultural and ecological contexts is to reconstruct cultural and ecological systems. Starting at the most basic level, each artifact is considered not as a time marker (as it is in the chronological approach) but rather as a result of and part of human activity and derived from the ecosystem that occurred in a particular position with which man had been associated.

Determining its particular position can be discovered by relatively simple means—careful in situ excavations to preserve the original association—but understanding exactly what activity it was a result of and what part of the ecosystem it came from presents more problems. Interdisciplinary data collection may yield information that tells where and in what part of the ecosystem the materials for the artifact were derived, and more important, it can establish a relationship between the cultural system and the ecosystem. Determining what activity the artifact was a result of is basically an attempt to reconstruct part of the technological subsystem. The most obvious mechanism for doing this is by ethnographic analogy; that is, establishing whether the artifact is similar to or the same as ones that ethnologists or others have recorded as being made or used by people by particular techniques. In some cases this is a valid technique for establishing hypotheses for reconstructing the technology involved, but in others there may be no comparable ethnographic analogies. Other types of analyses are necessary. One is by experiment: making and using the artifact or a replica fashioned by specific modern technicians. Another is by determining what other artifacts, debitage, or ecofacts are associated with this particular artifact in the same activity area or in the same archaeological occupation (component). This complex may give further insights into the technological subsystem by ethnographic analogy, by experiment, or by logic. Any conclusions reached are based upon two assumptions. One is that an artifact may be the result of or part of an activity that involved other artifacts, ecofacts, or products of the manufacturing process within a large cultural subsystem. Second, because artifacts were often manufactured in a relatively limited area, the end results, ecofacts, and tools of the trade are often spatially associated.

Ascertaining the use of the artifact or better determining the activity and the cultural subsystem that the artifact was involved in may also proceed by ethnographic analogy. However, since many artifacts may have had multiple uses, the determinations by ethnographic analogy must be considered a hypothesis and must be tested by experimental analysis: inspecting, often by microscopic techniques, the artifact and/or the associated artifacts, debitage, ecofacts, or features for attributes of use (scratches, nicks, polish, and so forth) and then comparing them with similar attributes made under known circumstances.[11]

This method need not apply just to artifacts that have obvious technological implications. Each piece of garbage, botanical and zoological, indicates something of subsistence activities, the elements of the ecosystem, the seasonality of settlement pattern activities, exchange activities, and so on. Burials also have many implications concerning past activities, particularly in the realm of kinship subsystems, rank and status subsystems, and religious activities, as do other features (firepits, architectural remains, and the like). Each artifact is a reflection of activities during human occupancy and thus helps determine the human activities and behavior during specific occupations and their relationships to the ecosystem.

Cultural-Historical Integration

Defining the Component   Determining the associational relationships of human activities, in the jargon of the archaeological trade, is often called defining the archaeological component. A component represents a specific occupation where people undertook activities in a specific space during a moment in time or during a time period sufficiently short so that no major interruptions took place in their activities or their cultural system or subsystems.[12] This means that there will be a cluster of artifacts and ecofacts representing human activities by one or more individuals in specific places.

Excavation will lead to a determination of the extent of the area covered by the artifacts that the inhabitants were using. Sometimes these artifact clusters will be fairly close to each other, and it becomes difficult to determine whether the clusters are merely activity areas within one component, or occupation, or two separate components. Understanding the temporal factors of each of the clusters, either in terms of years or even seasons, may assist in solving this dilemma. (This is one good reason why chronological studies should precede contextual ones.) But if the chronological studies show that the clusters are contemporaneous, the dilemma must be attacked in another manner. One way is to analyze the artifacts of the clusters so as to determine the activities and/or cultural subsystems they represent. If the activities or the cultural subsystems appear to be related sets of activities or cultural subsystems composing a larger cultural system or part thereof, it seems safe to assume that those closely spaced contemporaneous clusters probably were part of the same component or occupation. If the reverse is true, then they may be considered separate components. Thus, one of the major purposes of defining the component is to be able to determine what cultural systems or parts of cultural systems were in existence in specific spatial locations at particular periods of time; heuristically these can be referred to as moments in time.[13]

Defining the Cultural Phases   The other major purpose of defining the component is to establish cultural phases, a relatively stable and complete cultural system that existed in a geographical locality, region, or area for a relatively well-defined period of time. Here we move to a slightly higher level of abstraction, for phases may be composed of one or more well-defined components. I would reserve the term "complex" for a cultural system that is relatively incompletely defined by the archaeological record in the components. Further, I would find the concept of a subphase useful. Although the cultural system as a whole may be relatively stable for a given period of time, there may be minor changes within it such as in pottery types, or other artifact types, that while being good time markers do not immediately change the structure or basic stability of the cultural system.

A phase can be established by studying the artifacts, ecofacts, or debitage representing activities of various subsystems from one or more components to see if a relatively complete cultural system can be defined. In rare cases a single component may have artifacts, ecofacts, debitage, and other cultural features that represent most of the activities within the majority of cultural subsystems of the whole system; most do not. This means that to establish most phases, a series of comparisons of the materials from a number of components must be undertaken to show in terms of assemblage similarities that the components are of the same cultural systems and to supplement and augment the parts of the cultural systems that may occur at any of the related components of the cultural phases.

My concept of a cultural phase is much broader than that utilized by the majority of my colleagues. In fact, many of the cultural phases of Canada, including the ones I have defined, should be called complexes, and the majority of the phases of Mexico and Peru, except mine in Tehuacan and Ayacucho, might best be classified as subphases.

Defining the Ancient Environment   There still remains the problem of environmental or ecosystems studies, literally the *physical contexts* or *ecocontexts* of the social contexts. Two kinds of analysis are germane to these studies. On a more general level are paleoecological studies of the environments of each of the localities of each component of each phase. The work of determination can proceed from the earlier data collection phase of the contextual study when information was gathered about the modern environment of the area (or region or locale) being investigated; it also requires the use of the interdisciplinary approach but with a slightly different emphasis. Although many procedures are possible, one that has been successful involves the formulation of past botanical-climate changes from modern ecological analogues, dated sequences of soil, pollen studies, comparative botany, zoological evolutionary changes, geological studies of land forms and minerals, paleoclimatology, and so on. This means determining a sequence of ecosystems of the geographical unit or units under consideration, and then a temporal correlation of this ecological sequence with the cultural sequences. On the component level, the cultural changes are correlated with the general ecological changes and with changes within the microenvironment or microenvironmental zones.

The second kind of analysis involves the study of ecofacts and artifacts derived from the environments found in the various components and the derived sequential phases. The data gathered may supplement the paleoecological studies and confirm the previous correlations of the paleoecological and archaeological sequence; they may also give direct or indirect evidence about the relationship between the cultural systems and ecosystems throughout the sequence. This kind of study is integrative in its orientations and may lead to better interpretations on the cultural-historical integration level of study.

Defining the Sequence of Phases, Horizons, and Interaction Spheres The next level of study is the lower-level interpretations of cultural-historical integrations in which the chronological and contextual studies are amalgamated into various forms of synthesis. The result should be the construction of a sequence of cultural systems (phases) and ecosystems not only for the regional level but for the regions within an interaction sphere, which may vary considerably with time.

To define the interaction spheres at various time levels, one must determine the cultural exchanges between each regional sequence of cultural systems. This may be done by a number of techniques: ideas and concepts that may have diffused from one region to another, horizon styles, trade objects, and evidence of actual migration or movements of people. Clusters of evidence of exchanges between the various contemporaneous phases or cultural systems of the regional sequences of the interaction spheres thus become the basis for setting up horizons (or periods).

Defining the Traditions   One other aspect is of prime importance: determining changes in traditions, both through and between the phases and within the phases themselves. Each of the various subsystems of the cultural systems represents a tradition at least during any single phase and is related to the phase in some sort of feedback relationship. These feedback systems between the various traditions represented by the cultural subsystems may be negative during the life of a cultural phase or cultural system; that is, the input is equal to the output, but they can also be positive. A positive feedback system is one where the input is not equal to the output or vice versa. Further, this disequilibrium of input and output (positive feedback) between two or more subsystems or traditions may result in one or more subsystems changing into a new kind of tradition. When this happens, the relationships between the various subsystems change, and perhaps even the systems themselves change, thus forming a new cultural system or phase. Thus, the synthesis of the culture systems or phases should include descriptions of the various traditions and relationships of these traditions to each other—basic necessities to the analysis of cultural-historical integrations.

Determining Hypotheses Concerning Cultural Change

General Analysis   The purpose of such an analysis is to derive hypotheses about the necessary and sufficient conditions that have brought about the event of one cultural system or phase changing into another. A new cultural system comes about when one or more subsystems has changed before the other interrelated ones to such a degree that not only do the relationships between them change but the subsystems themselves change. Thus, the first changing subsystem (or subsystems) or tradition (or traditions) is the sufficient condition or triggering cause that brings about the event of one phase changing into another.

One method for deriving these sufficient conditions is to analyze the traditions within each of the phases of each fully reconstructed sequence of an interaction sphere. Such a complete cultural-historical integration is not necessary for deriving, somewhat deductively, hypotheses about why cultural systems change, however. In fact, a sequence of two systems with well-defined traditions in a single locale or region would be sufficient for setting up a hypothesis about what causes one kind of cultural system to change. However, the more complete cultural-historical integrations do have certain advantages; the hypothesis may be more sophisticated and general, and one may not fall into the trap of deriving a hypothesis of a unicausal nature if in fact the causes were of a multiple nature. In other words, while it may be that cultural system A develops into cultural system B because of condition 1, the cause of system B's changing into system C may be conditions 2–3, and system C's changing into D may be due to conditions 1–3, etc.

Deriving Sufficient and Necessary Conditions of System Changes
The exact technique or method for deriving triggering causes has not been fully explored, and attempts in this direction have not been very sophisticated or quantifiable, particularly those attempting to discern information or behavioral flow.

One method to determine the sufficient conditions of change of a system is to compare the elements, flow, or relationship of the early stable part of the life span of a system with the later or final part of the system when it is unstable and about to turn into another one. Those late-changed elements that do not allow the older system to continue and precede the changes leading to the next system may be considered causes or conditions for that system to change.

What new methods will be developed to determine necessary causes or prerequisite conditions remains to be seen. About all we can do now is to compare sequential systems with each other and discover the necessary conditions by discerning what factors, subsystems, or traditions that are important in the evolved conditions were present in the ancestral system. For example, corn, which became domesticated and was a major part of the horticultural-agricultural activities of a cultural system (called the Coxcatlan phase) was already present—albeit in a wild and almost unused form—in the preceding phase. Thus, the existence of corn

or at least other plants that could be domesticated became a prerequisite or necessary condition for the development of the Coxcatlan system.

Most of my hypotheses have been derived from a deductive
approach, but an inductive approach can also be used. In the deductive approach the hypotheses are obtained from the analysis;
in the inductive approach the hypotheses are tested against the
analyzed data. The latter approach, particularly as used by many
archaeologists, tends to be unicausation oriented, so the possibilities of multicausation are poorly studied. Thus, the analysis
of very short local sequences or analysis by the inductive approach
to derive hypotheses about why cultural systems change has some
inherent weaknesses methodologically.

So far, few attempts have been made to phrase cultural-
historical integrations in such a manner as to allow analysis for
hypothesis building, so it is far too soon to speak concretely about
all the kinds of methods or approaches that should be utilized.
For the moment, I recommend an analysis of long, very complete
cultural-historical integrations. There may not be many of these
at present, but at our current rate of archaeological investigation,
this situation should improve rapidly.

Testing Hypotheses by the Comparative Method

The final step in our becoming scientists is even more difficult. We lack hypotheses about cultural change from well-analyzed
cultural-historical integrations in a number of independent interaction spheres, and there has been little thought given to how to
use the comparative method for hypothesis testing. First there is
the whole question of just how comparable the things being compared are. For example, is the cultural-historical integration in
interaction sphere I that sees cultural system A in ecosystem X
change into system B in ecosystem Y because of conditions 1 and 2
really comparable with independent interaction sphere II, which
sees cultural system A in ecosystem X change into cultural system
B in ecosystem Y because of conditions 1 and 2? Once such relationships are established, the question still remains how many
comparisons are necessary to change a hypothesis into a generalization.

In fact, how valid is the whole comparative method for hypothesis testing? Right now, we have few answers to these queries, as well as to many more I have not mentioned, but at least now we are beginning to ask some of the right questions. Tighter case studies, discussion, and thought should lead to plausible and adequate answers. When this happens, archaeology truly will become a science of past human activities.

REFERENCES

1. F. NAGEL, *The Structure of Science* (New York: Harcourt, Brace, Jovanovich, 1961).
2. EUGENE P. ODUM, *Fundamentals of Ecology* (Philadelphia: Saunders, 1971).
3. KENT FLANNERY, "Archaeological Systems Theory and Early Mesoamerica," in B. J. Meggars, ed., *Anthropological Archaeology in the Americas* (Washington, D.C.: Anthropological Society of Washington, 1968).
4. G. WILLEY and P. PHILLIPS, *Method and Theory in American Archaeology* (Chicago: University of Chicago Press, 1958).
5. A. KROEBER, *Cultural and Natural Areas of Native North America* (Berkeley: University of California Press, 1939).
6. WILLEY and PHILLIPS, *Method and Theory*.
7. Ibid.
8. R. S. MacNEISH, A. NELKEN-TERNER, and I. W. JOHNSON, *The Prehistory of the Tehuacan Valley*, vol. 2: *The Nonceramic Artifacts* (Austin: University of Texas Press, 1967).
9. I. ROUSE, *Prehistory in Haiti: A Study in Method* (New Haven: Yale University Press, 1939).
10. MARK LEONE, ed., *Contemporary Archaeology* (Carbondale: Southern Illinois University Press, 1972).
11. S. A. SEMENOV, *Prehistoric Technology* (London: Cory, Adams, and Mackay, 1964).
12. D. S. BYERS, ed., *The Prehistory of the Tehuacan Valley*, vol. 1: *Environment and Subsistence* (Austin: University of Texas Press, 1967).
13. R. S. MacNEISH, *The Science of Archaeology?* (Hamilton, Ontario: D. G. Seldon Printing Limited, 1976).

4

On Being an Archaeologist

AFTER AN INITIAL PERSONAL DESCRIPTION OF MY DEVELOPMENT IN archaeology, as well as progress in the field itself, I outlined the ideal steps that archaeology might take from data collection to becoming a science: making generalizations or laws about cultural change. Although I have dealt with actual accomplishments, nowhere have I attempted to trace an actual archaeological investigation by carrying through these ideal stages. In these final chapters I shall try to show how one can move through these ideal five stages of development. The problem I will consider is one I know extremely well—the origin of agriculture. After a brief description in this chapter of how I became involved with this problem (specifically with the corn problem), I shall consider data collection concerning this problem both in Tehuacan and in Ayacucho. Then in the final part of this chapter, I shall pass on to the next stage—descriptions of chronologies and cultural contexts in the relevant time periods in Meso-America and the Andes, two of the four basic areas in which agriculture developed. In this chapter I will be dealing with getting and describing the data basic to the solution of the problem of the origin of agriculture.

In chapter 5, I will move on to the next higher level of abstraction—making the cultural-historical integration of the data I know best from Tehuacan, Mexico. In the last part of the chapter, I shall attempt to analyze these detailed data and derive some hypotheses about how and why agriculture began in this pristine area of development. The final chapter is the obvious methodological outcome of this endeavor, and I will attempt to test these hypotheses by comparing them with data from not only Meso-America but the Andes and Near East. With these data you can judge yourself how close we are to being a science of archaeology and how well my proposed methodology works.

THE PROBLEM OF THE BEGINNING OF AGRICULTURE

How the Corn Hunt Began

My concern with the problem of the origins of agriculture began one hot afternoon in January 1949 on the dirt streets of Los Angeles in the Sierra de Tamaulipas. It had been a long uphill walk back from Nogales Cave in the Canyon Diablo after closing down that dig. When I had left La Perra Cave late that afternoon two days before because we were finding nothing chronologically very new, my orders to Alberto Aguilar, one of my supervisors, were to be careful because there might be more preserved plant remains, to clean up the walls of our test, draw the profiles, load up the equipment and take it back to Los Angeles, and pack the jeep so we could move out of the Sierras. Alberto had just met me on the trail outside of Los Angeles and his answer to my questions: "Did you bring the equipment and specimens and was the jeep packed?" had been a deadpan "No."

My next question was, "Why the devil didn't you?" (or equivalent thereof in Spanish).

"Because I found what you hoped we might find."

"What was that?"

"Hard to explain."

By this time we were approaching the jeep, which obviously was unpacked, so my next statement was, "It better be good or you'll walk back to Panuco." A big grin broke out on his moon-shaped face, and he said, "Esta muy bueno!" and with that he ran into the house and returned with a box labeled "northwest corner of square N15SW5, depth 14 inches."

As I opened the box, I reflected that other artifacts from a depth of fourteen inches were certainly preceramic—some 3,000 or 4,000 years old. Then there it was! A fragment of a woven mat and three tiny corncobs tied with a string. Preceramic corn had never before been found in Meso-America.

Needless to say, we did not leave the Sierra de Tamaulipas. Instead we spent the next six weeks excavating La Perra Cave—literally peeling off from vertical faces layer after layer of pre-served plant remains, including more tiny corncobs. At this time, these were certainly the earliest corncobs excavated thus far in Mexico, and although few believed me for years to come, they seemed to be earlier than those that came from Bat Cave in the U.S. Southwest. If I was correct, then my finds were concrete evi-dence that corn had spread from Mexico to the United States, and although not even I really understood it then, I was thereafter in-volved in the hunt for the origins and spread of corn agriculture in the New World, and trying to discern how and why corn started anywhere.

During the next three years, I had this material dated by Libby, sent the corn to Paul Mangelsdorf, raised money, hired a crew, and bought equipment for research in southwest Tamauli-pas—an area I knew had caves with preservation.

Throughout much of December 1953, we worked hard and were successful in finding sites, but we never quite found the dry caves with very old preserved plant remains, including corn, that we needed. After all, the finding of even one is a thousand-to-one chance. Fortunately in my preparatory notes, there was a reference to a cave in Canyon Infiernillo in the Sierra Madre in southwest Tamaulipas. Here in 1937, a man named Guerra had guided Javier Romero and Juan Valenzuela of the Instituto Nacional de Anthropologia y Historia to this region where they had found mummies and possible preserved materials.[1] My notes indicated that the climate was right in this region for plant preservation in caves, and, what is more, it geographically had a good possibility for many more caves.

So, besides looking for caves, we also sought a man called Don

Ignacio Guerra who lived in our territory and who had been Romero's and Valenzuela's guide back in 1937. Finally, we caught up with him at his ranch near Ocampo celebrating Christmas. We had a glass or two of his fiery mescal, explained our interest in the caves he had reported to Romero long ago, and before nightfall we were making plans to visit the caves next day. We had only gone out for a visit, so we were ill prepared for the memorable days ahead.

The first day, we rode some thirty miles on horseback. This was particularly trying for us since we were not accustomed to the wooden saddles of the mountain rancheros. To top the very rough day, it was cold and rainy that night, and we were without tents or waterproof sleeping bags.

The next day we survived another fifteen miles, and then we camped in a flea-infested shelter on the mountain top, reputedly just above the cave. The following day we searched in vain, all day, for the trail to the cave, but the thick thorny brush had overgrown it since 1937. That night two local ranchers saw our fire, dropped in for a visit, and immediately recognized Don Ignacio as that famous revolutionary (bandit?) leader.

"Could they help us? Did they know about the caves?"

"Oh yes, they were right over there, and they would come back tomorrow and show them to us."

Although I had some doubts about this, as well as about the characters of these well-armed men, Don Ignacio assured me they were reliable. He then served us all a mighty draught of mescal and put his faithful .38 automatic under his pillow and bid them and us a fond "buenos noche." Both gestures relieved our spirits, and we too slept well, in spite of sore feet, sore rear ends, and flea bites.

Sure enough, the banditos returned in the morning and took us to two magnificent caves where looter holes revealed that these caves had beautiful stratigraphy and abundant preserved plant remains. We had found what we sought way ahead of schedule. Now we could start our excavations, set up our field lab, and maybe find a few more good caves in our spare time.

After a month or so of preparation, crew members Dave Kelley, Peter Grant, and Peter Pratt, and I began excavation in Romero Cave (Tc 247). It was unbelievable; there were seventeen beautifully stratified layers, lots of artifacts, and literally tons of preserved remains—baskets, mats, whittled sticks, string, feces, plant remains, and so on. We used our La Perra technique and it worked like a charm, but we began to notice new, significant information that was to modify our digging techniques and our recording of the data.

As we stripped off our floors, it became apparent that there were concentrations of certain kinds of artifacts on different parts of the floor. For instance, on floor II, the chips and cores were concentrated in two one-meter squares in the southeast part of the floor, and four end scrapers and eleven whittled sticks were found in three squares to the northeast; the mats and string occurred around the fireplace in the center, and so forth. In other words, the people who had been busy doing different things on the cave floor were doing them in different areas of the floor. Our recording of artifacts by five-foot squares was just not exact enough. Instead we would have to record them by subsquare or by their in situ location if we were to work out exactly what their tool kit was for each activity. This meant that in addition to traditional cross-sectional drawings of the vertical profiles of the stratigraphy, we should be making exact plans of each floor as we dug it. When we started doing this, it became apparent that the feet and inches system for recording was very cumbersome; next time we would switch to the metric system.

Gradually, as the crew learned my digging techniques, I left Dave Kelley to dig Valenzuela Cave (Tc 248), which had nine stratified layers. Much later we dug Ojo de Agua Cave with its twelve stratified zones, and Peter Pratt and I went to the southern part of the Sierra de Tamaulipas to do survey. With our survey techniques sharpened by experience, sure enough we found more good caves and we set to work digging them.

The digging was going great, and we were to find lots of material in beautiful stratigraphy, but I was running around like a madman doing too many things at once—survey today, Peter's digs in Sierra de Tamaulipas for the next three days, then a glance at the lab, then off to Dave's digs in the high mountains of southwest Tamaulipas for a few days, and in-between times doing accounts, buying supplies, and getting things shipped off to experts. Gradually it dawned on me that my problems were not technical but basically managerial. Eventually I shifted off the accounting and supply problems to Peter Grant. This worked fairly well, but obviously what I really needed was a full-time administrator who spoke Spanish and was a sort of "old China hand." Gradually, June Helm began to look after the lab, but I still spent a great deal of time doing cataloging and putting numbers on washed specimens. What I needed was a full-time trained specialist in archaeological analysis with whom I could spend considerable time working on crucial problems that would help direct the digging operations in progress.

Eventually we worked out a sequence of nine archaeological phases from 7000 B.C. to 1750 A.D. (with a few gaps in it, of course), which were associated with abundant plant remains. Somewhat to our surprise, our corn was of a different primitive—Bat Cave or pre-Chapalote—highland race and not really as old (about 2000 B.C.) as our primitive Nal-tel lowland race (2500 B.C.) from the Sierra de Tamaulipas. Thus, our new evidence from southwest Tamaulipas was of a negative sort: This area was not where corn was first domesticated.

Narrowing the Search

One conclusion seemed assured, however: early corn remains now available dating between 2000 B.C. and 3000 B.C. (from two areas of Tamaulipas, and from Swallow Cave in northwest Mexico and Bat Cave in the Southwest) were all north of the center of the origin of corn. Therefore, corn must have been domesticated well before 3000 B.C.—and it was a long slow process. There was no Neolithic revolution but a Neolithic evolution in the domestication of corn. But the question was, How far south did corn originate? Could it be that it really came from Peru, as Mangelsdorf and Reeves, the botanical corn experts, had conjectured a long time ago?[2] Since I am a practical fieldman who could find dry caves, the answer seemed to be to look somewhere between Peru and Mexico.

Both Honduras, which had some dry areas and where the people who had worked at Copan had reported caves, and the Zacapa Valley of Guatemala, which Dr. A. V. Kidder had reported as being very dry, seemed like good ideas. In 1958 I was off to Honduras, and I looked around Copán. There were good caves but no preservation and no preceramic; so I went on to Tegucigalpa (good caves, some preceramic, no preservation) and then to

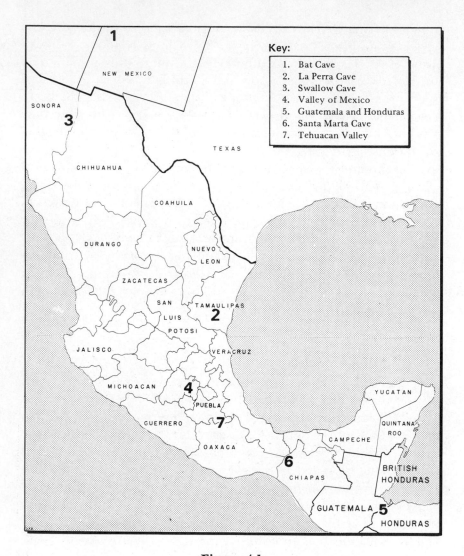

Figure 4.1

The search for early maize in the southwestern United States and Meso-America.

the Comayagua (poor caves, some plant preservation, no preceramic).

After this discouraging stint, I moved into the Zacapa Valley of Guatemala with about the same results. In the high part of the valley in the tropical rain forest, plant preservation was impossible although there were lovely caves; in the dry bottom of the valley where preservation was possible and where we did find preceramic remains, there were no caves.

I next decided to try a little farther north in Chiapas on the border of Guatemala where caves had been reported and where one of them had yielded a preserved textile. I briefly explored around Comitán and Ciudad de las Casas, where there were caves, but the climate was too wet for preservation, and then decided to try one named Santa Marta, which Fred Peterson had found near Ocozocoautla de Espinosa. It was a huge cave, and Peterson's initial test indicated there were stratified preceramic layers. He had found well-preserved bone and stone without pottery, and I thought perhaps there might be a few patches of preserved plant remains.

The stratigraphy of the cave was almost perfect, and we found ten stratified layers, five of which contained many preceramic tools and bones dating from between 7000 B.C. and 3500 B.C. But more important to the corn problem than discovering these first preceramic remains in southern Mexico was the Chiapas pollen profile, which showed corn pollen in the upper five strata but none in the ones older than 3500 B.C. Corn, therefore, was no older down there than it was in the excavations in northern Tamaulipas in Mexico. In fact, it seemed that Chiapas was too far south, while we knew our earlier studies had indicated that northern Mexico was north of the original center of domestication. But at least we were narrowing down the north-south perimeters of where the corn story might begin.

We now knew that corn had been domesticated north of Chiapas and south of our work area in Tamaulipas, Mexico. Further, Sears's analysis of pollen from the Valley of Mexico showed domesticated corn in layers that he dated at about 4000 B.C., as well as in layers perhaps 80,000 years old.[3] Therefore, we could push the northern border still farther south. We had some other facts to help us, for Mangelsdorf's studies of the archaeological corn we had sent him indicated that the wild ancestor probably was a highland grass that might have flourished best in a dry and high environment. A brief perusal of the maps of the area between Mexico City and Chiapas revealed only three major high dry valleys: southern Oaxaca, Tehuacan in southern Puebla, and the Rio Balsas in eastern Guerrero. This was where we should head next.

Hitting the Corn Problem Jackpot

I'd been in Oaxaca many times and had seen some caves. At the end of the 1959 Chiapas season, we had stayed overnight in Tehuacan and had even crawled into a couple of caves on our way into town. On this brief first visit to Tehuacan, I had been pleased to see an old friend of mine from my days in Yucatan, Ricardo Gutierrez, who was now the assistant manager of the Hotel Peñafiel in Tehuacan. Thus, in 1960 around Christmas, after a brief look around Mitla in Oaxaca for caves with only limited success (later investigations using many times more research money were to get the same results), I returned to Tehuacan to see Ricky Gutierrez and we talked into the night about my search for early corn. He arranged for Luis Vasquez, the director of the Museum of the Revolution in Puebla, to help me in my search. Vasquez and a willing amateur archaeologist, Juan Armenta, equipped me with tools, sleeping bags, assorted information about Tehuacan, and, of course, those necessary letters of introduction to all the local Tehuacan authorities. They also lent me their museum's proudest possession, "El Monstro," a 1949 Lend-Lease U.S. Army commando truck. Although better lent than leased, it was a damn good vehicle once the gardening crew of the hotel and I had pushed it in the morning from its perch in front of the hotel so that it could start. With a little bit of luck and careful parking on a hill it would run all day, almost anywhere, and through and over almost any trail.

On the first foray, along the highway between Chazumba and Huajuápam de León, in Oaxaca, we visited sixteen caves, but all were in volcanic deposits too porous to allow for the preservation of vegetal material, although some had preceramic materials. Four other large caves south of Huajuápam near the Pan-American Highway were equally unproductive. A second trip netted four caves near Zapotitlán in Puebla and one just past Tequixtapec, Oaxaca. The latter, and another one near Zapotitlán, had indications of preceramic stratigraphy and possible preserved organic remains, but both were very small. We also found five near El Riego just north of Tehuacan, three just northeast of town along the highway to Veracruz, and three just one kilometer south of Tehuacan. All had preceramic possibilities, but they were not ideal for finding the million-to-one shot—early corn. They were either too wet, had no deep stratigraphy, no preserved plants, or no pre-ceramic.

After looking at thirty-six sites unsuccessfully, I was begin-ning to get discouraged, but there was one more possibility. The local schoolteachers of Puebla had filled out a series of question-naires, and three of these forms mentioned caves in the general area of Tehuacan. The first two caves, one near Altepexi and another east of Ajalpan, revealed little of interest. The final cave, Ajuereado, was located south of a town called Coxcatlan. On Jan-uary 21, Señorita Martinez, who had filled out the form, arranged for a guide, Pablo Bolanos, and her brother Hector to take me to this cave ten kilometers south of Coxcatlan along the edge of the mountains. After a hot, sweltering walk southward through the mesquite and agave, we arrived in front of the cave, and even from a distance it appeared to have exciting possibilities. It was very wide, on a cliff facing north away from the direction of the rain, had a wide talus slope of potentially deep refuse, and was very dry. The surface collection—including chipped stone artifacts, the rock shelter's large size, and the preserved vegetable material, which turned up from under the covering layer of goat dung—indicated that this was a site that had to be tested.

For six days we dug a two-meter-by-two-meter square to a depth of about two meters using a trowel, spoon, and paintbrush This hole was located in back of a large rock roughly in the center of the cave. All the material we uncovered by trowel and spoon was taken out by bucket and put through a half-inch mesh screen. As time went on, we got less and less on the screen and more in the excavating. Slowly but surely we peeled off the occupation of five soil zones and many different strata. Starting at the top we had some Post-Classic remains (700–1500 A.D.), and under it some Classic (0–700 A.D.), and a little bit of Formative (0–500 B.C.), then a sterile layer, and then a thick dark layer, which was obviously preceramic (before 2500 B.C.). On January 27, Pablo stood up from his scratching in the lower layer, reached over to my sorting screen, and dropped a tiny corncob on it. "Is this what you're looking for, Señor?"

I blinked and said, "Where did you find that?"

"Over there in the corner," said Pablo, pointing to the deep-est and darkest part of our test in the northeast corner of the square. I got down in the trench and with a trowel and paintbrush

began cleaning off the area. After a couple of minutes I brushed
out a tiny corncob from the stratum. I was beginning to sweat
now, and before I started to dig again, I looked at the wall of the
stratigraphic cut to see if it might somehow be intrusive.

No way! So clutching the valuable dehydrated corncob in my
left hand, I started cleaning again, struck a small flat rock, cleaned
around it with a paintbrush—and there, sticking out from under-
neath the rock was another minute corncob.

I stood up and told the men we were finished digging. They
looked perplexed, so I said I'd pay them for the full week. We
packed up everything, I took some pictures, finished the profile
drawing, made a map of the cave, and we left.

I dropped the workers in the town of Coxcatlan, drove to
Tehuacan, sent Paul Mangelsdorf a telegram, and then went to
the bar of the Hotel Penafiel to tell Ricky all about it. The big
push was on! We had found the earliest corn and this time, after
all the years of doing wrong things, we were going to run a project
that was as perfect as I could manage.

After January 27, there was no more digging, but we explored
the valley where we were about to start our intensive investigations. We also officially informed the authorities in Mexico City
about our finds.

Then I went back to Ottawa and made a quick visit to Paul
with my precious cobs to show him we had finally been successful.
He agreed that these were what we had been looking for, and we
should now set about making specific plans for our really major
research.

DATA COLLECTION

The first aspect of our research was data collection. Here
rather than presenting data collection for only Tehuacan with the
description of ethnologies and cultural contexts in Tehuacan and
Tehuacan's place in the cultural-historical integrations in Meso-
America coming first and then doing the same thing for Ayacucho,
I shall compare data collection in Tehuacan with that in Ayacucho. Our techniques and methods in the latter case were mere
developments from the former.

Survey

In both areas our initial endeavors were archaeological reconnaissance after we had delimited the area somewhat as to its ecozones. (See figure 4.2.) In Tehuacan, we had to find specimens of preserved corn in dry caves. Thus, the area we chose to investigate after some preliminary study and driving around was one that had fewer than 800 mm of rain annually and that overlapped with areas that had both Monte Alban and Mixteca-Puebla pottery, as

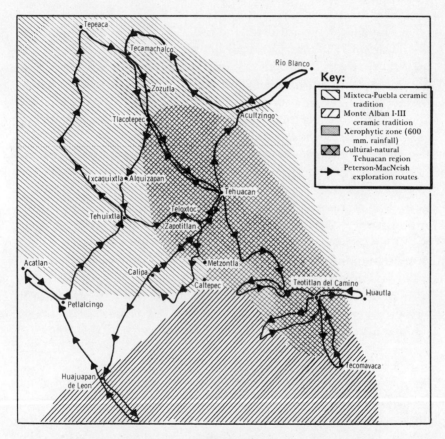

Figure 4.2

Map of the Tehuacan region, showing routes of initial exploration, the Mixteca-Puebla ceramic tradition, the Monte Alban ceramic tradition, and the xerophytic vegetational ecozone. The overlapping of the three zones defined our area of investigation.

well as preceramic materials older than 3000 B.C. in caves.[4] The area we chose was not very well defined, ecologically speaking.

In Ayacucho, there was no such problem, for the valley was ringed with mountains over 4,000 meters high; all microenvirons within it were distinctive and well defined and had similar preceramic and ceramic remains, and all were somewhat different from other adjacent valleys.[5]

In Tehuacan, I worked with Fred Peterson on survey for the first couple of months, and then he carried on alone for the next sixteen. The survey was conducted on a very pragmatic basis, and he moved from one village or town base of operations to another, from one end of the valley to the other. Forms for each site were filled out, and the materials for each site were bagged. The survey moved rapidly, and the catalogs of the bagged material never kept pace. The main purpose was to find sites with stratified remains, preferably preceramic, so a complete sequence of the valley could be obtained, and second, to get a sampling of the kind of sites that existed at all periods in the valley. Generally, those sites that Peterson had found with potentially stratified deposits I returned to for testing. No archaeological survey had ever been done previously in the valley.[6] Our original survey represented, at best, a sort of random sampling, and only about 456 sites were discovered although they contained over 1,200 occupations.

The reconnaissance in Ayacucho was very different from many standpoints. First, considerable survey had been done in the valley by members of the University of Huamanga as well as by me before our project began. Second, we had come to realize from our previous findings in Tehuacan the importance of microenvironments and scheduled seasonal occupations in the origin of agriculture. Thus we attempted to find stratified sites in each microenviron that would yield complete sequences of seasonal occupations. Using Tosi maps of life zones, we subdivided the valley into seven zones more or less compatible with them and surveyed for a sample of the kinds of sites for each period accordingly.[7] This survey was well planned. Angel Garcia Cook coordinated the efforts of as many as eight well-trained students, kept the survey records, and used aerial photography in a sophisticated manner. Further, our laboratory had a full cadre, so cataloging kept up with the survey, and decisions on whether to excavate were based on laboratory analysis of the survey materials, as well as on skilled testing of the sites. We discovered about 500 sites, a much more adequate sample than we had for Tehuacan.

Ironically enough, although this better-done Peruvian reconnaissance discovered sites that upon excavation yielded better cultural sequences in five of its six microenvironments than our survey in Tehuacan, because of local climatic conditions, we did not find many caves with the crucial preserved plant remains. Four out of our five Tehuacan microenvironments yielded preserved plant remains.

Excavation

The archaeological reconnaissance was but the preliminary step in data collection that led to the all-important step of excavation. The techniques and methods for both areas were similarly well done, but our Andean endeavors benefitted from our earlier experiences in Meso-America. (Figures 4.3 and 4.4 show the excavated preceramic and early ceramic components from each microenvironment from Tehuacan and summarize the chronological results of our excavation.)

In Tehuacan our most complete sequence came from the microenvironment termed the alluvial slope, which had a thorn forest vegetation. Here we (mainly Melvin L. Fowler of the University of Wisconsin) dug Coxcatlan Cave with twenty-eight stratified zones and forty-two cultural occupations producing abundant artifactual and ecofactual remains that extended from 10,000 B.C. to the present.[8] What is more, twenty-eight of the stratified occupations came from the crucial period before 2500 B.C. and contained many wild plant and early domesticated plant remains. Also dug nearby was an open site (Ts51) with two floors of the period from 5000 to 6000 B.C., which underlay a floor dated at about 3000 B.C., which in turn was under strata with later ceramic remains.

Another microenvironment with excavations that gave data of the period pertinent to our problems of initial domestication was called the canyons and the dissected alluvial slopes. In this area, we excavated three sites; the most important of these was Purron Cave, where we uncovered twenty-seven stratified zones, which represented thirty-one occupations, giving us an unbroken sequence from 6600 B.C. to 1000 B.C. with some artifactual and eco-

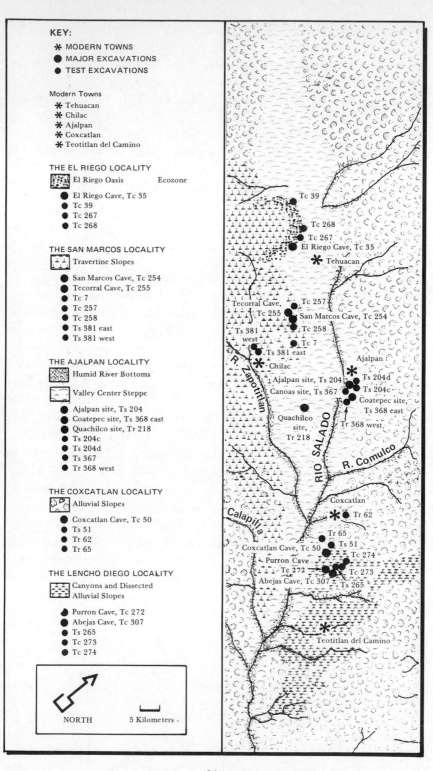

KEY:

✳ MODERN TOWNS
● MAJOR EXCAVATIONS
● TEST EXCAVATIONS

Modern Towns
✳ Tehuacan
✳ Chilac
✳ Ajalpan
✳ Coxcatlan
✳ Teotitlan del Camino

THE EL RIEGO LOCALITY
El Riego Oasis   Ecozone
● El Riego Cave, Tc 35
● Tc 39
● Tc 267
● Tc 268

THE SAN MARCOS LOCALITY
Travertine Slopes
● San Marcos Cave, Tc 254
● Tecorral Cave, Tc 255
● Tc 7
● Tc 257
● Tc 258
● Ts 381 east
● Ts 381 west

THE AJALPAN LOCALITY
Humid River Bottoms
Valley Center Steppe
● Ajalpan site, Ts 204
● Coatepec site, Ts 368 east
● Quachilco site, Tr 218
● Ts 204c
● Ts 204d
● Ts 367
● Tr 368 west

THE COXCATLAN LOCALITY
Alluvial Slopes
● Coxcatlan Cave, Tc 50
● Ts 51
● Tr 62
● Tr 65

THE LENCHO DIEGO LOCALITY
Canyons and Dissected
Alluvial Slopes
● Purron Cave, Tc 272
● Abejas Cave, Tc 307
● Ts 265
● Tc 273
● Tc 274

NORTH   5 Kilometers

factual remains.[9] Nearby Abejas Cave yielded seven cultural strata from about 6800 B.C. to 4800 B.C. with many artifacts and bones; four underlying strata between 3200 B.C. and 2500 B.C. had artifacts, bones, and a few perishable vegetal materials. The other site excavated (Ts365) was an open camp with one occupation at about 4000 B.C.

One other subarea with a fairly good sequence, although there was a gap in it from about 2500 B.C. to 1100 B.C., was the travertine slope environmental zone.[10] One cave (Tc255) had a lower stratum containing artifacts and bones dated at about 6800 B.C., and an open site (Ts381) had a huge roasting hearth about 8,000 years old. Another had a pithouse dating from about 2800 B.C. One small cave (Tc254) had stratified remains with limited amounts of artifacts but a good sample of preserved plant remains. The earliest level, zone F, was about 7,000 years old. Zone E above it was dated at 4150 ± 200 B.C., zone D was dated at 3300 ± 250 B.C., and zone C was dated at 1025 ± 200 B.C.

From the other environmental zone within the travertine slope zone, dubbed the El Riego oasis, three other excavations gave us a sequence from about 2500 B.C. to about 7500 B.C.[11] The more complete excavation from El Riego Cave gave us abundant artifacts and some bones from three superimposed layers. Layer 6 was about 9,000 years old, layer 5 about 8,000 years old, and layer 4 about 6,000 years old. The other excavations were merely test dug in arbitrary levels; the lower levels (8 and 9) were about 10,000 years old, levels 6 and 7 were about 8,000 years old, and levels 4 and 5 were about 5,000 years old.

Excavations from two other environs yielded less stratigraphic data.[12] In the humid river bottoms area, two excavations at the Ajalpan site yielded seven stratigraphic zones from about 900 B.C. to 1500 B.C., while in the Coatepec site (Ts368) there were only four superimposed occupational layers between about 1100 B.C. and 900 B.C. The survey also yielded thirteen surface components that probably ranged in time from 2500 B.C. to 9000 B.C. The other environmental zone, the valley center steppe, had no excavations that directly pertained to the preceramic periods, although the

Figure 4.3

◄ *The Tehuacan Valley, showing principal towns, major excavated sites, and tests in the ecozones.*

ENVIRONMENTAL ZONES / Phases	CANYONS & DISSECTED ALLUVIAL SLOPES — Excavated Sites			Surface Components	ALLUVIAL SLOPES — Excavated Sites		Surface Components	VALLEY CENTER STEPPE — Excavated Sites	Surface Components	HUMID RIVER BOTTOMS — Excavated Sites		Surface Components	TRAVERTINE SLOPES — Excavated Sites				Surface Components	EL RIEGO OASIS — Excavated Sites			DATES
	Tc 272	Tc 307	Ts 365		Tc 50	Ts 51		Tc 50		Ts 204 (Zones C-H)	Ts 368e (Zones J-K3)		Tc 255	Tc 254 / Ts 381w	Ts 381e			Ts 35	Ts 39	Tc 266	
Ajalpan	Zone J			Ts 15					Ts 4			Ts 2046		Zone C						Tc 266	1000 B.C.
Purron	Zone KI, Zone K			Ts 15																	2000 B.C.
Abejas	Zone L, Zone M1, Zone M, Zone N1, Zone N	Zone B, Zone B1, Zone B2, Zone C		Ts 273	Zone VIII, Zone XI, Zone X	Zone C				Ts 204, Ts 367, Ts 368			Zone D	Zone B1	Ts 388, Ts 375, Ts 386, Ts 253	Levels 4-5		Zone D	3000 B.C.
Coxcatlan	Zone O, Zone P, Zone Q1, Zone Q	Zone C, Zone D			Zone XI, Zone XII, Zone XIII		Ts 156			Ts 204, Ts 367, Ts 368			Zone E, Zone F		Ts 371, Ts 373, Ts 376, Ts 326, Ts 385, Ts 338, Ts 348	Layer 4			4000–5000 B.C.
El Riego	Zone R, Zone S, Zone T, Zone U	Zone D1, Zone D2, Zone E, Zone F, Zone G, Zone H			Zone XIV, Zone XV, Zone XVI, Zone XVII, Zone XVIII, Zone XIX, Zone XX, Zone XXI, Zone XXII	Zone D, Zone E				Ts 204, Ts 367			Zone B		Ts 377,256, Ts 323,379, Ts 374, Ts 384, Ts 252, Ts 387, Tc 390	Levels 6-7	Layer 5		6000–7000 B.C.
Ajuereado					Zone XXIII, Zone XXIV		Tc 391	(Pleistocene) Zone XXV, Zone XXVI, Zone XXVII, Zone XXVIII	Ts 343	Ts 204, Ts 368, Ts 500, Ts 380, Ts 383		Zone C			Ts 372	Levels 8-9	Layer 6		8000–10,000 B.C.

Figure 4.4

Sequences of excavated and surface preceramic and early ceramic components in the environmental zones of the Tehuacan Valley.

Figure 4.5

Initial excavations in San Marcos Cave (Tc254) viewed from the west.

Figure 4.6

Burials A–E of Layer 1 of El Riego Cave (Tc35w) as seen from the north.

first four occupations of Coxcatlan Cave at Pleistocene time probably saw that cave located within the earlier, much-expanded
grassland zone. Also, only two survey sites found in that zone were
relevant to the period of early plant domestications.

In spite of our limitations of data collection for stratigraphic
sequences in all microenvironments, we do have a very complete
sequence for the area as a whole documented by thousands of
artifacts and tens of thousands of ecofacts. (See figure 6.2.) One
process that made this possible was that our laboratory analysis of
artifacts and ecofacts was going hand in hand with excavation, and
in many cases the information yielded formed the basis for policy
decisions about excavations and excavation techniques. One of
these laboratory techniques was in the line of radiocarbon determinations, which was under the direction of Dr. Frederick
Johnson.[13] As we excavated, we sent out carbon samples from the
lowest, middle, and upper strata of the excavation. We got the
dates back within a few weeks and on a bracketing technique
gradually put together a long unbroken sequence of dates. Often
within the dated brackets there would be long, temporal gaps, and
we would dig in layers between the bracketed dates or selected
strata or sites based on artifactual analysis until we found floors
with carbon specimens that dated in the gaps. The decision of
what carbon sample to send was based upon our laboratory analysis of artifacts.

Collecting good chronological data was made possible by having artifactual analysis and cataloging taking place along with the
excavation: thus the lab was a fundamental part of the data collection process. However, both the laboratory analysis for chronology and the contextual studies were dependent upon good digging techniques and accurate recording of our findings. These
were much the same in both Tehuacan and Ayacucho. Since it
would take a ponderous volume to describe them, I will mention
only a few of the salient procedures.

Generally, for each site that we excavated, which had been
given a survey number, we first made a contour map and set up a
one-meter grid system; each square of the grid system was given a
number based on the north-south grid coordinates. Next, we dug
an initial square or trench into the center of the site by trowel
from above with a conscious effort to remove and record each artifact as to its position in each square and stratum or substratum.

Once this initial sounding was completed to the bottom of the archaeological deposit, we then shifted our technique, for we felt that we could have good control at defining the cave stratigraphy if we could excavate it by trowel, spoon, or paintbrush from a vertical profile that clearly showed all the nuances of the strata. The first step in this direction was a thorough study of the walls of our sounding to determine the strata, which were given a number. Then drawings and photographs were made of these profiles along the grid lines. We continued this process until we had long scrolls of profiles for every grid line in every direction. When the stratigraphy was complex or special features were encountered, we made other profiles. These good records of the strata were supplemented by soil and pollen samples from each one.

The recorded profiles and the excavation of them from a vertical face or various vertical faces done by using our La Perra alternate square technique (see figure 4.10) and the cataloging of materials by strata gave us good vertical control of the data. Our system for excavating each square by one stratum at a time and recording the material accordingly also gave us our horizontal control. In this system we stripped off from a vertical face each stratum, discernible floor, or the like, one after the other. Square description forms recording the data of each stratum or zone, as well as the artifacts and ecofacts and features in them, were then filled out. Sometimes floorplan drawings or photographs supplemented the written record about the specific stratum at that specific square, and a general diary was kept of the overall operations, as well as various records for special purposes. We were attempting to record every artifact, ecofact, and feature as to its specific position in and on a stratum. The correlation of these horizontal data by square of every item in and on a particular floor could give all the contextual data about a particular occupation or group of occupations. Thus, our excavation techniques and records were yielding information that would be susceptible to descriptive and analytical studies on our next level of abstraction, which would give us cultural chronology and cultural reconstructions.

In Ayacucho, as in Tehuacan, reconnaissance was followed by excavation. Figures 4.11 and 4.12 show the excavated components for each microenvironment and the chronology for this area.

The archaeologic data collection in Ayacucho was much more complete because of our larger and better organized laboratory

Figure 4.7

*Excavation in the east end of Coxcatlan Cave (Tc50) show-
ing its stratigraphy in the area of E10.*

Figure 4.9

*Even in this deep pit at Coatepec (Ts368) the excavation is
under perfect control through tracing of zones and location
of corner posts.*

Figure 4.8

◄   *The south E3 profile (left) and east part of S8 profile, showing the zones of Purron Cave (Tc272).*

Figure 4.10

*Alternate square excavation technique in the central portion
of Coxcatlan Cave (Tc50).*

where the analysis of excavated materials kept pace with the actual
field excavation. Our most complete sequence came from a subzone, the thorn scrub of the microenvironment thorn forest, where
five rock shelters were excavated (Ac100, Ac102, Ac244, Ac217,
and Ac240). (See figures 4.13 and 4.14.) The seven lowest zones of
Pikimachay Cave belonged to three phases—Pacaicasa, Ayacucho,
and Huanta—that were dated in carbon 14 time in the period from
9000 B.C. to 20,000 B.C. The lowest component from Ac102 was
roughly about 9,500 years old, the lowest from Tc244 (zone G) was
about 8,200 years old, and another (zone F2) from Ac100 was about
8,800 years old. In the period from 5800 B.C. to 4400 B.C., there
were six other floors from Pikimachay Cave (Ac100), as well as
another (zone F) from Ac244, while zone VII of Ac100 was dated
at 5610 ± 150 B.C. In the period from 4400 B.C. to 3100 B.C., there
were two more floors from Ac100, a floor from Ac102, and zone D
from Ac117 that dated at about 3200 B.C. The final preceramic
phase from about 3100 B.C. to 1750 B.C. again saw four floors from
Ac100 and one each from Ac244 and Ac240. The first ceramic
period up until 1000 B.C. was represented by but a single floor from
the latter cave. There are about another fifty excavated floors
from more recent times to the time of the Spanish conquest from

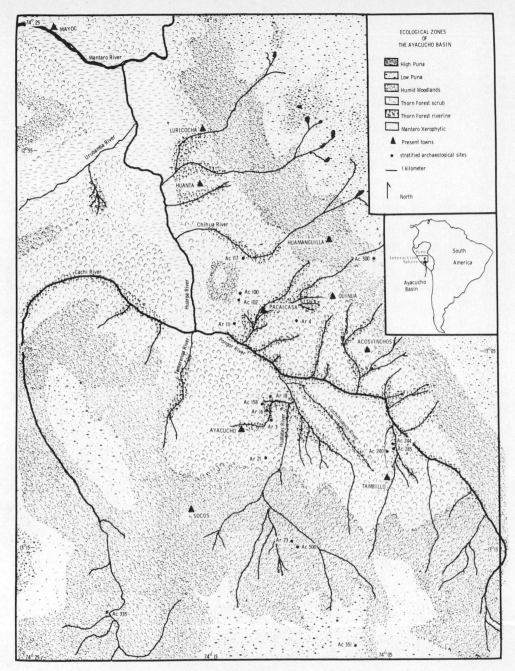

Figure 4.11

The major excavated archaeological sites in the ecological zones of the Ayacucho Basin—a typical highland zone of ecological diversity.

ENVIRON-MENTAL ZONES	XERO-PHYTIC ZONE	THORN FOREST										HUMID WOODLANDS			LOW PUNA			HIGH PUNA	DATES
		RIVERINE SUB-ZONE			SCRUB SUB-ZONE														
Phases	Surface Compo-nents	Excavated Sites Ac 158	Excavated Sites Ac 18	Surface Compo-nents	Ac 100 south room	Ac 100 central room	Ac 100 north room	Excavated Sites Ac 102	Ac 244	Ac 117	Ac 240	Surface Compo-nents	Excavated Sites Ac 335	Ac 500	Ac 23	Surface Compo-nents	Excavated Sites Ac 300	Ac 351	Surface Compo-nents	Surface Compo-nents	
Wichqana Andamarka	Ac 52, Ac 406, Ac 421	Zone G, Zone H, Zone J, Zone K, Zone L	Ac 141, Ac 143, Ac 316, Ac 304, Ac 142, Ac 243, Ac 330, Ac 241, Ac 144, Ac 125, Ac 62, Ac 131, Ac 331, Ac 34, Ac 356								Zone G	Ac 337, Ac 234, Ac 444, Ac 223, Ac 223, Ac 320, Ac 319, Ac 308b, Ac 303, Ac 306, Ac 235			Zone 191-192, Zone 194-195, Zone 196	Ac 500b, Ac 378b, Ac 384b		Zone C	Ac 300D, Ac 300E, Ac 351a, Ac 4976	Ac 5016, Ac 504	1000 B.C.
Cachi	Ac 395, Ac 393, Ac 390, Ac 108, Ac 109, Ac 40, Ac 400, Ac 401, Ac 411, Ac 417b, Ac 420, Ac 422, Ac 423	Zone Ib, Zone Ic, Zone Ie, Zone Id, Zone Ie, Zone D	Ac 558, Ac 147, Ac 194, Ac 195, Ac 315		Zone F, Zone G, Zone H	Zone VI	Zone L			Zone H	Ac 386, Ac 370, Ac 371b, Ac 375, Ac 120, Ac 268, Ac 273, Ac 239, Ac 348, Ac 350, Ac 168, Ac 161, Ac 166, Ac 170, Ac 308a		Zone 191	Ac 267, Ac 284, Ac 360, Ac 380		Zone C1, Zone C2	Ac 308b, Ac 497a	Ac 498	2000 B.C. / 3000 B.C.
Chihua	Ac 404, Ac 401, Ac 438, Ac 417, Ac 427, Ac 422b, Ac 420	Zone Id, Zone Ig, Zone Ih1-2, Zone Ih, Zone Ii, Zone Hav, Zone II	Ac 364, Ac 374, Ac 147, Ac 292		Zone VII, Zone VIII, Zone X	Zone VI	Zone D	Ac 396, Ac 390b, Ac 372, Ac 371a, Ac 324, Ac 280, Ac 269			Ac 179, Ac 165, Ac 378, Ac 309, Ac 384	Zone C south	Ac 3516, Ac 496	Ac 501a	4000 B.C.
Piki	Ac 413, Ac 130, Ac 117, Ac 422, Ac 328	Zone III, Zone IIb, Zone IIa, Zone IIa1, Zone VI, Zone V, Zone IV, Zone VIIa, Zone VII, Zone VIa, Zone VIII, Zone IX, Zone IXa, Zone X	Ac 22, Ac 198		Zone K, Zone I, Zone V, Zone W	Zone I, Zone VII	Zone F	Ac 390a, Ac 101, Ac 296, Ac 169, Ac 188, Ac 172, Ac 176, Ac 208, Ac 174, Ac 20		Zone F	Ac 371	Zone D	Ac 300a	Ac 500, Ac 499	5000 B.C.
Jaywa	Ac 158a	Zone XI, Zone XIa, Zone XII, Zone XIIa, Zone XIII	Ac 2		Zone 12		Zone G	Ac 369, Ac 270, Ac 242, Ac 204a		Zone C, Zone D, Zone E, Zone F, Zone G, Zone H	Ac 204	Zone C north	Ac 351a	Ac 502	6000 B.C. / 7000 B.C.
Puente		Zone XIV			Zone VII		Ac 305, Ac 306	Zone I, Zone J, Zone 11, Zone 12, Zone 13, Zone K				8000 B.C.
Huanta			Zone h										10,000 B.C.
Ayacucho			Zone h, Zone h1										12,000 B.C.
Pacaicasa			Zone i, Zone d										16,000 B.C.
			Zone i, Zone k										20,000 B.C.

Figure 4.12

Sequences of excavated and surface preceramic and early ceramic components in the environmental zones of the Ayacucho Basin.

this zone. In fact, this area has the longest unbroken cultural sequence in the New World, and it compares favorably with any known in the Old World.

The other subzone of the thorn forest, called riverine, yielded even more bone and archaeological remains, but of a slightly shorter period. Most of these materials came from thirty-five stratified floors from the Puente site (Ac158) that ranged in time from about 7200 B.C. to 1800 B.C. Most of these floors were carbon 14 dated. One ruin yielded four floors of the early ceramic period from 1750 B.C. to 1000 B.C.

Figure 4.13
Pikimachay Cave (Ac100) from the east.

The humid woodlands also yielded an unbroken sequence from 9000 B.C. to 1500 A.D. with the most abundant material coming from the Jaywa site with twelve floors from 9000 B.C. to 5800 B.C. A smaller cave (Ac500) yielded three floors at about 5200 B.C.,

Figure 4.14
Stratigraphy in the south room of Pikimachay Cave.

Figure 4.15

The Puente site (Ac158) in the desert zone (left). Stepped trench method of excavation at the Puente site (right).

Figure 4.16

Stratigraphy at the Puente site.

Figure 4.17
Looking northward at Jaywamachay (Ac335).

4000 B.C., and 2500 B.C., and the Chupas ruin (Ar23) had seven floors in the period from 17,500 B.C. to 1000 B.C. The other slightly higher environmental zone, the low puna, also had a long sequence represented by lesser materials from two caves, Ac300 and Ac351, with zone C of Tc300 at about 13,900 B.C., zones C1 and C2 at about 1900 B.C. and 2600 B.C., zone C of Tc351 at 1500 B.C. No sites were dug in the high puna zone (because our earlier ecological studies did not indicate it was a separate zone from the low puna), but even here survey gave a site between 7000 B.C. and 6000 B.C., one at about 5000 B.C., one at about 3800 B.C., another at 2500 B.C., and two between 2000 B.C. and 1000 B.C. The other environmental zone that just barely impinged on our area of research, the so-called xerophytic zone, had no excavations in it, but there were twenty-nine survey sites between 7100 B.C. and 1000 B.C.

Our fine ecologic studies of highland Peru were matched by equally complete excavated archaeological materials, giving stratified sequences documented by many artifacts, debitage, and bone for most of the environmental zones. Unfortunately preservation of plant remains occurred only in the thorn forest zone, and even

Figure 4.18

Jaywamachay east-west profile (left). Jaywamachay north-south profile (upper right). Excavation technique at Jaywamachay (lower right).

here they were rare in the periods before 4000 B.C. Pollen studies now being undertaken may be of assistance in filling this gap in our knowledge. Thus, there were deficiencies in our much better planned data collection in Ayacucho that match our relatively un-

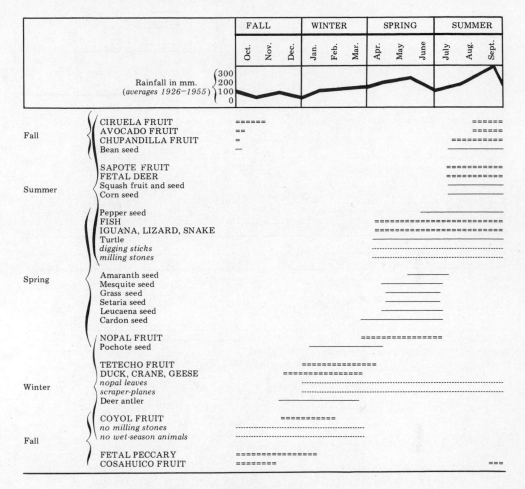

Figure 4.19

Seasonal indicators in the Tehuacan Valley (7400 B.C. to 850 B.C.).

planned data collection at Tehuacan, which had abundant plant remains for most of its 10,000-year overall sequence.

Interdisciplinary Data Collection

Our initial step also included interdisciplinary ecofact collections. In Tehuacan, in terms of scheduling, much of this work actually followed the excavation, but in terms of methodological chronology, it was really part of the initial stage of our researches. C. Earle Smith of the University of Mississippi came to the valley to

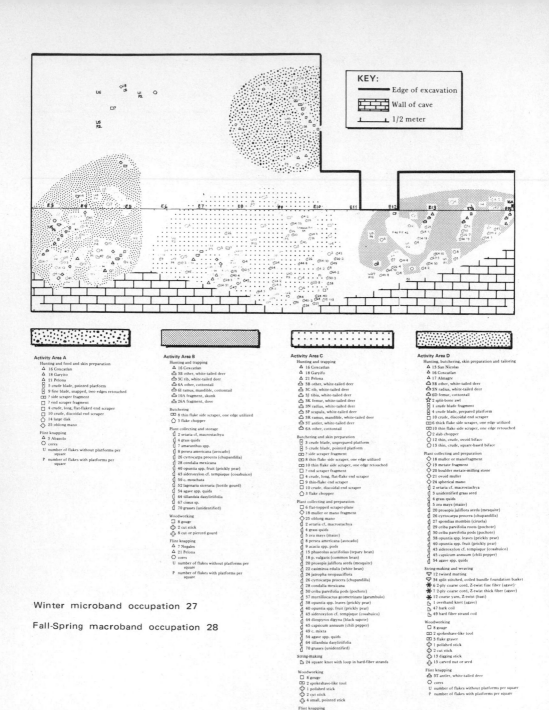

KEY:
━━━━ Edge of excavation
▨▨▨ Wall of cave
├─┴─┤ 1/2 meter

Activity Area A

Hunting and food and skin preparation
△ 16 Coxcatlan
△ 18 Garyito
△ 21 Pelona
◨ 5 crude blade, pointed platform
◨ 9 fine blade, snapped, two edges retouched
◨ ? side scraper fragment
□ ? end scraper fragment
□ 4 crude, long, flat-flaked end scraper
□ 10 crude, discoidal end scraper
◇ 14 large disk
◇ 25 oblong mano

Flint knapping
△ 5 Abasolo
○ cores
U number of flakes without platforms per square
P number of flakes with platforms per square

Activity Area B

Hunting and trapping
△ 16 Coxcatlan
△ 3B other, white-tailed deer
△ 5C rib, white-tailed deer
△ 6A other, cottontail
△ 6I ramus, mandible, cottontail
△ 10A fragment, skunk
△ 26A fragment, dove

Butchering
◨ 8 thin flake side scraper, one edge utilized
◇ 3 flake chopper

Plant collecting and storage
◖ 2 setaria cf. macrostachya
◖ 4 grass quids
◖ 7 amaranthus spp.
◖ 8 persea americana (avocado)
◖ 26 cyrtocarpa procera (chupandilla)
◖ 28 condalia mexicana
◖ 40 opuntia spp. fruit (prickly pear)
◖ 43 sideroxylon cf. tempisque (cosahuico)
◖ 50 c. moschata
◖ 52 lagenaria siceraria (bottle gourd)
◖ 54 agave spp. quids
◖ 64 tillandsia dasyliriifolia
◖ 67 cissus sp.
◖ 70 grasses (unidentified)

Woodworking
□ 8 gouge
✚ 2 cut stick
✚ 8 cut or pierced gourd

Flint knapping
△ 7 Nogales
△ 21 Pelona
○ cores
U number of flakes without platforms per square
P number of flakes with platforms per square

Activity Area C

Hunting and trapping
△ 16 Coxcatlan
△ 18 Garyito
△ 21 Pelona
△ 3B other, white-tailed deer
△ 5C rib, white-tailed deer
△ 5J tibia, white-tailed deer
△ 5K femur, white-tailed deer
△ 5N radius, white-tailed deer
△ 5P scapula, white-tailed deer
△ 5R ramus, mandible, white-tailed deer
△ 5T antler, white-tailed deer
△ 6A other, cottontail

Butchering and skin preparation
◨ 3 crude blade, unprepared platform
◨ 5 crude blade, pointed platform
◨ ? side scraper fragment
◨ 8 thin flake side scraper, one edge utilized
◨ 10 thin flake side scraper, one edge retouched
◨ ? end scraper fragment
□ 4 crude, long, flat-flake end scraper
◇ 9 thin-flake end scraper
□ 10 crude, discoidal end scraper
◇ 3 flake chopper

Plant collecting and preparation
◖ 6 flat-topped scraper-plane
◇ 18 muller or mano fragment
◇ 25 oblong mano
◖ 2 setaria cf. macrostachya
◖ 4 grass quids
◖ 5 zea mays (maize)
◖ 7 acacia spp. pods
◖ 8 persea americana (avocado)
◖ 15 phaseolus acutifolius (tepary bean)
◖ 18 p. vulgaris (common bean)
◖ 20 prosopis juliflora seeds (mesquite)
◖ 22 casimiroa edulis (white bean)
◖ 24 jatropha neopaucifflora
◖ 26 cyrtocarpa procera (chupandilla)
◖ 28 condalia mexicana
◖ 30 ceiba parvifolia pods (pochote)
◖ 37 myrtillocactus geometrizans (garambulo)
◖ 38 opuntia spp. leaves (prickly pear)
◖ 40 opuntia spp. fruit (prickly pear)
◖ 43 sideroxylon cf. tempisque (cosahuico)
◖ 44 diospyros digyna (black sapote)
◖ 45 capsicum annuum (chili pepper)
◖ 49 c. mixta
◖ 54 agave spp. quids
◖ 64 tillandsia dasyliriifolia
◖ 70 grasses (unidentified)

String-making
◖ 24 square knot with loop in hard-fiber strands

Woodworking
□ 8 gouge
◨ 2 spokeshave-like tool
✚ 1 polished stick
✚ 2 cut stick
✚ 4 small, pointed stick

Flint knapping
○ cores
U number of flakes without platforms per square
P number of flakes with platforms per square

Activity Area D

Hunting, butchering, skin preparation and tailoring
△ 13 San Nicolas
△ 16 Coxcatlan
△ 17 Almagre
△ 3B other, white-tailed deer
△ 5N radius, white-tailed deer
△ 6D femur, cottontail
✩ 2 split-bone awl
◨ 1 crude blade fragment
◨ 4 crude blade, prepared platform
□ 10 crude, discoidal end scraper
◨◨ 6 thick flake side scraper, one edge utilized
◨◨ 10 thin flake side scraper, one edge retouched
◇ 2 slab chopper
◇ 12 thin, crude, ovoid bifacc
◇ 13 thin, crude, square-based bifacc

Plant collecting and preparation
◇ 18 muller or manofragment
◇ 19 metate fragment
◇ 20 boulder metate-milling stone
◇ 21 ovoid muller
◇ 24 spherical mano
◖ 2 setaria cf. macrostachya
◖ 3 unidentified grass seed
◖ 4 grass quids
◖ 5 zea mays (maize)
◖ 20 prosopis juliflora seeds (mesquite)
◖ 26 cyrtocarpa procera (chupandilla)
◖ 27 spondias mombin (ciruela)
◖ 29 ceiba parvifolia roots (pochote)
◖ 30 ceiba parvifolia pods (pochote)
◖ 38 opuntia spp. leaves (prickly pear)
◖ 40 opuntia spp. fruit (prickly pear)
◖ 43 sideroxylon cf. tempisque (cosahuico)
◖ 45 capsicum annuum (chili pepper)
◖ 54 agave spp. quids

String-making and weaving
▽ 12 twined matting
▽ 34 split stitched, coiled bundle foundation basket
✳ 6 2-ply coarse cord, Z-twist fine fiber (agave)
✳ 7 2-ply coarse cord, Z-twist thick fiber (agave)
✳ 12 coarse yarn, Z-twist (bast)
▽ 1 overhand knot (agave)
▽ 47 bark coil
▽ 49 hard fiber strand coil

Woodworking
□ 8 gouge
◨◨ 2 spokeshave-like tool
◨◨ 3 flake graver
✚ 1 polished stick
✚ 2 cut stick
✚ 13 digging stick
✚ 15 carved nut or seed

Flint knapping
△ 3T antler, white-tailed deer
○ cores
U number of flakes without platforms per square
P number of flakes with platforms per square

Winter microband occupation 27

Fall-Spring macroband occupation 28

Figure 4.20

Activity areas of zone VIII of Coxcatlan Cave (Tc50), Tehuacan Valley.

undertake botanical survey in the summer after the end of our first season. Hugh Cutler of the St. Louis Botanical Gardens and Tom Whitaker of the United States Department of Agriculture came in the spring of 1962 to study the squashes, as did Eric Callen, of Mac-Donald College at McGill University, to study archaeological human feces. Lawrence Kaplan of the University of Massachusetts came that fall to study the beans, and slightly later Paul Mangels-dorf and Walton Galinat, both of the Harvard Botanical Museum, undertook their corn studies. In 1963 Kent Flannery undertook zoological survey in the valley; J. Schoenwetter did pollen and ecological studies; and R. C. Drake studied land snails. All these studies pertained to ancient subsistence reconstruction and modern ecosystems.

Other specialized information came from a variety of sources. Geological studies of the Tehuacan Valley were made by Jean Brunet of the Centre National Recherche Scientifique Français au Mexique. Geographical studies of the region were made by Douglas S. Byers of the R. S. Peabody Foundation. Prehistoric and modern irrigation systems were investigated by Richard B. Woodbury, acting head of the Smithsonian Office of Anthropology, James E. Neeley, and Aubrey W. Williams, Jr., of the University of Maryland. James E. Anderson, now of McMaster University, undertook a study of the morphologic features of the human skeletal remains taken from the excavations. Most of these studies took place in 1964 and continued after the field project closed. At various times information was collected concerning the ethnohistory and ethnography of the Tehuacan Valley by Carmen Cook, Aubrey W. Williams, and Robert Chadwick. In 1965 and 1966 Douglas S. Byers undertook geographical and hydrographic studies of the Tehuacan Valley, and it was at this time that the interdisciplinary studies were coordinated.[14]

Although our Tehuacan interdisciplinary studies gave fine results, they were not as well organized as those from Ayacucho, which are still to be completed.[15] In Ayacucho, botanical survey began during the first year of our survey in the winter dry season and continued in the second year in the summer wet season. The actual archaeological specimens were classified in our third season under the direction of Barbara Pickersgill of the University of Reading. Zoology followed a similar course with Kent Flannery of the University of Michigan making wet season collections be-

tween the second and third field seasons, while Elizabeth Wing of
the Florida State Museum collected during the dry part of the
third field season. During this third season, Kent Flannery re-
visited Ayacucho and coordinated his data with Wing and also
collected climatological and ethnographic information. In the second season, Nathaniel Rutter of the Geological Survey of Canada
undertook geological, geomorphological, and soil studies, as well
as collecting pollen for J. Hopkins and Charles Schweger at the
University of Alberta. During this season, Grayson Meade made
further geological studies, as well as paleontological ones, and he
also shipped fossil bone material to B. Patterson of the Museum
of Comparative Zoology at Harvard University. The late Eric
Callen started the study of the human feces and other botany investigations in the second season, which were concluded by
Vaughn Bryant of Texas A&M University in the third season.
In addition to these field studies, Barbara Pickersgill arranged for
various specialists to study our limited domesticated plant remains: Whitaker, the cucurbits; Kaplan, the beans; Stephens, the
cotton; and Galinat and Mangelsdorf, the corn.

As important as the field data collection was a coordinating
conference held at the end of the third season, where the microenvironments of the Ayacucho Valley were defined on the basis of
rainfall, temperature, elevation, topography, soils, flora, and fauna.
There were indications that with our pollen and soils studies, we
could determine the fluctuations in the distribution of the environmental zones through a 10,000-year period. Thus, our ecosystem studies in Ayacucho were a decided improvement over
what we had attempted in Tehuacan.

CULTURAL DESCRIPTIONS

Having touched upon the preliminary step in archaeological
investigations, data collection, let us pass to the second step, the
preliminary analysis and description of the materials collected at
Tehuacan and Ayacucho. We were concerned with two major
problems: analyzing the artifacts and ecofacts so that a sequence
could be defined and described, and analyzing these same ma-

terials so that the human activities with interrelated ecological contexts could be described for each step in this sequence.

Defining the Chronology

Tehuacan   The chronology of the area was defined first. In Tehuacan, we began with a study of the large sample of artifacts from the twenty-eight stratified zones of Coxcatlan Cave. For convenience in studying this large amount of materials, they were divided into a series of *morphological classes*—that is, classes of objects with a series of characteristics or attributes in common. On the grossest level, the artifacts were divided into chipped unifaces, chipped bifaces, ground stone, bone, antler, shell, copper, wooden baskets, mats, sandals, cordage, knots, bark cloth, textiles, ceramic vessels and figurines, and spindle whorls. Because of the large amount of chipped stone tools, these were further subdivided: unifaces worked laterally, unifaces worked terminally, bifaces with points on one end and facilities for hafting, other bifaces without these characteristics, and unifaces made from polyhedral nuclei. The first three of these subclasses often were called by popular functional names for convenience: side scrapers, end scrapers, and projectile points. In these chronological studies we were not concerned with functions but rather with changes in stylistic features and various manufacturing techniques.

In terms of actual procedures, the artifacts of the various classes were laid by the zones of Coxcatlan Cave. Then they were studied to determine which attributes of the various artifacts in each class were good time markers. Occasionally the chi-square statistical formula was used to determine which characteristics were significantly different through time. These significant attributes we have termed *modes*. Artifacts having a cluster of modes and attributes became our types—basically, artifactual time markers. Then percentile trends of the various types for the twenty-eight sequential zones of Coxcatlan Cave were established. Next, the same process was undertaken with the artifacts from the other stratified sites, the types refined, and their various zones aligned in chronological order along with those of Coxcatlan Cave on the basis of the artifact percentile trends. Eventually all sixty of the excavated zones before 1000 B.C. were aligned in chronological order on the basis of two hundred or so temporally aligned artifact types. In addition, the approximately forty surface-collected sites were temporally ordered in the same manner. The final step in the sequential artifactual studies was the comparison of artifact types in a series of sequential zones to determine the sequential clusters of types. These became the basis for our establishment of nine artifact clusters or archaeological phases from before 10,000 B.C.: Ajuereado, El Riego, Coxcatlan, Abejas, Purron, Ajalpan, Santa Maria, Palo Blanco, and Venta Salada. Of these, the first six are the most pertinent to our studies of early agriculture because after 900 B.C. (Santa Maria), the domestication of corn and most other plants had been completed.

Somewhat on the basis of the establishment of these sequential zones and sequential phases by artifact studies, approximately seventy-two charcoal or vegetal specimens were selected to be used for radiocarbon determination to date the six earliest phases, as well as various zones within them. These, of course, were dated in radiocarbon time, not sidereal years, but recent research has allowed these radiocarbon dates to be transferred into true year dates. We now estimate that the Ajuereado phase existed from earlier than 10,000 B.C. to about 7800 B.C., El Riego from 7800 B.C. to 5800 B.C., Coxcatlan from 5800 B.C. to 4000 B.C., Abejas from 4000 B.C. to 2860 B.C., Purron from 2860 B.C. to 1700 B.C., and Ajalpan from 1700 B.C. to about 900 B.C.

The dates can also be applied to our evidence of changes in the ecosystem since most of our information comes from data collected in our cave excavations. In the caves there is evidence of change to modern fauna at about 8000 B.C. with the horse, antelope, giant turtle, large jackrabbit, various kinds of rodents, and probably mammoth becoming extinct in the Tehuacan Valley. This evidence, plus geological studies, suggests that perhaps during the Pleistocene the Tehuacan Valley was slightly wetter and cooler than it is now; thus the humid river bottoms were more extensive, and the grassland steppes expanded at the expense of the thorn forest vegetation in the alluvial slope and the Sonora-like desert vegetation in the travertine slopes. Studies of the vegetal materials, faunal remains, geography, and geology from 8000 B.C. to the present suggest no major ecological change. Therefore, besides having a quite complete cultural sequence for Tehuacan, we also have information about changes in the ecosystem, small as they may have been.

Ayacucho   Our studies of the changes in the Ayacucho ecosystem were very different, not only in terms of the techniques and methods but also in terms of the results. Although we made geographical, geological, zoological, and botanical studies for determining ecological changes of excavated materials in Ayacucho, our soil and pollen studies were very different from anything attempted in Mexico because of better scientific techniques. A minor aspect of this method was obtaining three 9,000-year-long pollen profiles from the low puna, thorn forest scrub, and thorn forest riverine. Augmenting these studies were analyses of buried soils, as well as the pollen in them, at over 150 stations in different parts of the valley to determine the kinds of flora that formed each of these soil horizons. When this study is completed, we should know the geographical distributions of the ecosystems of each environment zone during every period of the last 10,000 years. At present, all we know is that the Pleistocene glaciation ended about 11,000 years ago and that it was followed by a cooler and wetter period than at present, which gradually dried up by 3000 B.C.; this dry period lasted until about 1000 A.D. when the modern dry conditions started.

Thus, the rather different methods achieved a chronology of ecosystems for both Ayacucho and Tehuacan; our method of achieving a chronology of artifacts and zones was much the same, however. Perhaps the only difference in Ayacucho was that we supplemented our typological studies with a computer cluster analysis of artifact attributes and confirmed our determination of cluster of types into phases by the use of a factor analysis program. The phases defined between 9000 B.C. and 1000 B.C. (called Puente, Jaywa, Piki, Chihua, Cachi, and Andamarka) are pertinent to our early agriculture studies. There were also three earlier phases: Pacaicasa, Ayacucho, and Andean bifacial complex.

On the basis of our chronology of artifacts and zones, we selected thirty-five carbon samples for radiocarbon determinations, and these dated in radiocarbon time twenty-six strata as well as the six pertinent Ayacucho phases. In sidereal years these are Puente from 9000 B.C. to 7700 B.C., Jaywa from 7700 B.C. to 6600

B.C., Piki from 6600 B.C. to 5100 B.C., Chihua from 5100 B.C. to 3700 B.C., Cachi from 3700 B.C. to 2100 B.C., and Andamarka from 2100 B.C. to 1000 B.C.

The conclusions of the chronological analyses of the materials from both Tehuacan and Ayacucho seem to be on a firm footing.

Reconstructing Cultural Contexts

One of the next considerations in this type of descriptive study in Tehuacan concerned the reconstructed ecosystems and man's exploitation of them. Early in these endeavors, our interdisciplinary scientists analyzed the modern flora and fauna to determine seasonal indicators, and their efforts were rewarding. About thirty reliable indicators were found, such as tetecho fruits occurring in December and January; migratory cranes and Canadian geese being in the valley from December through February; pochote flowering from February through March; mesquite, amaranth, and seteria seeds in the spring; turtle, snakes, lizards, and iguana coming out of hibernation during the spring and summer months; corn, beans, and squash fruiting in the late summer; and a variety of fruits maturing in the fall. (See figure 4.19.) Then the ecofacts from each zone were studied to determine in what season or seasons the zones or floors were occupied. This study not only yielded information about the duration of the occupations, but the location of occupations when taken in conjunction with the seasonality of the occupations allowed us to reconstruct annual movements and their scheduling of the exploitation of various microenvirons seasonally.

Further studies of the ecofacts from each occupation gave us information about what aspects of the microenvironments were being utilized. Perhaps the most important facet of these studies concerned the edible floral and faunal data that allowed us to reconstruct the sustenance of each occupation. Basically we attempted to take all the garbage, both plant and animal, from a single zone and transfer it into comparable units of food (liters of food or, ideally, kilocalories). We analyzed animal bones, derived minimum numbers of animals killed for food, then calculated the liters of meat yielded by each animal. We also estimated the liters of wild and domesticated plant foods and studied the human feces for the relative amounts of food that were consumed. These two combined measures thus gave relative proportions of foods in the diet of the inhabitants of each occupation, and comparisons of the sequential occupations showed relative trends in the amounts of food from animals, wild plants, and domesticated plants. Of particular importance were the trends in domesticated plants, for more intensive studies by botanists revealed changes caused by cultural as well as biological mechanisms that gave basic information about the actual process of plant domestication. These materials are unique because of the excellent archaeological preservation in the Tehuacan Valley.

We are attempting to make the same kind of studies for the Ayacucho region of Peru, where our reconstruction of the past ecosystems may eventually be accomplished more precisely than in Tehuacan. Studies of the seasonality for Ayacucho are dependent mainly upon animal remains, but there are indications that many occupations will be dated as precisely as those from Tehuacan. Since we have many more preceramic sites surveyed as well as excavated components from more microenvironments in Peru, our knowledge of the relative duration of occupations, seasonal movements, and scheduling should be even better estimated. Study of the ecofacts from the various Peruvian occupations should also tell us much about some of the elements of the ecosystems of the various microenvironments that were being utilized. Our estimates of the diet of the inhabitants of each occupation in Ayacucho cannot be done as well because the plants and human feces are not so well preserved, although we have thousands of animal bones. Zoological studies of these bones, which include camelids (guanaco, llama, and alpaca) and guinea pigs, may also be relevant to understanding the process of animal domestication.

These contextual studies of the elements of the ecosystem that were used for food lead into a consideration of the activities that were concerned with obtaining these resources and their preparation into edible food. Food preparation activities, subsystems within the cultural system, required various kinds of artifacts as tools. The pointed, bifacial, chipped objects with bases amenable to hafting, on the basis of ethnographic analogy, were considered to be projectile points. Further study of these points revealed morphological differences, which, compared with points of primitive peoples, showed that some were similar to those used on jabbing and hunting lances, hurling atlatl darts, shooting arrows, and so forth. Wood objects, such as those with slots, hooks, or grooved bent twigs, were so obviously similar to ones used by primitive peoples that they could be readily identified as lance shafts, atlatl throwing sticks, or traps. The grinding stones were also compared with tools of primitive people and, on the basis of ethnographic similarities, could be classified (mortar, pestle, muller, milling stone, metate). The butchering tool kits of primitive people were also compared with artifacts from our zones or floors, and then some of the bifaces were classified as choppers, some as unifaces and blades, and some as meat knives.

The next process was to correlate tools reflecting subsistence activities and food preparation with the actual food remains for each floor or zone. This was a way of testing our hypothesis about the use of tools as derived from ethnographic analogy by actual association on the floors. For example, the occurrence on the same floor of bones of deer, often hunted by primitive people with points that we thought on the basis of ethnographic analogy were lance points used for hunting, did seem to indicate the probability that the points were used in hunting and that the deer had been hunted with a lance tipped with these type points.

The final aspect of this study of the artifacts themselves in Tehuacan was an attempt to classify the rest of the artifacts on every floor as to their use, as well as their method of manufacture. For example, on the basis of ethnographic analogy, terminally retouched unifaces were thought of as having been end scrapers often used in skin scraping activities, but they were also objects made by knocking out a large flake of flint from a bifacial core by percussion with a hard hammer and then retouching them on the end dorsally by pressure flaking, the end product of certain kinds of flint knapping activities. In the end, we derived from this sort of study of the artifacts and ecofacts for each floor or zone evidence of a whole series of possible activities of the ancient inhabitants, as well as some guesses about their tools and the end products of the activities.

Quite by accident we discovered one other technique for determining the use of some of these artifacts when Tony Nelken undertook a functional classification of the grinding stones. We discovered that not only could we derive ideas about their use from comparing them with similar tools used among primitive

people but that these archaeological tools often had evidence of
wear, indicating how they were used. For instance, the milling
stones and mullers, particularly the broken and used-up ones, had
circular scratches on them, indicating the grinding had been done
horizontally with a round and round motion; the metates and
manos had longitudinal scratchings, indicating back and forth
grinding. Here was a way to check our concept derived from
ethnography.

By the time the Tehuacan fieldwork was coming to a close in
1964, we had begun to feel that using analogous ethnographic data
for interpreting archaeology, including artifact use and ancient
activities, led not to definite or probable conclusions but only to
hypotheses that had to be tested. In our later endeavors in Ayacucho we had a rather different attitude and methodology concerning this second level of contextual studies, even though our studies of the ecosystems, chronology, and data collection were much
the same. In Ayacucho our artifacts and ecofacts and fragments
removed in the resharpening of artifacts were examined with a
microscope and by microscope photography for deformation and
breakage from various kinds of use or kinds of manufacture. The
evidence of use or manufacture was then compared with a series of
artifacts we had made and used in various ways to get a characteristic indicating use or manufacture, a process that might be called
experimental analogy. For example, for chipped stone we were
able to determine by experiment characteristics indicating drilling
something hard, drilling something soft, piercing or punching
something hard, piercing soft, cutting or whittling hard or soft,
scraping hard or soft, sawing hard or soft, chopping hard or soft.
We also did something similar for the ground, pecked, and polishing stones, bones, and vegetal artifacts. Also we used an expert
flint knapper, Carl Phagan, to chip stone tools from a wide variety
of materials by a large number of techniques and noted the characteristics on the debitage indicating different techniques of manufacture. Phagan, with an assistant, then examined a statistically
selected random sample of debitage and artifacts from various
squares from many floors for evidence of use and manufacturing
techniques. Both of these studies then became the basis for testing
the hypothesis about the use and manufacture derived from ethnographic analogy of every artifact from every floor or zone in the
Ayacucho excavations. One of the results is that many artifacts,

which ethnology would tell us had single definite uses turned out to have multiple uses. For instance, some small, triangular unifaces with their bases unifacially retouched and edges adapted to scraping (which ethnography would indicate were skin scrapers) showed not only end wear caused by scraping something soft like skins but also wear on their corners from drilling and/or cutting something hard or soft, and use wear on their sides for cutting and/or sawing something hard or soft. In fact, my impression from this study is that preceramic man, rather than making specialized tools for a single task, preferred to have a sort of boy scout knife that could be used for multiple tasks. Eventually our studies of artifacts and ecofacts from Ayacucho will show with a high degree of probability in what activities most of the artifacts were involved because the hypotheses from ethnographic analogy were being tested by conclusions from technological or experimental studies.

We also gradually developed one other technique for testing hypotheses about the use of artifacts. Even in my 1954 excavations in the Sierra Madre of Tamaulipas where we uncovered many ecofacts and artifacts on well-defined floors, probably representing a single occupation, it was apparent that artifacts were not randomly distributed over these floors but appeared in clusters or concentrations. Further, the artifacts or ecofacts in these clusters often seemed to be related in terms of actual activities. For example, four round stone pebbles with pecked ends, antler tines with nicked ends, possible hammerstones, and antler flakers occurred along with 95 percent of all the chips, flakes, and nodules of flint in the southwest corner (four square meters) of one cave. Ethnographic analogy would suggest the hypothesis that the round, pecked pebbles were hammerstones, and the nicked and antler tines were flaking tools for flint knapping; technological study of the pecking on the hammers, scratches on the antler, and platforms and bulbs of percussion on the flakes or the cores would tend to confirm the hypothesis that they were used in such an activity because all features were like those that resulted from specific flint knapping activities derived in modern experiments. The hammers, antler tines, flakes, and cores were all found in a nonrandom cluster, strongly suggesting that they were related and, what is more, probably interconnected with a similar activity, in this case flint knapping.

Because of our earlier Tamaulipas observation of this sort, when we began digging in Tehuacan, we made considerable efforts to determine the cluster of artifacts and ecofacts on each floor and to discern the activities that were undertaken in each of these areas. Further, we compared the seasonal indicators of each activity area to determine which activity areas were contemporaneous with each other. Thus our floors became specific occupations with a series of interrelated and interdependent activities—in other words, our occupations were cultural systems or parts of cultural systems (see figure 4.20). Each occupation was composed of a series of cultural subsystems or traditions or elements that were regularly interacting together and were interdependent in forming a unified whole or a system or part of a system, a specific moment in time and space. When we compared an adequate series of components or occupations from various seasons and locations with each other and found them to be similar, we classified them together as an archaeological phase. What we really were doing was combining a series of interrelated and interdependent cultural subsystems into a large cultural system or part of a cultural system. Thus the final result of our contextual studies in Tehuacan has been the ability to describe a sequence of cultural systems interacting with and independent of various ecosystems.

In Ayacucho, our contextual studies are not so complete as those of Tehuacan, but attempts have been made to plot and define activity areas on the more numerous floors. Thanks to Robert Vierra, we have done this plotting not by hand drawing but by the use of computers. We plan to define these clusters and their elements by various computer programs, such as cluster analysis, factor analysis, and nearest neighbor. Whether our interpretations of the activities of each floor or descriptions of the interrelated cultural subsystems that occurred in each period will be any better remains to be seen.

CONCLUSION

Our basic descriptions from Tehuacan have reached a stage where some sort of synthesis can be undertaken on the cultural-historical integrative level. For Tehuacan we can describe the se-

quence of ecosystems and cultural systems, along with the sequence of technological traditions or elements that developed
within them or evolved through them. Although our other Meso-
American data are limited, we can relate these interrelated sequences to others that occurred in the various contemporaneous
horizons or time periods within the fluctuating interaction sphere
of Meso-America.

Such synthesis can lead to testable hypotheses that may become the basis for formulating generalizations about human activities. Both these tasks—synthesizing information about human
activities and establishing explanatory statements about the reasons for these activities—mean that the archaeologist has moved
onto a high plane of abstraction. In fact, the archaeologist has
stopped being a technician and detective of the past and hand-
maiden to anthropology and history and has begun to try to be a
scientist.

REFERENCES

1. Javier Romero and Juan Valenzuela, *Expediciona La Sierra Azul
   Ocampo, Tamps* (Mexico: Anales del Instituto Nacional de Anthropologia y Historia, 1945).
2. P. C. Mangelsdorf and R. G. Reeves, "The Origin of Maize:
   Present Status of the Problem," *American Anthropologist*, n.as. 47,
   no. 2 (1945).
3. Paul Sears and K. H. Clisby, *Palynology in Southern North
   America*, pt. 4: *Pleistocene Climate in Mexico*, Bulletin of the Geological Society of America, vol. 66 (1955).
4. R. S. MacNeish, *The Science of Archaeology?* (Hamilton, Ontario:
   D. G. Seldon Printing Limited, 1976).
5. R. S. MacNeish, F. A. Peterson, and K. V. Flannery, *The Prehistory of the Tehuacan Valley*, vol 3: *Ceramics* (Austin: University of Texas Press, 1970).
6. Edward B. Sisson, *First Annual Report of the Coxcatlan Project*.
   (Andover, Mass.: R. S. Peabody Foundation, 1973). Ed Sisson is
   doing further survey in the Coxcatlan area.
7. Joseph A. Tosi, *Zonas de Vida Natural en El Peru*, Instituto Interamericano de Ciencias Agricolas de la OEA Zona Andina,
   Boletin Tecnico, no. 5 (Lima, 1960).
8. M. L. Fowler and R. S. MacNeish, "Excavations in the Coxcatlan
   Locality in the Alluvial Slopes," in MacNeish, ed., *Prehistory,*

vol. 5: *Excavations and Reconnaissance* (Austin: University of Texas Press, 1972).

9. R. S. MacNeish and Angel Garcia Cook, "Excavations in the Diego Locality in the Dissected Alluvial Slopes," in MacNeish, ed., *Prehistory,* vol 5.

10. R. S. MacNeish and Angel Garcia Cook, "Excavations in the San Marcos Locality in the Travertine Slopes," in MacNeish, ed., *Prehistory,* vol. 5.

11. R. S. MacNeish and Angel Garcia Cook, "Excavations in the Locality of the El Riego Oasis," in MacNeish, ed., *Prehistory,* vol. 5.

12. R. S. MacNeish and F. A. Peterson, "Excavations in the Ajalpan Locality in the Valley Center," in MacNeish, ed., *Prehistory,* vol. 5.

13. F. Johnson and R. S. MacNeish, "Chronometric Dating," in MacNeish, ed., *Prehistory,* vol. 4.

14. D. S. Byers, "Climate and Hydrology," in MacNeish, ed., *Prehistory,* vol. 1: *Environment and Subsistence.*

15. R. S. MacNeish, A. Nelken-Terner, and Angel Garcia Cook, *Second Annual Report of the Ayacucho Archaeological-Botanical Project* (Andover, Mass.: R. S. Peabody Foundation, 1970).

5

On Growing Up:
From Archaeologist
to Social Scientist

THE NEXT TWO LEVELS OF INVESTIGATION ARE THE MAKING OF A PRE-
historic cultural-historical integration for the Tehuacan region of
the Meso-American nuclear area and then analyzing these sum-
marized sequential data to see if we can derive hypotheses about
why plant-domestication, agriculture, and village life started. As a
start to our description of the cultural-historical integration of
Tehuacan, let us consider its environmental background on a
more general level (Meso-American and then specifically—the
Tehuacan Valley).

ECOSYSTEMS OF MESO-AMERICA

In summaries of the fuller cultural sequence for Tehuacan up
until the stage when agricultural village life began at between

about 2000 B.C. and 1000 B.C., it is necessary to consider not only the Tehuacan Valley ecozones but the environment of Meso-America as a whole. Obviously the Tehuacan Valley is only a region or subregion of one of the many natural regions, subareas, or life zones of the Meso-American nuclear area. Robert C. West has divided Meso-America into nine major regions with some twelve subdivisions within two major superregions.[1] His classification is based in part upon the correlations of interrelations of hydrography, soils, topography, rocks and minerals, climate, floral and faunal factors, and ecofactors. I have adapted West's divisions to reflect the archaeological sequence in ancient times (10,000 B.C. to 1500 B.C.). (See chapter 6 for a fuller discussion of my classification.)

The two major divisions of West's classification are the tropical highlands and tropical lowlands. The tropical highlands superregion has five regions or subareas within it: the Sierra Madre Occidental and the Sierra Oriental (my subarea 8), the Sierra and Mesa del Sur (subarea 6), the southern highlands (my subarea 5), the dry interior tropical basins, with the Rio Balsas and Valley of Ciapas subdivisions (subarea 4), and the mesa central, with an arid and rain-shadow subdivision within it (my subarea 7). The Tehuacan Valley is in one of the more southerly arid rain-shadow subdivisions within subarea 7. The other major division is the tropical lowlands, which has three major regions: the Caribbean gulf-lowlands (subarea 2) and the Pacific lowlands (subarea 3). The former has five subdivisions within it and the latter has three subdivisions, mainly because of topographic and soil factors for the climate and hydrography and much of the flora and fauna are quite similar. The third region would be the dry subtropical lowlands of Tamaulipas (subarea 1).

A nuclear area (sometimes mistakenly called a center of domestication) has a number of definite characteristics. First, the regions or subareas are relatively close together, so there is potentially relatively easy communications or movement of objects, ideas, or people from one to any of the others. Even preliminary studies of such items as obsidian artifacts in Mexico indicate that movement occurred frequently for at least the last 11,000 years; future study will yield even more evidence of this.[2] Second, botanical studies reveal that many wild relatives of domesticated plants of the area are confined to this nuclear area; thus, a good characteristic of a nuclear area is the existence of many plants (and animals) within it that have the potential for domestication. Third, although our geographical and paleoecological studies are woefully inadequate, it would appear that in the period before man domesticated plants, there has been only one major ecological change: a shift from a Pleistocene climatic period to a Recent period.

Although this change may have resulted in the extinction of certain fauna in the Tehuacan Valley, it mainly concerned slight shifts of boundaries of the present microenvironments, only slight changes in the annual temperatures, and perhaps the loss of only a few millimeters of annual precipitation. The final characteristic is that these centers show considerable ecological diversity of a relatively dichotomous nature. At one end are the lowlands, which have relatively large amounts of rainfall, high temperatures, and not well-marked seasons (perhaps only a rainy season and dry season with the latter being not very dry). Such regions, while having a number of microenvironments, often paralleling the coasts or river valley for considerable distances, have in each one of them a large number of plant and animal (including marine) foods that would allow man to exist fairly securely without regard to season or much sophisticated technical knowledge. The Ocos area, studied by Flannery and Coe, with nine or so microenvironments, each rich in food, would be an example of this sort of zone, which might be termed one of lush (in terms of food) uniformity.[3] Each coastal region, whether northwest, southeast, or north (on the Gulf Coast) from Ocos, tends to repeat the same seven to nine microenvironments in seemingly endless monotony.

At the opposite end of the scale are regions like Tehuacan, which have great seasonality and a series of microenvironments that yield wild food resources, including some potentially domesticable plants, in each season. In such a zone, man, with little technical equipment, could not exist without shifting his base of operation, and perhaps abode, to other microenvirons with every season. Each part of the valley basin would also have different rainfall patterns, elevations, soils, flora, and/or fauna. Thus, there would be great ecological diversity within each region and also between each region or highland subarea. This considerable diversity lessens with the drop in elevation.

ECOZONES OF THE TEHUACAN VALLEY

The ecozones of the lenticular Tehuacan Valley, some seventy kilometers long and twenty kilometers at its widest, are not only examples of a region or subarea of great diversity and limiting resources but the background within which each sequential phase existed. I shall describe them in terms of their individual elements or components, although obviously each is a type of ecosystem in which the elements are interconnected by various kinds of energy and physiochemical flow.

El Riego Oasis

The first of these, the *El Riego oasis* ecozone, existed in the northwestern flanks of Tehuacan Valley surrounded by the travertine slopes ecozone to the south and west and the valley steppe ecozone to the north and east. The zone itself is roughly a ten- to twelve-kilometer crescent shape and is never more than a kilometer wide bulging eastward toward the grassland steppes and in a cliff from three to forty meters at the foot of the travertine slopes. The underlying rocks of this cliff are limestone, but mineral-laden water from springs in these strata has encrusted the face of these cliffs with contorted layers of travertine, within which are a series of niches, tunnels, and caves. The talus below the cliffs is gravelly with boulders of chert and other siliceous pebbles useful for making flint tools, and the flat below it contains deep, well-watered alluvial soil good for agriculture. Although the zone has very limited rainfall—less than 500 mm during brief showers in June and August—and warm temperatures ranging from 1°C in the winter to as much as 40°C during the rest of the year, it is a well-watered area with lush vegetation because of the springs. Some studies indicate that the water table has fallen steadily since the Pleistocene, so once it was an even lusher and wider zone. In fact, stray finds suggest that mammoth and mastodon once inhabited the zone.

Its vegetation is green throughout the year in contrast to the rest of the valley, which is dusty brown for the October to June rainless season. This floral system includes leaf trees (such as mesquite, guaje, tule, and ciruela), fruit trees, prickly pear and organ

Figure 5.1

Excavations in the locality of the El Riego oasis.

cactus, and agave, along with dense patches of weeds and grasses. In terms of man's food, agave leaves and opuntia fruits are available in the winter, grass and amaranth seeds and mesquite beans occur in the spring, other seeds and some fruits reach fruition in the wetter summer, and ciruela plums and chupandilla and cosahuico fruits are edible in the fall.

As might be expected with these available plant and water resources, animal foods are equally available throughout the year; they include deer, peccary, skunk, raccoon, gray fox, gopher, rabbit, opossum, snake, lizard, turtle, iguana, and a wide variety of rats, mice, birds, and insects. Some of these inhabit the area all year round, although the concentration of these animals is less in the fall and winter than in other seasons when they can spread out to the more amenable ecozones. The El Riego oasis is a particularly good dry season habitat for man; it could be occupied all year round except for the fact that it is very small and could never provide large amounts of food for large groups for any length of time.

Travertine Slopes

The *travertine slopes* subregion encompasses the El Riego oasis and occupies the northwest one-sixth of the valley. It is a roughly sloping area that rises west of the central valley steppes, which contain many low hills of sandstone and limestone that have been cut by canyons draining into the central valley Rio Salado. These rocks have some deposits of flint and onyx that are useful to man, and they also have salt seeps, a very valuable human commodity. Soils, except for small alluvial deposits in the bottoms and on the terrace of the canyons, are extremely thin and heavily travertine (lime) impregnated. This condition, in conjunction with very limited rainfall (less than 400 mm annually that falls in summer showers) and temperatures ranging from 13°C to 45°C (very hot), make for a Sonoran-like desert vegetation, including yucca, barrel cactus, organ cactus, spiny mala mujer, agave, palm-like bushes, a few thorny trees, some grasses, and probably once wild corn. These yield edible food only during the brief wet seasons, which is the only time that many animals are found in the ecozone (deer, peccary, rabbits, skunks, gray fox, gophers, mice, rats, birds,

Figure 5.2

Excavations in the San Marcos locality in the travertine slopes.

and hibernating reptiles such as turtles, snakes, iguanas, and lizards). Thus, without technology, this barren environment gives man usable foods for a few weeks in the wetter summer months, although the onyx, flint, and salt make it profitable for visits at any time.

Valley Center Steppe and Humid River Bottoms

The finding of bones of antelope and horse in Pleistocene deposits of the travertine slope suggests that during that period it was much smaller in size and that the *valley center steppe* ecozone, now to the east and south, had contracted out of it. The ecozone now runs north and south through the relatively level center of the Tehuacan basin (some seventy kilometers) and, depending on the width of the valley floor, is from one to ten kilometers wide. It is bisected by and surrounds still another ecozone, the *humid river bottoms,* which is the area of the Rio Salado and its banks, as well as those of its major tributaries.

Both zones, locationally and topographically similar, have the same amount of annual rainfall—between 400 mm and 600 mm, falling in the summer—and an average annual temperature

Figure 5.3
The north end of the plaza of the Quachilco site (Ts218) in the valley center steppe, as viewed from the southeast.

Figure 5.4

View of Coatepec (Tc368) in the humid river bottoms from the west, with Ts368w trench in the foreground. Ts368e is indicated in the background.

between 19°C and 24°C. Here the resemblances end, for the humid river bottom areas have permanent water and deep, fertile, alluvial soils with resultant lusher and distinctive biotic assemblages. The sides of the rivers have a form of gallery forest of leaf trees, including many fruit trees and thorny mesquite trees. The canopy, often with Spanish moss on it, hangs over thickets of river cane, marsh weeds, and various kinds of grasses. A wide variety of animals, rare or absent in other valley environs, include teal, crane, and killdeer in the dry winter season, and dove, quail, mud turtle, fish, and green iguana in the wet season. Animals common to the rest of the valley—such as opossum, cottontail rabbit, deer, peccary, skunk, raccoon, hawk, black iguana, lizard, snake, and fox— seem to be more common in this riverine environment during the dry season. Mammoth, as well as horse and antelope, probably existed in this subregion, which expanded farther up the tributaries of the Rio Salado during the Pleistocene. From many standpoints this environment is the best one for year-round living in the

valley, particularly in the dry season when other microenvironments yield little food and animals have been forced out of them
because of the dry conditions.

This relatively desirable environment stands out in marked
contrast to the valley center steppes that flank it on either side.
Most of this ecozone lies west of the Rio Salado and north of the
river's confluence with the Rio Zapotitlan. Its soils are shallow
and heavily impregnated with salts and travertine. These soils and
the limited amounts of seasonal rainfall create a barren grassland
spotted here and there with agave, opuntia, mesquite, and an
occasional tree legume. Food from these plants is available mainly
during the spring. Jackrabbits and kangaroo rats are the dominant
fauna of the locality; night hawks and owls prey on them and, in
the wet parts of the year, there are opossum, deer, and fox. During
the Pleistocene the size of the area was much expanded and was
probably a major habitat of the horse and antelope on a year-
round basis. Occasional salt seeps probably had considerable value,
but, generally, the area after the Pleistocene could support, without agriculture, few people except in the spring and early summer.

In Coxcatlan Cave in the alluvial slope faunal remains of
steppe animals such as horse, antelope, and jackrabbit suggest that
this steppe subregion was probably the dominant ecozone of the
valley during the Pleistocene, partaking of not only part of the
present travertine slope ecozone but much of the alluvial slope
ecozone, which is now the valley's dominant zone.

Alluvial Slopes

The alluvial slopes ecozone exists to the east and northeast
of the steppes and extends well up the slopes of the Sierra Madre,
to the west of the Rio Salado and steppe area in the south and
southeastern part of the valley (which extends up into the Mixtec
hills), and even surrounds part of the travertine slope to the west
and northwest. Topographically, although it exists on the gentle
slope of the valley, it also occurs along the many arroyos and on
the erosional remnants and hills that protrude out of the valley
slopes. Its sandy and gravelly alluvial soils cover a variety of
minerals, flinty rocks, rocks useful for building, and some salt deposits. Rainfall ranges from 400 mm to 800 mm, with most of it

Figure 5.5

Excavations in the Coxcatlan locality in the alluvial slopes.

falling in the brief periods at the beginning and at the end of the summer. Temperature varies with the season but ranges from over 50°C in the hot summer months to occasional frosts on the colder winter nights. These factors make for a distinctive vegetational assemblage, typically a canopy of thorny trees and scrubs interrupted by only occasional patches of grass or fruit trees along the arroyos or moister sections.

Deer, coyote, puma, bobcat, peccary, skunk, fox, and rat are found during most seasons. Turtle, lizard, iguana, dove, and owl appear during the wet season and crane and duck during the winter.

Foodstuffs are seasonal. Agave, opuntia, and tetecho fruits, and a few animals and birds are available in the winter. In the spring, this assemblage is augmented by grass seeds and pod foods, as well as more animals. Summer is the best season, for there are more seeds, fruits, game, and reptiles available. During the fall, the seeds and animals disappear but various plums, tuna, and other fruits reach fruition. In summary, then, it was the summer and fall when food was abundant; in the spring, man could barely manage to eke out a living. Only the winter presented major problems as energy expended for food may have just barely equaled the energy obtained from those foods.

Narrow Canyons and Dissected Alluvial Slopes

The alluvial slopes ecozone surrounds still another small ecozone in the southeast portion of the valley: the *narrow canyons and dissected alluvial slopes* ecozone. It is characterized by many formations of rock, with only a few minerals useful to man. Only the flanks of the arroyos and talus slopes of the mesa and hills have soils, and these are sandy and rocky.

Daily average temperatures range from about 4°C in winter to about 45°C in the summer, and rainfall is between 500 mm and 800 mm per year. None of the arroyos has permanent water, but raging torrents of predominantly run-off water occur during the May–June or September peaks of the wet season.

Low thorn scrub, cacti, agave, and occasionally fruit trees grow in the canyons. Higher elevations carry agave and organ cactus and sometimes thorn tree or bush.

The faunal assemblage is about like that of the surrounding alluvial slopes. Generally, wild foods, both plant and animal, are

Figure 5.6

Excavations in the Lencho Diego locality in the dissected alluvial slopes.

most abundant during the spring and wet seasons, and game is relatively easy to find during the dry seasons. Food, however, is limited and does not encourage long stays in the subregion.

From these descriptions of the highland zone of harsh diversity, it should be readily apparent that primitive man without agriculture and after the Pleistocene could eke out a living only by making well-scheduled trips from one ecozone to the next in exactly the right seasons. However, our cultural story starts before these environmental restrictions were either so harsh or varied. In the Pleistocene epoch when seasonality may not have been so great, the gallery forests along the waterways were more extensive, and the central grasslands and mountainside oak-pine forests were expanded at the expense of the thorn forest and other xerophytic ecozones. Even more important, there are good indications that megafauna such as at least mammoth and mastodon existed, and various animals (such as extinct horse, antelope, wolf, jackrabbit, and extinct giant turtle) were much more numerous than after the Pleistocene.

TEHUACAN CULTURAL PHASES

It was in this rather different environment where we find the remains of the earliest archaeological phase or cultural system. It is defined on the basis of over twenty components. Seven of these (called early Ajuereado) are in the Pleistocene and date roughly between 10,800 B.C. and 8800 B.C. in sidereal time. The others would be of late Ajuereado times–8800 B.C. to 7800 B.C. sidereal time and from about 8100 B.C. to 7000 B.C. in radiocarbon time. Much earlier remains at the Tlapacoya site in the Valley of Mexico and at Valsequillo near the city of Pueblo have been uncovered that date back more than 20,000 years. Moreover, comparative data suggest that earlier materials existed in Mexico, perhaps going back 50,000 years. Thus, the beginning of man's story in Tehuacan, perhaps the first two stages of his development, are as yet unknown. However, as far as the present problem is concerned, it makes little difference, for our earliest Ajuereado remains are thousands of years before plant domestication or the origins of agriculture in Meso-America.

Ajuereado Phase: 10,000–7000 B.C.

Our reconstruction of the cultural system of the Ajuereado phase is based upon a study of only about 150 artifacts, 400 or 500 fragments of debitage, and fewer than 1,000 ecofacts, about 20 of which were plant remains (the rest were bones).

Settlement Patterns   Of the over twenty occupations we discovered, only ten came from excavations. Identification of the seasonality at these brief occupations indicated they ranged from a few days to less than three weeks, but this can be estimated for only twelve components. Two of these were dry season encampments in the oasis zone, two were wet season occupations in the travertine slopes, two dry and two wet camps were in the alluvial slopes with its thorn forest, three wet and two dry occupations were in the expanded Pleistocene grassland or steppes, and three wet and maybe one dry camp were in the lusher humid river bottoms. All occupations were by microbands (three or fewer families).

Subsistence   Certain of the activities of its cultural system are related to the surrounding ecosystem; these are called the *techno-subsistence subsystems*. Many of these activities (which might be considered a single technology) persisted in varying popularity throughout the 3,000 or so years of the period, and some—such as flint knapping—lasted thousands of years into the following phases; thus, they can be classified as tradition. However, for the moment, we are concerned with reconstructing the cultural systems in what might be heuristically considered a moment, an event, or a single period of time, so we shall talk of them as subsystems or activities with an emphasis on their being interconnected in terms of energy flow.

One of the most important subsystems or activities from a standpoint of energy input and output was lance ambushing of horse, antelope, deer, and perhaps other large mammals (mammoth included). The tools used were wooden lances tipped with leaf-shaped, flint-chipped projectiles. Probably whole families or even groups of families undertook such activities. In terms of energy flow, the experiments by Don Crabtree and others suggest that chipping the points, making the string, obtaining the gum

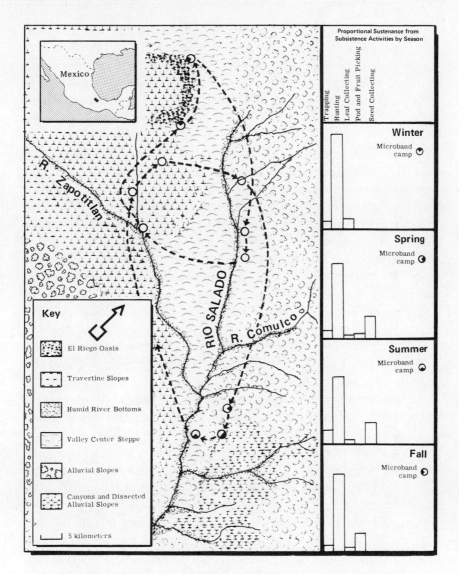

Figure 5.7

Ajuereado phase (10,000 B.C. to 7000 B.C.) with estimates of proportions of sustenance from subsistence activities of season (right column) and the distribution of seasonal microband camps with their hypothetical wanderings that form nomadic microband communities in the microenvironments of the Tehuacan Valley (left column).

to secure the tips, and fashioning the wood for the lances would have probably taken only a couple of hours of work, or 300 (2 hours × 150 calories each) to 400 (2 hours × 200 calories each) calories of energy. Therefore, an eight-hour hunt by perhaps as many as five or six men using 150 to 200 calories each may have only taken some 6,000 (150 calories × 5 men × 8 hours) to 9,600 (200 calories × 6 men × 8 hours) calories; but the slaying of only a single horse would have yielded some 80,000 to 100,000 calories of edible meat.[4] Even if we consider a hunting party of one boy and two men, expending a total of 500 calories per hour over an eight- to ten-hour period, the killing of one horse per four or five hunts would have been very profitable business in early Ajuereado times. The caloric expenditure would have been 16,000 to at most 25,000 calories in return for 80,000 to 100,000 calories of meat. In fact, for every calorie expended in hunting, three to six calories would be obtained from the meat killed. A study of the bones from the occupations suggests this activity may have yielded as much as 50 percent to 60 percent of the inhabitants' sustenance in the early part of the phase and 30 percent to 40 percent in the latter part of the phase. It was done throughout the year in most microenvirons.

Another important subsistence option, which also decreased throughout the phase, was rabbit drives done by the whole group in all environs throughout the year with probably even less equipment, perhaps just a few clubs or rocks.

One of the options that increased in importance after the extinction of animals at about 8000 B.C. would have been stalking big game using atlatl darts tipped with tanged or bulky projectile points. Our study of activity areas of various floors at various sites suggests that this was carried on throughout the year in most microenvironments. Other subsistence options utilized even less, though found in every environment in every season, would have been trapping small game, collecting small game, and cutting opuntia or agave leaves. Two other minor options could be done only in the wet season in certain environs: seed collecting and fruit picking. Nevertheless, for all these minor options or activities, the equipment necessary was relatively easy to make, although it did take considerable technical skill. Also, these minor options would not have been possible without a considerable accumulation of ecosystem knowledge. It is my opinion that these two factors only came into being among primitive man in Tehuacan near the end of the Pleistocene.

Closely connected with the subsistence activities were a series of food preparation subsystems: various butchering techniques by choppers and flakes with cutting edges, barbecuing or hot-rock roasting techniques, and (late in the phase) pounding food by pestles in mortars and circular grinding of seeds by pebbles in flat rocks with a concavity. Again, the tools used were simple. There is little or no evidence of storage of food.

Technology   Various other activities involved manufacturing the tools needed. Flint knapping, an important one, was accomplished mainly by a few simple percussion techniques, although a pressure technique was sometimes utilized. Other tools were pebble hammers and antler tine retouchers. There was some woodworking, though only a little log cutting, perhaps by unhafted pebble choppers. There was more working of sticks by scraping, shaving, and sawing by flint blades or flakers, spokeshaves, denticulated end or side scrapers, and gravers. A few bone tools, awls, and antler flakes were manufactured by whittling, perhaps using tools just mentioned, as well as by slicing, probably using burins. The bone awls and flint gravers suggest that some tailoring of skins was done, and the many haftable end scrapers suggest animals were fleshed and skins scraped by a few simple techniques. Whether sewing of any sort occurred is difficult to determine, but string was made by rolling chewed fiber of agave. Perhaps a few simple nets and twined baskets or bags were made with this string or sinew. Perhaps a few objects, like obsidian Plainview points, were obtained by the indirect procurement system, trade.

Social and Value Systems   Our occupations suggest that people lived in family groups. Microbands moved in a relatively random manner chasing game. They changed their abode often without regard to season and had no well-defined territories. In other words, they were nomadic microbands. Other aspects of their social life are difficult to determine, but we could guess on the basis of ethnographic analogy that there was a division of labor and status based on skill, age, and sex, some sort of exogamous marriage and kinship system, weak leadership, and some sort of a limited ceremonial system (we found a fragment of burned human jaw). Of their system of values we know nothing.

There was considerable energy available for such endeavors as thinking, passing on information, social systems behavior endeavors, and leisure—all activities above and beyond the technosubsistence activities. In fact, the Ajuereado had considerable leisure time: about 30 percent to 40 percent of their energy was available for nonutilitarian activities. There is confirmation of this hypothesis in the research of ethnographers, who often write about the large amounts of leisure time available to hunters and gatherers.

Summary   Our Ajuereado energy system does not show that these early hunters ate predominately vegetable food or did little meat hunting or collecting like many modern Bushman hunter-gatherers do and which many ethnographers hypothesize were analogous to people of the upper Pleistocene or American Paleo-Indians. In fact, our Ajuereado susbsistence activities do not seem directly analogous to any modern desert people but are more like those of the Eskimo.

The Ajuereado data tend to show that technosubsistence activities were extremely similar in each season of the year with heavy emphasis on hunting and large amounts of meat consumption and these subsistence techniques have an energetic efficiency rate of about 4 (that is, for every calorie spent in hunting, they got four back from the meat of animals they killed). Their nomadic microband settlement pattern required that considerable energy be utilized in group travel, and there was a relatively limited number of technological energy expenditures or energy used in exchange of goods, ceremonials, or making storage facilities. In fact, within our sequence this model is distinctive from all the ones that follow it, but it is sufficiently general and nonculturally bound so it might be compared with other models of early hunters in other regions where agriculture evolved. This is obviously important to the energy systems concept. As we shall see shortly, the real value of this model is apparent when we analyze the life span of a culture or energy system, for here the energy flow material clearly shows the causes of the break-up of a specific energy system and its development into a new one.

Ajuereado Cultural Relationships   It appears that this Ajuereado energy and cultural system existed during the early lithic horizon from roughly 10,000 B.C. to about 7,000 B.C. in carbon 14 time. There are a few other related finds in Tamaulipas, Querétaro, Hidalgo, the Valley of Mexico, Oaxaca, and Guatemala that seem to be of this general horizon. Because of their limited nature, however, it is difficult to determine the interaction sphere in which the Ajuereado culture system was involved. Probably its sphere was like that of the so-called Cordilleran tradition and not only existed in much of Mexico and Central America but extended up the west coast into the United States and perhaps even into Canada. It probably was contemporaneous with the Llano-Plano and Folsom interaction spheres in the Great Plains and the U.S. Southwest, as well as some sort of Archaic interaction sphere in eastern North America.

El Riego Phase: 7000–5000 B.C.

The Ajuereado developed into the El Riego cultural system, which existed from about 7800 B.C. to about 5800 B.C. sidereal or solar time (or 7000 B.C. to 5000 B.C. in carbon 14 time). The 3,000 artifacts, thousands of pieces of debitage, and about 2,000 ecofacts from the fifty or so occupations uncovered (only about twenty from the surface) give a sound basis for reconstructing this system.

Settlement Patterns   Two dry season encampments came from the El Riego oasis, and five similar camps came from the humid river bottoms. There were also four wet season occupations from the latter and a single one from the grassy steppes. The travertine slopes have two wet season occupations and two possible dry season camps. From the excavation of Coxcatlan Cave, we have many occupations from the alluvial slopes ecozone: five from the summer, four from the spring, three from the fall, and three from the winter; four of these were multiseason. The dissected alluvial slopes had seven spring encampments, two summer ones, and a single winter occupation.

Subsistence Activities   These data, coupled with a study of subsistence systems, indicate the occupation of certain microenviron-

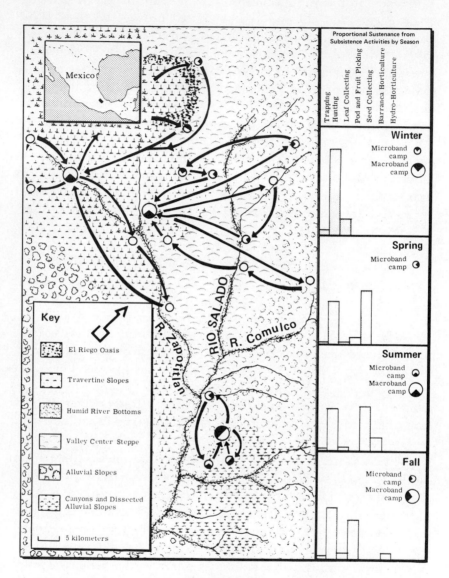

Figure 5.8

*El Riego phase (7000 B.C. to 5000 B.C.) with estimates of pro-
portions of seasonally scheduled subsistence activities (right
column) and the distribution of seasonal micro-macroband
camps with their possible cyclical movement that form
communities of seasonal micro-macrobands in territories
within the microenvironments of the Tehuacan Valley (left
column).*

ments or ecozones in certain seasons. A study of the materials seems to indicate seasonally scheduled subsistence options for certain environs—a major shift from the Ajuereado system. Dart stalking was a major subsistence activity along with minor frequencies of lance ambushing in the winter (although both were important throughout the year). As a tradition it seems little changed from Ajuereado times except that a wider variety of projectile point types was used. The other two winter subsistence options—trapping and leaf cutting—both very minor, continued in small amounts throughout the year. These practices were little changed from what they were in Ajuereado times, although nets may have been used in addition to spring snares, and leaf-carrying equipment may have included carrying loops, nets, and baskets. Seed collecting, as important as hunting, did not begin until the spring and continued into the summer, as did fruit picking, which was a minority subsistence option until the fall when it was the equal of hunting. Some seed storage was done at this time. Although rabbit drives seem to have disappeared in middle Ajuereado with the extinction of the Pleistocene jackrabbit, in the main the El Riego subsistence options were about the same as those of Ajuereado, but they occurred in very different proportions and were neatly scheduled.

Only two new subsistence options occurred very late in El Riego: seed planting, which had grown imperceptibly out of seed collecting and occurred as a majority option only in the summer, and fruit pit planting, which occurred as a minority option in the fall. One might speculate how the process of annual migration, which saw a shift from seed collecting to seed planting, began as man returned seasonally to some seed or fruit area each year. This work would have led to some clearing, enrichment, and improvement of the habitat of the seeds and fruits, which, with man's selection of larger seeds for food, would have led to changes in the seed and fruit population, some of them possibly genetic. Eventually the process may have led to the use of the domesticates (genetically changed food plants) and finally to some planting of individual seeds (amaranth, chile, mixta squash) or pits (avocado) in some kind of plots or gardens (horticulture). Another practice that would have developed is storage, which made life more secure in hard times or bad years and allowed larger groups to come together and stay longer at particular spots. This concept of storage might in fact be well considered the necessary conditions for the advances that were to take place in later cultural or energy systems.

However, in spite of these two new subsistence options, subsistence technology and tool kits were little changed. This was not true of food preparation activities, butchering and barbecuing excepted. Bones were crushed up by new chopper types and pebble hammers to make bone gruel. Food, particularly leaves, was roasted in special large pits. Seeds were ground round and round in milling stones by mullers and also ground back and forth by manos in metates. Seeds and nuts were pounded into a more palatable form in three different kinds of mortars (bowl, tecomate, and flaring rim) by conical, long, and cylindrical pestles. These five activities were usually done during the spring and/or summer.

Technology   A number of other new activities were undertaken in spring and summer. One was making ground stone tools by gouging, pecking, and grinding using chipped flint tools. Another was making marginella shell beads by piercing them with chipped stone drills or gravers. Also, paint (possibly red) was ground up in small hemispherical dishes. String or yarn, though still handmade, often of chewed agave fibers, now also was made of soft bast fiber and often was woven into two-ply cord and four-ply rope. A number of these were knotted, and some knotted nets, as well as knotless nets, were made into bags. Others were woven into twined baskets, blankets, bags, or kilts. Coiled baskets with interlocking or noninterlocking stitch were also manufactured.

Other activities similar to those of Ajuereado were done throughout the year, but some new techniques and tools of the trade were slightly different. Bone tools now included three kinds of awls, needles, hammers, and flakers. They were not only whittled and sliced but scraped, sawed, and drilled. Woodworking was much the same, but some sticks were ground to points, and flint gouges were now used. Skins were also fleshed by a new wide assortment of bifaces, blades, and side scrapers, and they were scraped by new, small, haftable scraper types, as well as large scraper planes. Flint knapping continued some of the older techniques with the same tools, but abrader hammers and antler hammers were used for new percussion techniques on prepared platforms, and retouching techniques were more widely used.

Social and Value Systems   Trade increased slightly, but it was still of the indirect procurement type. A study of the occupations reveals three times as many people as in the previous phase. There were now thirty-one microband encampments and ten macroband occupations by the last half of the El Riego phase. (By macroband I mean groups of three or more nuclear families.) Sites also clustered geographically in groups, suggesting some sort of band territoriality. This settlement pattern type has been called *seasonal micro-macroband* system. Ethnographic analogy with Great Basin groups suggests that El Riego had patrilineal exogamous bands and status division of labor based on skill, age, and sex. Leadership was weak and transitory. Five complex burials in Coxcatlan Cave, a cremated female in El Riego Cave, and a flexed female in Purron Cave suggest elaborate rites and rituals, perhaps directed by a shaman. Unfortunately the burials were not complete enough to confirm our hypotheses on the kinship system.

Summary   The energy system model for this phase is unique and shows different energetic efficiencies and kinds of energy flow for each of the four seasons of the year. The energetic efficiency rate, which rose to 5 or 6, has many ethnographic analogies to desert hunters and gatherers (particularly at Great Basin) with their high consumption of calories from gathered plants and large amounts of energy expended in their collection in certain seasons, when their energetic efficiency often went well over 10. Again in terms of comparison our preliminary studies of El Riego show it can be grouped with certain hunters and gatherers and separated from others not in these so-called centers of domestication. However, one major attribute of the use of the energy system model of this time period is that it shows what factors caused the system to evolve into a new one.

El Riego Cultural Relationships   Other excavated sites of this horizon are not numerous in Meso-America and the adjacent United States, but there are enough to guess that there were at least four interaction spheres at this time. Probably a large desert culture extended over much of Mexico and the western United States (of which El Riego is a part), another Archaic sphere existed in Texas, an Archaic one was in the eastern United States, and a Plano one occurred in the Great Plains and prairies.

Coxcatlan Phase: 5000–3400 B.C.

On the basis of continuity of the racial type, as well as artifact type, the Coxcatlan phase seems to have developed out of El Riego at about 5000 B.C. and continued until about 3400 B.C. in carbon 14 time (5800 B.C. to 4000 B.C. in sidereal time). Although there are more artifacts, debitage, and ecofacts in Coxcatlan components than in El Riego to use in reconstructing the cultural system, fewer occupations (twenty-four) occurred.

Settlement Patterns   This fewer number of occupations may seem to indicate a diminution of population, but, in fact, it does not, for twelve of the occupations were macrobands and all were for two or more seasons (in the travertine slopes, one spring–summer and one fall–winter occupation; in the steppes, a single spring–summer occupation; in the humid river bottoms two fall–winter and four spring–summer encampments; in the alluvial slopes one spring–winter occupation, as well as a summer–winter camp; in a canyon of the dissected slopes, a spring–summer open site). The twelve microband occupations were much the same as those of El Riego, but one in the alluvial slopes lasted from spring to fall, one in the travertine slopes was spring and summer, and the other three were just of the summer. The other single season microband occupation occurred in the oasis (two dry seasons) camps in the Lecha Diego Canyon (one summer, two spring, and two winter camps).

The Coxcatlan subsistence system was much like that of El Riego in terms of seasonal scheduling. Winter was still the time of hunting, mainly by the dart stalking technique as well as a little lance ambushing, but a new hunting technique came into being that used thin points with serrated edges and sharp barbs; man could wound an animal and then trail it until it bled to death. Leaf cutting and trapping also occurred in this season, and all three activities carried into the rest of the year in very diminished amounts. Seed collection was still important in the spring and summer. Fruits and pod picking started in the spring and became dominant by the fall, when fruit trees also yielded some produce. Except for the trail and bleed projectile points, the technical equipment remained about the same.

There is one major difference from the previous period: the

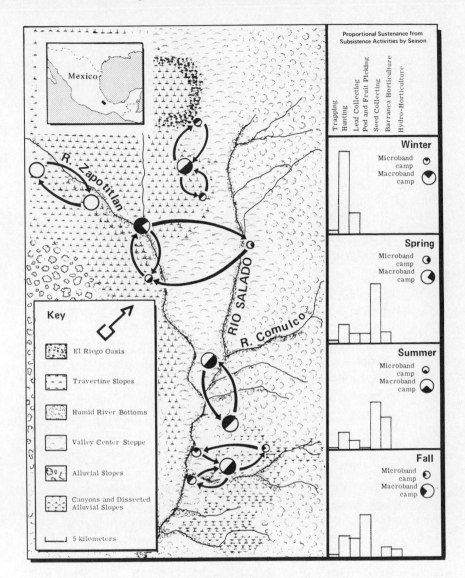

Figure 5.9

Coxcatlan phase (5000 B.C. to 3400 B.C.) with estimates of proportions of seasonally scheduled subsistence activities (right column) and the distribution of seasonal micro-macroband camps with their possible cyclical movements that form communities of seasonal macro-microbands in territories within the microenvironments of the Tehuacan Valley (left column).

planting of cultivars or domesticates in the spring or summer, which yielded storable surplus foods for at least the summer season. Unlike the previous periods, a wide variety of plants were used, among them corn, common beans, chupandilla plums, white and black zapotes, mixta and moschata squash, gourds, avocados, chile peppers, and amaranths.

There is considerable evidence that corn was first domesticated in or near Tehuacan and that it definitely did not evolve out of teosinte, its nearest wild relative with the same chromosome number.[5] The evidence that it came from Tehuacan (or nearby Oaxaca) is that corn (and Oaxaca corn pollen) is earlier here than anywhere else. That corn did not evolve out of teosinte is clearly indicated by a restudy by Walton Galinat and Louis F. Randolph of what was originally called wild maize.[6] This study shows (as does figure 5.10) that some of the earliest maize could well be a prototype of both later corn and teosinte for it has low row numbers (like teosinte), wide capsules (like teosinte) but many spikelets (like corn), and soft glumes (like corn and never occurring in teosinte). The next corn in our sequence is more like later maize developments, and it is only in latest Coxcatlan times and in the following Abejas phase that we have wild maize with many teosinte characteristics, or tripsacoid corn, which probably is some sort of a cross between maize and teosinte, or wild maize type, with teosinte tendencies. It seems very probable that teosinte evolved about this time from one of the earlier maize types. Obviously our sample from Tehuacan is small, but all the evidence there is leads me to the above interpretation.

The inhabitants thus had more storable foods, which allowed them to spend more than one season in one spot in bigger groups. They also began pounding their food in new kinds of stone bowls and grinding it back and forth in better-made metates with a number of different kinds of manos. Butchering of animals and cooking were done much as they were in the previous periods, but the tradition of making bone gruel by pounding was going out of style.

Technology   Many of the year-round activities, such as woodworking and boneworking, were the same as those of El Riego, although more kinds of products were manufactured. Flint knapping was only slightly changed; there was more pressure flaking

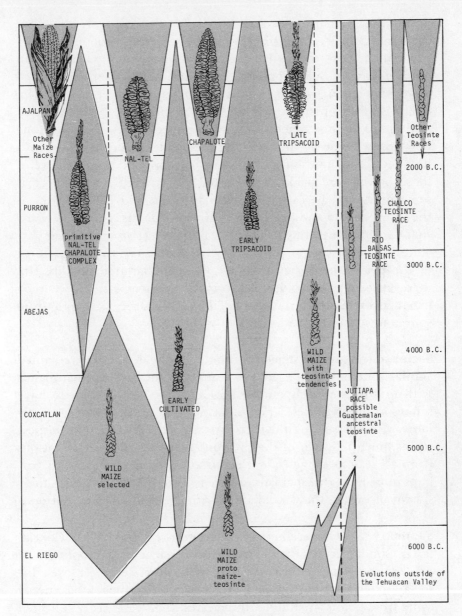

Figure 5.10

Sequence of archaeological corn in the Tehuacan Valley from El Riego to Ajalpan times showing possible relationships with teosinte.

and indirect percussion with an anvil. Most of the tools used were the same. Other technological activities occurred throughout other parts of the year, unlike El Riego when they usually occurred in specific seasons. String making, knotting, and weaving remained about the same, although split stitch coiled baskets appeared. Shells were still pierced, and the people still made paint. Ground stone tools became much more numerous, and some of the stone bowls were made by first gouging them into shape (possibly with flint tools) and then grinding them into finished form. Many of these bowls were made of imported volcanic tufa, and there is some indication by caches of obsidian, flint, and tufa, as well as the many new domesticated or cultivated plants, that a new exchange system pertained. This is called *direct procurement:* raw materials were transported directly by individuals from the source to the place where they were locally manufactured and distributed. Of course, the older indirect procurement system, whereby products or raw materials passed through a series of hands from source to consumer, still operated.

Social and Value Systems   The settlement pattern remained similar, but now there were as many macrobands as microbands with multiseason occupations; however, bands still seem to have some sort of territories. The system is called *seasonal macro-micro-bands.* Reconstructing the social system is difficult, but we suspect it was much like that of the previous El Riego phase. Cremations from all seasons suggest more elaborate rites and rituals and perhaps more powerful shamans. There is little we can say about their system of values, the flow of information, or other emic matters.

Summary   The preliminary energy system model for Coxcatlan is similar to El Riego: energetic efficiency was about 6; 30 percent to 40 percent of total expenditures were left over for social activities, thought, and/or leisure; and much food energy came from plants (including stored ones) that were easily collected efficiently. The model appears radically different because of longer spring–summer periods at bigger occupations. In fact, the Coxcatlan peoples had basically only three seasons per year, not four. For comparative purposes an energy flow model for this incipient agricultural group should be of great value, but again the early and late Coxcatlan energy system when compared reveals the factors in the late Coxcatlan model that are connected with the conditions leading to change into the Abejas system, mainly a new exchange system resulting in more domesticates and the growing of plants for storage.

Coxcatlan Cultural Relationships   More material from this period has been uncovered from other parts of Meso-America. A preliminary study of these still relatively meager remains suggests there were four or five interaction spheres. One was in central southern Mexico; it is called the Tehuacan sphere, and the Coxcatlan phase was part of it. In this sphere the exchange of domesticated plants was a major element of the interactions. Another sphere, northeast Mexico, may have extended into southern Texas. A third, the Big Bend sphere, was in north central Mexico. A fourth seems to have extended out of the U.S. Southwest into western Mexico and has been called Cochise. The fifth has not been defined but excavations from Veracruz hint that still another base camp, called Palma Sola, existed. This type was oriented toward a more sedentary exploitation of marine life along this coast or both the Pacific and Atlantic coasts. Perhaps all of these spheres had some contact with each other and should be considered subspheres, but only more research will determine this relationship.

Abejas Phase: 3400–2300 B.C.

The Coxcatlan phase seems to have developed into Abejas, 3400 B.C. to 2300 B.C. carbon 14 time (4000 B.C. to 2800 B.C. sidereal time), without major intrusions of new peoples. Although there were about as many artifacts, debitage, and ecofacts from Abejas as from Coxcatlan and two more occupations (twenty-six), the basis for reconstructing the Abejas cultural system is not quite as good because none of the three possible hamlets in the humid river bottoms was completely excavated.

Settlement Patterns   Most of our relevant information comes from three winter, one spring, one spring–summer, and one fall–spring microband camps and a single spring macroband camp in the canyons of the dissected alluvial slopes and four multiseason occupations and two winter and one year-round microband camps from the alluvial slopes. Three spring–summer macroband occupa-

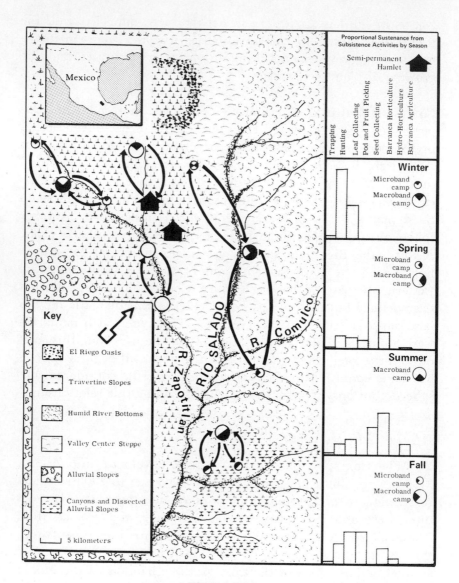

Figure 5.11

Abejas phase (3400 B.C. to 2300 B.C.) with estimates of pro-
portions of seasonally scheduled subsistence activities (right
column) and the distribution of their hamlets and macro-
band camps that were the bases for the seasonal microband
and macroband camps, forming communities of central
based bands within the microenvironments in the Tehaucan
Valley (left column).

tions in the travertine slopes also gave some information, as did the four spring–summer macroband camps in the humid river bottoms and the two fall–winter camps in the El Riego oasis ecozone.

Subsistence Activities   Most of the information on Abejas subsistence, which comes from the four multiseason camps in the alluvial slopes and from the one in the travertine slopes, indicates that the seasonal scheduling of this subsystem was much like that of Coxcatlan. Trapping and leaf cutting were minor activities throughout the year, hunting dominated in the winter, seed collection was most important in the spring and summer, and fruit picking and hydrohorticulture were more important in the fall. The planting of seeds of the same Coxcatlan plants plus tepary beans in gardens was only slightly more popular in the spring, summer, and perhaps fall than it was in Coxcatlan times. Now, however, there was an increasing emphasis on planting new, more productive corn types of hybrids. Some large concentrations of corn in certain activity areas in association with digging sticks, plus the occurrence of many of the larger sites near the fertile flats, suggest that crops were beginning to be sown in fields (*barranca agriculture*). Also, cache and storage pits suggest that some seasonal surpluses were grown for longer periods of occupancy of sites, as well as to allow greater security.

Because of better food supplies, most of the macrobands (twelve) could remain in one place for two or more seasons. In addition, there were three year-round occupied hamlets with pithouses. We believe that eleven microband camps (six of which were for a single season) represent groups who worked out from the larger home base sites. Thus, we have classified their settlement pattern as being the *central-based band* type.

In spite of a slightly larger population, a new settlement pattern, and a subsistence pattern that produced some surplus, the food preparation activities changed little. The butchering techniques, cooking, storage, and pounding and grinding round and round of foods were about the same. The back and forth grinding method was still used, but now large real metates and manos used by two hands occurred. Also, for the first time there is some evidence that food was boiled in stone bowls.

Technology   Many of the previous year-round technological activities continued: boneworking, fleshing, scraping, and tailoring. Although our sample is poor, there is a suggestion that less energy was expended on these activities, perhaps because of a greater use of woven fabrics. Woodworking remained about the same, using whittling, sawing, and grinding techniques on small sticks. Polished and rubbed pebbles seemed to be new tools used for the latter activity, and one pit was carefully carved. One difference is that now logs (perhaps for house construction) were chopped beaver fashion with a type of adz, perhaps the flake and discoidal choppers hafted or unhafted. The other year-round activity, flint knapping, continued the use of the older four or five traditions, but a new one started at this time: making fine (often obsidian) blades by pressure flaking neatly made conical cores with a prepared striking platform.

Of the other technological activities that occurred from spring through fall, some, such as string making, knotting, and making twined mats, continued in much the same way. So did the making of ground stone objects and the grinding of paint, although sometimes it was done on flat slab palettes. Disk stone beads were made in a new manner: stone cylinders were ground into shape, drilled from opposite ends, and then sawed into disc beads.

Perhaps the most important technological innovation for Abejas concerned the construction of pithouses. Pits were dug some five or six meters long, three meters wide, and one meter deep, perhaps using wooden slab shovels, and poles were cut for the tentlike roof frame. The poles were tied or laced together and finally covered with a brush roof, perhaps treated in a thatchlike manner.

Social and Value Systems   Foreign objects suggest trade, of both the direct procurement and indirect procurement type. Cremations in a few winter sites suggest that some sort of ceremonial system still adhered. Clusters of artifacts inside the pithouse and outside indicate a division of labor based on sex. However, until either large macroband camps or hamlets, as well as many burials, are excavated and then analyzed, it is almost impossible to reconstruct the Abejas social system. The value system is also unknown.

Summary   Energetic efficiency climbed to almost 8, in large part because of the beginning of barranca agriculture of new corn hybrids in late Abejas. This subsistence activity had an energetic efficiency of between 15 and 20. The Abejas systemic model is distinctive because it had two basic parts: a short dry season when storage products were consumed, and the rest of the year when food was produced and collected. The preliminary research on energy on this phase requires considerably more study and has many difficulties, not the least of which is that the ethnographic record has few, if any, analogous examples showing people just beginning to use agriculture.

Abejas Cultural Relationships   There are also difficulties in terms of relationships for, peculiarly enough, sites in this horizon in Meso-America are less numerous than in the previous horizon. There still seems to be a central Mexican interaction sphere, which included the Abejas phase, but how far south of Tehuacan it extended is unknown. There also is a northeast Mexican interaction sphere, which might be called La Perra, and a northwest Mexican interaction sphere that extended out of the U.S. Southwest. From the Palo Hueco site in central Veracruz, as well as Puerto Marquez and at Laguna del Chantuto on the Pacific Coast, there is a hint of a hamlet shell mound interaction sphere. Whether there are still other spheres in southern Meso-America or south-central Mexico is unknown. It might be noted that while there is considerable interaction inside each sphere, there also was some interaction between the Shell Mound and central Mexican spheres.

Purron Phase: 2300–1500 B.C.

Developing out of the Abejas phase was the Purron phase, 2300 B.C. to 1500 B.C. carbon 14 time (2800 B.C. to 1800 B.C. sidereal time). Unfortunately, the Purron phase is represented by only three cave occupations—a winter microband camp and two summer camps—and it is very probable that the dominant settlement type was akin to a hamlet system. Although we know these groups augmented their subsistence systems with considerable barranca corn agriculture and were using a new technological system—the making of pottery—our basic information is so meager that I will not attempt to reconstruct its cultural system. Instead I shall pass on to a consideration of the Ajalpan phase from 1800 B.C. to 1100 B.C. sidereal time.

Ajalpan Phase: 1500–850 B.C.

Our sample of Ajalpan artifacts, debitage, and bones is very large, but we have plant remains from only two small cave sites. We found few burials and were unable to test any hamlets adequately so our reconstruction of this culture system leaves much to be desired.

Settlement Patterns   We tested only sixteen occupations: Twelve hamlet sites found in the humid river bottoms; a hamlet site and a summer–fall macroband camp in a canyon of the dissected alluvial slopes; a hamlet in the steppes (perhaps originally along the waterway); and a spring–summer camp in the travertine slopes.

Subsistence Activities   Our analysis of bones suggests that hunting was still the major subsistence activity in the winter. Projectile points were mainly of the dart stalking or trail and bleed type, and there was little or no lance ambushing. Trapping and leaf cutting occurred occasionally during the winter, as well as during the rest of the year. While seed collecting may have occurred in the spring and summer along with a little hunting, trapping, leaf cutting, fruit picking, and growing some domesticated plants in gardens or fields, the major activity and source of food seems to be growing improved corn in river bottom fields. This subsistence agriculture probably gave the Ajalpan people sufficient food to last them all year long and allowed them to live in sedentary hamlets. During the fall further barranca agriculture, as well as fruit picking, collecting of domesticated fruits from gardens, and some of the other activities may have taken place. Basically, however, this was a single season economy with major amounts of energy involved in barranca agriculture in the spring and summer. The rest of the year yielded only foods to supplement the basic corn surpluses.

The technological equipment necessary for this system was little different from that of the previous periods. In addition, the equipment necessary for preparing food was little different, as were the methods, although more back and forth seed grinding was

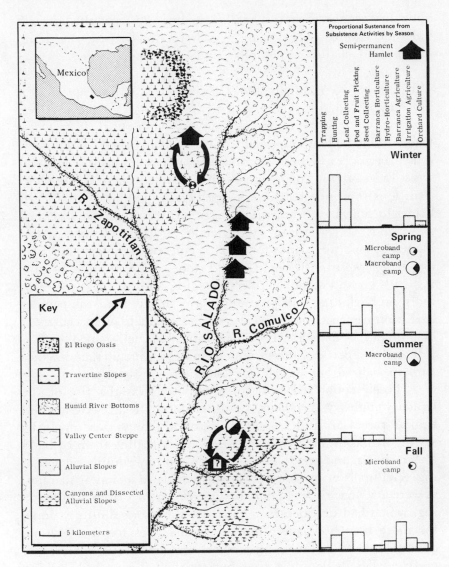

Figure 5.12

Ajalpan phase (1500 B.C. to 850 B.C.) with estimates of proportions of subsistence activities that were basically food producing at all seasons (right column) and distribution of semipermanent sedentary hamlets or villages and the seasonal microband and macroband camps for planting and harvesting in the microenvironments of the Tehuacan Valley (left column).

done in metates with two-handed manos. Perhaps the greatest differences were using ceramic vessels for food storage, cooking, steaming in small-mouthed ollas, and eating from dishes.

Technology   Although the technological equipment for a much-improved subsistence system showed only minor changes, other activities of the technology showed major shifts. In fact, the whole technical tempo seemed to have suddenly sped up. Further, much seemed to be done on a year-round rather than a seasonal basis. Even in flint knapping, which continued many of the older traditions, three new techniques appeared for making fine obsidian blades by pressure or indirect percussion (by soft hammers) against new kinds of conical or double-ended cylindrical cores. Also, blades became the blanks for making fine end scrapers and disks by further pressure flaking. Ground stone tools produced by sawing with ground stone, abraders, gouging and drilling with flint tools, and grinding and polishing with various kinds of pebbles gave rise to many new types of tools, often made of special rocks or minerals, such as adz, celts, fine truncated, bell-shaped, or flat-iron handled pestles, saucer, oblong, and basin metates, and manos with specialized handles and/or triangular cross-sections.

Closely connected with these activities was the rise of the lapidary industry. Pendants, beads, earplugs, atlatl weights, and similar pieces of jadite or other imported stones were made by sawing blanks into their desired forms, then drilling them by hand or bow drills, and finally finishing them off by grinding or polishing. Shell tools or ornaments were also made in a similar manner, as were a wide variety of bone tools or ornaments. Even skin working, which had declined in popularity, was more skillfully done, for there were now fine obsidian blade knives for the fleshing, delicately made haftable end scrapers for cleaning the skins, and more needles, drills, and curing tools for the tailoring and working of the skins. It would appear that this decline in skin working was at least partially caused by the rise of a fairly sophisticated textile industry. Now, yarn, string, cord, and rope were made by rolling or twisting hard and soft fibers by hand, and some cotton was spun by the use of the spindle whorl. Many kinds of knots were utilized. Twilled mats were often woven from agave strands, and split-stitch baskets, as well as twined fabrics, were made. Also, there is some evidence of cloth weaving (probably often with cotton yarn) on simple one-over-one belt looms. Much of the weaving, which now employed various kinds of bone or wood tools, such as heddles, spatulas, and weaving picks, may have been done for making blankets or cloth. (A study of the figurines, mostly female, reveals a little evidence of only the briefest cloth; rather they show elaborate headdresses or hats.)

Another set of new activities in the ceramic industry was much concerned with style, as well as a whole new set of techniques. Special clay was now kneaded to special consistencies, then made into vessels of a number of forms (about ten) by the coil technique, stick polished or brushed over, then often decorated (usually by red or black paints), and fired in some sort of bonfire-like kiln. In addition to clay vessels, figurines were made by modeling from two cylindrical masses, hand modeled into hollow or solid types, or made in final form by a gingerbread-like technique (attaching the various separate modeling body parts into their final form). Whistles, ocarinas, animal effigies, and stamps were made in a similar manner. Some of these, like the pots, were decorated by incising in the wet clay or by painting. In addition, throughout Ajalpan refuse we found many fragments of slab paint palettes indicating yet another activity: making red paint for ceramics, houses, fabrics, and probably faces and bodies.

Social and Value Systems   That some of the raw materials for paint, particularly the specular red hematite, as well as many vessels and some figurines, were obviously imported has implications for the social system. The large amounts of pottery, particularly types like Ajalpan fine red and Coatepec red on buff, indicate that a whole new exchange system had come into being along with the continued use of the older type of indirect and direct procurement. This new folk *market exchange* system involved specialized or semispecialized producers, special agents of exchange (merchants), formal mechanisms of distribution (some sort of markets), and relatively unspecialized consumers. Also, during the final parts of the Ajalpan phase there were hints from the lapidary products and many foreign figurines from the Olmec area on the coast that still another exchange system was being inaugurated, which became more popular in the following Santa Maria phase. This *socioceremonial exchange* system was carried on by full-time specialist producers (in jewelry and religio-figurines), specialized agents of distribution or redistribution (priest-traders or special ceremonial functionaries), formal mechanisms of distribution in certain ceremonies or social occasions (such as marriages and birth rites), and specialized consumers and members involved in the ceremonies. Obviously, not only material goods but ideas, concepts, and elements of the value system were also disseminated by the system.[7]

Another set of mundane activities or interconnected cultural subsystems has important implications that concern the reconstruction of the Ajalpan social system: the architectural complex. On the simplest level of the complex are the woodworking activities, many of which do not concern architecture, such as the cutting, scraping, and sawing with flint tools of small sticks to make a variety of wooden tools used in other activities. These are much like those of the Abejas phase. The cutting of cane for house siding, the working of logs for house frames with ground stone adzes and celts, and the weaving of thatched roofs are all new. Equally new is the making of daub, by mixing clay and grass, to plaster onto the cane lattice tied to log-based house sides. For the first time this wattle and daub was covered by fine clay plaster and then painted (often red). Another new development was the digging of post holes and bell-shaped refuse and burial pits. The houses of these villages were aligned in a well-planned linear manner and, in the late part of the phase, often had foreign (Olmec) figurine types that are panhousehold. This change indicates considerable social cooperation and control.

Studies of the individual houses also hint at other aspects of the social system. The finding of a male in a special burial pit with one of the Olmec figurines suggests that control was of a sacred nature, and there was a ranking system with certain full-time ceremonial leaders (possibly priests) who from both a secular and sacred standpoint were above the mass of the population. Clusters of artifacts suggest a division of labor not only based upon age and sex, but also upon a few full-time specialists with ceremonial orientations. Many of the houses yielded particular individualized figurine types, indicating that the household groups were special kin-aggregate groups with (figurine) sodalities. Though I hesitate to use the word *clan*, ethnographic analogy suggests these kin-aggregates behaved in much the same manner as did clans in terms of marriage, kinship, and integrative social behavior. Although our data are woefully inadequate, we have reconstructed some aspects of the social system at the Ajalpan phase. Further, the resemblance of their subsistence and technology as well as their social system to that of the idealized folk society of Robert Redfield suggests the value systems may be analogous.[8]

Ajalpan Cultural Relationships In terms of Meso-America, the Ajalpan phase seems to have existed in a horizon that has been found in many places and is termed the *early formative*. There seem to have been two main interaction spheres: a highland one (like Ajalpan) and a lowland one with a rather sophisticated way of life oriented around an Olmec cult. Studies of trade materials, stylistic horizon markers, and concepts involved in archaeological manifestation indicate some of the sort of interaction that occurred within and between these two spheres.

Other Phases

Our researches in Tehuacan have revealed development from an Ajalpan to a Santa Maria phase (900 B.C. to 150 B.C.) and then to a Palo Blanco phase (150 B.C. to 700 A.D.) and a Venta Salada phase, which saw the coming of the Spanish (700 A.D. to 1531 A.D.). However, Ajalpan represents the development of an agricultural village way of life, so this is the end of the story as far as our problem of determining how and why it came into being. Thus, rather than go on to describe these latter phases, I will instead analyze the Tehuacan sequence from Ajuereado to Ajalpan times to derive hypotheses as to why such a development took place.

DERIVING HYPOTHESES OF SYSTEMIC CHANGES

Two assumptions are basic. First, we are dealing with a system (or systems) that is a complex of elements directly or indirectly related in a causal network. The other is a corollary: a change in any element of the system (or systems) may change the whole system, and this initial changing element is the cause of the change or the condition under which one system changed into another.

Obviously, with the reconstructions of our Tehuacan systems, either cultural or energetic, as incomplete as they are, we will not be able to determine all the causes or conditions, but we do believe we can discern some of them.

From Ajuereado to El Riego

Analysis   We will first try to determine some of the sufficient conditions that caused the change from the Ajuereado to the El Riego cultural system. The method is a close scrutiny of the interconnected elements or subsystems that lasted through Ajuereado times from 10,800 B.C. to 7,800 B.C. (sidereal time). Although occupations representing early Ajuereado are woefully inadequate, there are strong suggestions that many subsystems or elements of traditions of this culture system lasted through this whole period relatively unchanged. Examples are the nomadic microband settlement pattern system, the trapping and animal collecting minor subsistence activities, all the techniques of the flint knapping activities, the bone and woodworking activities, the fleshing, scraping, and tailoring activities, the various butchering activities, and the indirect procurement exchange systems. Also, many elements of the ecosystem—such as the rocks and minerals, topographic features, locational factors, and rainfall pattern—carry through this period unchanged. None of these can be considered causative factors or sufficient conditions bringing about change in the Ajuereado cultural system.

Other elements, however, did change or come into being during the life span of these systems, and these are worthy of further examination. Lance hunting and rabbit drives subsistence subsystems, which were very important in the early part of the period, diminished in importance rapidly after 8800 B.C. The magnitude of this change becomes evident from an examination of the Ajuereado energy system. The energetic efficiency of lance ambushing that was responsible for 60 to 70 percent of the calories consumed in early times fell from about 4 to 2.5. Rabbit drives, which decreased from about 4 to 1, became even less profitable. Leaf and fruit collecting stayed about the same; both were minor in terms of energy input and output. Also staying the same in terms of energetic efficiency at about 6 or 7 was the dart stalking **system** used in hunting, although with the extinction of herd animals, probably the food consumption of animals (mainly deer) may have risen from about 10 to 25 percent calorically at the expense of decreases in meat from herd animals. Seed collection also may have increased in energetic efficiency, in large part because the inhabitants began collecting more seeds (including grass and cactus) with higher caloric values while continuing to expend about the same amount of calories picking these products. The making of ground stone tools, as well as the use of them, occurred only at the very end of the period, and, since these activities followed seed collection, they were obvious results; they can therefore be eliminated as causative factors.

As far as the ecosystem is concerned, horse, antelope, jackrabbit, giant turtle, and perhaps other animals disappeared about 8000 B.C. This change is thought to be correlated with a slight warming of the temperature, which apparently caused a change in vegetation as the grasslands shrank. It appears that the changes in the ecosystem and the loss of popularity of rabbit drives and lance ambushing are interconnected, perhaps in some sort of positive feedback system (where one changed the second and then it in turn changed the first one again, which changed the other) and that this interconnected systemic change was the major cause of the whole systemic change.

While this set of conditions explains the conditions changing the major Ajuereado subsistence activities, what about the other ones? Certainly the increased efficiency of seed collecting from about 6 to 13 must be considered, but basically this was not so much a new development as a development of an older technique, perhaps because more nutritious seeds were being picked, better bags and baskets that leaked fewer seeds were made, there was better positioning of base camp locations, and so forth. Fruit picking, leaf collecting, and trapping techniques during Ajuereado times may have also improved, and the development of more and better projectile points may have made dart-stalking hunting technique more amenable for greater use. Another energetic factor—not quite a subsistence option—also commenced during late Ajuereado: the storage of seeds for use in the dry seasons. All of these new and better (more efficient) subsistence options became important activities in El Riego times and as such might be considered necessary conditions for change, not sufficient or triggering ones.

Based on considerably shakier archaeological floor study evidence, Ajuereado populations (though always microband groups) were increasing during the life of the phase. However, since this increase does not seem to be much different from what happened in the El Riego phase and since the group was operating well below the carrying capacity of the land with a satisfying subsistence strategy, population pressure can be considered a necessary condition for change rather than a triggering one. In other words, these minor pressures made the system unstable and susceptible to change.

Other necessary conditions allowed the Ajuereado system to change into El Riego. These, of course, must be potential system elements that became important as part of the new cultural systems in El Riego, although they had existed in the Ajuereado system. Completely new, important systems of El Riego were barranca and hydrohorticulture, both of which required plants that were susceptible to becoming domesticates or cultivars. There is some suggestion that they existed during Ajuereado times in its ecosystem in terms of the wild avocados, wild mixta squash in the present-day ecosystem, and corn in pollen profiles of Ajuereado age in nearby Oaxaca. Another fundamental aspect of the El Riego cultural system was a seasonally scheduled subsistence subsystem, which required both an ecosystem with definite seasonality as well as considerable microenvironment diversity. Both existed in Ajuereado times as well as later.

Hypothesis   This analysis of Tehuacan can be stated in summary form to give a hypothesis that can be tested by independent comparative data. The formulation in general terms is:

If a cultural system like that of Ajuereado—which might be classified as a nomadic hunting microband type—has the following necessary conditions:

1. gradual but constantly increasing human populations who
2. live in regions with considerable ecological diversity with yields of different foods in different ecozones at different seasons of the year and when
3. some of the plants in the ecosystem could be domesticated and some of the animals tamed,

and the following sufficient conditions:

1. the development of a series of seasonally adaptive subsistence options with their necessary subsistence knowledge that coincides with
2. an ecosystem change that reduces the faunal subsystems (biomass) to such an extent that extensive hunting or animal collecting or a single subsistence option is no longer tenable,

then a cultural system like that of El Riego—which could be classified as a seasonally scheduled collecting microband-macroband type—may evolve.

From El Riego to Coxcatlan

Analysis   Now let us consider the development of the El Riego micro-macroband with a seasonally scheduled subsistence system into Coxcatlan, a cultural system with a macro-microband seasonally scheduled subsistence pattern with horticulture—still another optimizing type of subsistence strategy. Now the question becomes, Do the same conditions for change still pertain? The answer is that some of the necessary ones seem to continue but not the sufficient ones. Since much of Coxcatlan's subsistence was based on a seasonal schedule, the environmental factor still is a necessary condition, and since horticulture became even more important, there still had to be potential domesticates or cultivars, so some of the old prerequisites were still relevant.

A major new feature of the Coxcatlan system was the new direct procurement exchange system with the resultant changes in the horticultural system, as well as the occurrence of other activities brought in from the outside (such as string making, weaving, and the like). For this system to develop, the Coxcatlan phase had to be situated so that it had easy access to or communication with other zones with either great diversity or lush uniformity. Nevertheless, these would not have been sufficient to cause the shift from one system to the other, but it does become a necessary condition, allowing the subsequent systemic changes to happen.

To determine the sufficient conditions or causes for change, we must turn to an examination of the changes that took place within the El Riego system itself. Two new important subsystems developed about mid-El Riego times, roughly around 6300 B.C., plus or minus a couple of hundred years. One was the gradual emergence out of their seasonally scheduled plant gathering system to a system of planting cultivars or domesticates. The other was the occurrence of macrobands who lived in one spot for more than one season. A population increase seems to have occurred about the same time as horticulture developed, and both were interrelated, perhaps in a positive feedback manner since they occurred within the cultural system. However, since either one could have developed relatively independently (and probably did in some cases), I consider them two conditions for change rather than just one.

Hypothesis   The formulation of the necessary and sufficient conditions for a change from an El Riego type culture system into a Coxcatlan one can be stated as follows:

If a system with a micro-macroband settlement pattern and a seasonally scheduled subsistence system occurs in an ecosystem with the following necessary conditions:

1. plants that have the potential for cultivation and animals that can be domesticated,
2. great ecological diversity, and
3. easy communication and interaction with other areas of great ecological diversity or lush ecological uniformity

and if the following sufficient conditions occur:

1. the population of that system increases to a point where the equilibrium in terms of energy flow between the ecosystem and subsistence is upset and
2. horticulture (and perhaps tamed animals) gradually comes into being at about the same time,

then this system will evolve into one that has a macro-microband settlement pattern subsystem with a seasonally scheduled subsistence system with horticulture (or tamed animals): the Coxcatlan type of system.

From Coxcatlan to Abejas

Analysis   As far as the shift from this Coxcatlan system to the Abejas type system (with a central-based band settlement pattern and seasonally scheduled subsistence with extensive horticulture

and domesticated animals) is concerned, some of the same necessary conditions still pertain.

Population went back to a slow, steady increase and became
pressure for systemic instability rather than causes of change—in
other words, necessary conditions for change once again.

Other kinds of instabilities and change affected the very existence of the Coxcatlan system itself. One shows up in the energy
system studies as a very slight energetic increase, which was expended in the direct procurement exchange system that throughout the Coxcatlan life span was responsible for increasing amounts
of foreign plants—such as gourds, moschata squash, black and
white zapotes, and common beans—being used for horticulture
as well as new trade goods. Horticultural systems that had an energetic efficiency at 8 to 10 in El Riego times now increased to
15 or 20, the equal of efficient seed collection, but done where
man put his plants, not where nature scattered them. Going hand
in glove with this development was a gradual shift from storage
of wild seeds to the storage of domesticates, which resulted in
longer and larger seasonal occupations and greater security—
perhaps a necessary compensation for the risks an optimizing sort
of strategy involved in planting in an environment subject to
drought as well as planting new domesticates that might not be
adaptable to the new and/or different Tehuacan environment.
The direct procurement system with its horticultural increases
plus the effort of growing for storage against disaster seems to
have operated in a positive feedback manner that changed the
whole Coxcatlan system into an Abejas one.

Hypothesis   Thus if a Coxcatlan type of system has the following necessary conditions:

1.   an existence in a zone of great ecological diversity, which
     may have in it
2.   plants with the potential for cultivation and animals with the
     potential for domestication,
3.   easy access to other areas of great ecological diversity where
     plants have been cultivated,
4.   population increases making for systematic disequilibrium

and if the following sufficient conditions develope:

1.   stimulating interactions involving the exchange of cultures and domesticates because of the direct procurement exchange system, as well as
2.   a tendency to grow cultivated and domesticated plants for storage to compensate for the possible risks involved in an increased amount of horticulture,

then a system like Abejas will develop.

From Abejas to Purron and Ajalpan

Analysis   The final step in this evolution of the rise of agricultura village life—or, in my terms, the development of semipermanent hamlet settlement with an agriculture subsistence pattern, examples of which were much like that which must have existed in the rest of Mexico between 2300 B.C. and 1000 B.C.—developed out of the Abejas type. The conditions that brought about this cultural system were probably more complex, and some of the causal factors, particularly in the social realm, are more difficult to discern. Ideally, two studies should be done here: a study of the change from Abejas to Purron and then the changes from Purron to Ajalpan. But in fact, the data available on Purron are so poor that the stage must be jumped over to Ajalpan. However, even so let us attempt hypotheses, for we certainly cannot have hypotheses to test by being noncommittal or only destructively critical.

Many of the same prerequisite conditions still pertain: increasing sedentarism, accessibility to other developing regions, and great ecological diversity in the Tehuacan Valley. Although the population increases and the rise of the new settlement pattern type occurred in late Abejas times, it is difficult to decide if they were sufficient or necessary causes of change, particularly lacking the Purron systemic transitional change.

The potential sufficient conditions for systemic changes certainly include the rise of barranca agriculture. An energetic efficiency rate rise in horticulture from 15 to 20 to almost 30 is the most important change that took place in late Abejas time. In addition, the use of hybridized corn, along with the other factors, could well have been a significant condition leading to Purron. On a less firm base are two factors that were not present in Abejas times but seem to have occurred in earliest Ajalpan, hinting they developed in Purron and could have been sufficient conditions for the development of the Ajalpan type of cultural system. Both are exchange systems that show up suddenly as significant new energy expenditures that perhaps signal even more important social system shifts. The one that might have come first has been called the folk market exchange system. It might well have developed within Purron and might have tended to redistribute basic foodstuffs so that this new, more tribal social system could operate. The other that might have developed in late Purron times or earliest Ajalpan was probably diffused into the Tehuacan region from elsewhere and was integrated into the local system because of the need for some sort of a more cohesive force working to keep that sort of expanding society together. This second exchange system has been termed the socioceremonial system and probably not only was involved with the transfer of exotic goods over fairly long distances, but was much concerned with the transfer of emic information, such as religious knowledge, ceremonies, myth, ritual, and concepts of the cosmos.

Because the analysis here is so tentative, the hypothesis will also be tentative:

Hypothesis   If a culture type like Abejas—a home-based horticulture band type of society—exists in

1.   a region of great ecological diversity that
2.   has easy access and is part of an interaction sphere with other cultural types in areas of much uniformity, and
3.   if some of its cultivated plants are susceptible to hybridization, which increases energetic efficiencies,

and if the following sufficient conditions include:

1.   increasing population and sedentarism,
2.   increasing local exchange systems like the folk market type with redistribution of basic foodstuffs in time (seasonally) and space, as well as
3.   socioceremonial exchanges,

then an Ajalpan type of culture system—semipermanent hamlet communities with subsistence agriculture—may evolve.

CONCLUSION

This fairly long and complicated attempt to explain the development of the village agricultural system in the Tehuacan Valley in Mexico is not a unicausal model. The question to ask now is, Is this a particularistic model explaining a single happening, or is it a general statement that explains all corresponding happenings? The only way to decide this question is to test the hypothesis against other long sequences where pristine village agriculture developed independently, such as we have in Peru and the Near East. Thus we move into our final part of investigation: testing the hypotheses by the comparative method.

REFERENCES

1. ROBERT C. WEST, "The Natural Regions of Middle America," in R. C. West, ed., *Handbook of Middle American Indians,* vol. 1: *Natural Environment and Early Cultures* (Austin: University of Texas Press, 1964).
2. JANE WHEELER PIRES-FERREIRA, EDGARDO PIRES-FERREIRA, and PETER KAULICKE, "Preceramic Animal Utilization in the Central Peruvian Andes," *Science* 194 (1976).
3. M. D. COE and K. V. FLANNERY, "Microenvironments and Mesoamerican Prehistory," *Science* 143 (1964).
4. WU LEUNG, WOOT-TSEUN, *Food Consumption Table for Use in Latin America* (Bethesda, Md.: National Institute of Health, 1961).
5. JOHN PFEIFFER, *The Emergence of Society* (New York: McGraw-Hill, 1977).
6. W. C. GALINAT, "The Origin of Maize," *Annual Review of Genetics* 5 (1971).
7. R. S. MACNEISH, "Summary of the Cultural Sequence and Its Implications in the Tehuacan Valley," in R. S. MacNeish, ed., *The Prehistory of the Tehuacan Valley,* vol. 5: *Excavations and Reconnaissance* (Austin: University of Texas Press, 1972).
8. ROBERT REDFIELD, "The Folk Society," *American Journal of Sociology* 52 (1947).

6

On Trying to Be a Scientist

NOW LET US GET TO THE NITTY-GRITTY OF MY KIND OF ARCHAEOLOGY
—making generalizations about the conditions that led to certain
past events, which explain all corresponding or similar past happenings. My goal here is to formulate in general terms the necessary and sufficient conditions that led to plant domestication and
the concomitant development of village life that was a prerequisite to pristine civilizations. These generalized statements should
explain how and why village life developed in all areas of pristine
agriculture and civilizations: Meso-American, Andean, and Near
Eastern nuclear areas.

My method for deriving such generalizations was first to establish a complete sequence (a cultural-historical integration) in
an area or region where agriculture began. I did this for the
Tehuacan region of the Meso-American nuclear area. Next I
analyzed this sequence of events or cultural systems and ecosystems
(cultural phases and environments) to determine the conditions
that caused each one to change into the next. In other words, I
set up hypotheses about the necessary and sufficient conditions
under which the events (now cultural systems and ecosystems) lead-

ing to agriculture occurred in the Tehuacan Valley. Now, after putting Tehuacan in the slightly large arena of Meso-America, I shall test the hypothesis against data from the Near Eastern and Andean areas, where there were corresponding happenings—that is, the development of agriculture and the concomitant rise of village life leading to pristine civilization.

MAKING THE DATA COMPARABLE

One of the problems of testing hypotheses by the comparative method, or even analyzing the data to derive hypotheses, is that often the cultural-historical integrations are not correctly stated or included in the correct integration mechanisms: the concept of interaction sphere, horizon, tradition, and sequences of cultural phases or systems. Thus, before we can discuss the chronologies in the Meso-American, Andean, and Near Eastern areas (or interaction spheres or culture areas) in the relevant time periods, we must attempt to make them comparable.

One of the first steps in this direction is to attempt to discuss the three areas in terms of comparable spatial units, such as cultural areas, subareas, or interaction spheres. In this realm the data are so incomplete that any classification or unit of classification is at best a hypothesis—to be tested when more research is undertaken.

I began with a consideration of Tehuacan, which I know best. As I mentioned in chapter 5, West has classified the various ecozones of Tehuacan as being in one of thirty-one subdivisions of the natural areas of Meso-America: a subdivision of subarea 7, *arid rain-shadow strip,* of subarea 7, *the mesa central,* of the major area B, *tropical highlands and extratropical appendages.*[1] In my classification, with its various regional archaeological sequences, this same area became a subarea, which I renamed the *high mountain valleys.*

Now the question becomes what the other natural areas were of Meso-America that were related to our Tehuacan archaeological data of the relevant period, 10,000 B.C. to 1000 B.C. Here we are obviously limited by incomplete and inadequate investigations from many, in fact most, of West's various regions or areas. However, we do have some data that can be interlinked to show interactions in terms of artifact similarities with Tehuacan; what is more, these subareas cover much of the same ecological range as do those of West's. One zone with adequate relevant archaeological material is Tamaulipas in northeastern Mexico.[2] West classified it as subarea 4, *Tamaulipas subhumid lowlands of the extratropical dry lands,* and I made it my subarea 1, *dry subtropical lowlands.* Closely related to it are the more tropical Gulf lowlands: West's 11a, *Peten-Yucatán rain forest area;* 11b, *southern Veracruz-Tabasco rain-forest area;* 11c, *Las Tuxtlas;* 11d, *deciduous forest Veracruz;* 11e, *northern Yucatán;* and so on. Since these have many ecological traits in common and since we had only one adequate preceramic sequence, I included them all in my subarea 2, *tropical humid lowlands.*[3] Somewhat similar and less adequately represented archaeologically is the Meso-American narrow Pacific coast with slightly different ecozones; this became my subarea 3, *subtropical wooded lowlands.*[4] It included what West had called the *Pacific lowlands,* area 12, which had six subdivisions in it. My subarea 4, *dry lowland river basins and/or drainages,* is directly analogous to West's area 13, *dry interior tropical basins,* with its two subdivisions: 13a, *Balsas-Tepalcatepec basin,* and 13b, *Valley of Chiapas.* My materials from Santa Marta Cave were all there was archaeologically, but again, they had artifactual similarities suggesting interaction with Tehuacan.[5] My subarea 5, *low wooded mountain valleys,* is less well represented archaeologically and has different ecological zones from those West had put in his subarea 9, *highlands of northern Central America.*[6] My subarea 6, *medium high mountain valleys,* and West's area 8, *Sierra and Mesa del Sur,* were archaeologically represented in the relevant time slot by the Oaxaca Cave materials.[7] My final subarea 8, *mountain peaks and valleys or highest valleys,* includes West's subareas 5 and 6, *the Sierra Madre Occidental* and *Oriental;* here we had my Tamaulipas Sierra Madre archaeological cave materials from a not very high valley.[8]

West's categories were not intended to be cultural areas, and obviously, with so little known archaeologically, they do not serve very well as my ideal interaction spheres. Much work needs to be done to turn my subareas used here into spheres of interactions. At best, my subareas are hypothetical spheres to be tested by more adequate data.

As poor as they may be, however, they are better than we have for the Andean area. This is true because many regions of the Andes have relatively limited preceramic archaeological materials, and the best classification of natural areas is one by Tosi.[9] He defined thirty-four life zones based on the correlation of annual rainfall, evaporation, altitudinal levels, vegetational regions (such as desert, forest steppe, chaparral), and temperature regions (such as polar, frigid, temperate, subtropical, tropical). It is extremely difficult to directly relate these Andean life zones with our natural zones of Meso-America. However, on the basis of archaeological materials and their relationships or interaction with that of the Ayacucho region in subarea 6 where I worked, I have attempted to do this in the following charts and tables.[10] How well these hypotheses will stand the test of time and future research remains to be seen.

The problem of establishing comparable natural zones with the Near East is even worse. Butzer probably has the best division available.[11] His in part are vegetational, as are those of Flannery.[12] Butzer's divisions are: a, *high coniferous forests,* b, *deciduous and mixed forests,* c, *subtropical woodlands,* d, *grasslands,* e, *deserts,* and f, *semidesert.* Other works indicate that the subtropical woodlands can be divided into at least four divisions: *Mediterranean vegetation, Levant vegetation, Caspian vegetation,* and *hill flank grassland,* as well as *mixed forest* with parts of central Turkey as well as Kurdistan in the Iranian plateau. These additions bring the total to about twelve, but none are really comparable to either the Meso-American or Andean classification.

I have squeezed these zones into my eight subareas, however. Obviously we need some more studies to make for better uniform classification for the three areas. The list below is just a start, obviously hypothetical, but it does have the virtue of making the regions comparable, and a close examination may lead to some sort of generalization about the sort of environments agriculture originated in.

Subarea 1: Dry subtropical lowlands
    A.   Meso-America: Tamaulipas subhumid woodlands (A4)
    B.   Andes: Deserto tropical (d-T), maleza desertica tropical
          (mo-T); maleza desertica subtropical (md-ST), desierto
          montano bajo (d-mB); maleza desertica montano bajo

(md-MB), desierto subtropical (d-ST); chaparral bajo montano (bajo)

C.   Near East: Levant subtropical scrub woodland (not really a Meditarranean vegetation)

Subarea 2: Tropical humid lowlands

A.   Meso-America: Deciduous forest of northern Veracruz (11d), southern Veracruz-Tabasco rain forest area, Yucatán-Peten rain forest (11b)

B.   Andes: Bosque muy humedo tropical (bmh-T), bosque humedo tropical (bh-T), bosque seco tropical (bs-T); bosque muy humedo subtropical (bmh-ST), bosque humedo subtropical (bh-ST), bosque pluvial subtropical (bp-ST)

C.   Near East, Caspian, Black Sea: Coastal woodlands

Subarea 3: Subtropical wooded lowlands

A.   Meso-America: Cape region of Baja California (12g), volcanic lowlands of Central America (12d), coastal lowlands of southwestern Mexico (12e), coastal lowlands of Nayarit-Sinaloa (12f)

B.   Andes: Bosque muy humedo montano bajo (bmh-MB), bosque humedo montano bajo (bh-MB), bosque pluvial montano bajo (bp-MB), bosque muy humedo montano (bmh-M), bosque humedo montano (bh-M), bosque pluvial montano (bp-M), estepa montano (e-M), desierto montano (d-M), maleza desertica montano (md-M)

C.   Near East: Eastern Mediterranean wooded coast

Subarea 4: Dry lowland river basins and/or drainages

A.   Meso-America: Dry interior tropical basins (13), Balsas-Tepalcatepec basin (13a), Valley of Chiapas (13b)

B.   Andes: Bosque espinoso (be-T), bosque muy seco (bms-T), bosque seco subtropical (bs-ST)

C.   Near East: Tigris-Euphrates grasslands

Subarea 5: Low wooded mountain valleys

A.   Meso-America: Highlands of northern Central America (9)

B.   Andes: Estepa espinosa montano bajo (ee-MB), chaparral alto montano bajo (ca-MB)

C.   Near East: Hilly flanks of the Tigris

Subarea 6: Medium high mountain valleys

A.   Meso-America: Sierra and mesa central (8)

    B.   Andes: Bosque espinosa subtropical (be-ST), bosque seco montano bajo (bs-MB)

    C.   Near East: Anakova or Karfsten basin

Subarea 7: High mountain valleys

    A.   Meso-America: Mesa central arid rain-shadow (7)

    B.   Andes: Tundra pluvial alpino (pmh-SA), tundra humedo alpino (md-SA), tundra muy alpino (ph-SA)

    C.   Near East: Deciduous and mixed forest mountains of the Near East and Greece

Subarea 8: The mountain peaks and (highest) valleys

    A.   Meso-America: Tropical highlands and extratropical appendages (B), Sierra Madre Occidental (5), Sierra Madre Oriental (6), tropical extension of the Sierra and eastern plateau escarpment (6a)

    B.   Andes: Tundra pluvial

    C.   Near East: Coniferous forest mountain zone.

The other major mechanism for making our data comparable is a temporal one. Here the concept of a horizon is extremely useful for placing the various sequences of phases with their traditions in chronological order. More important, the horizon characteristics may be classified in such a way as to make them comparable in the three areas under discussion.

My establishment of the horizons was based upon my Tehuacan sequence, but I later modified it and extended it because of new and early culture types I uncovered in Peru. The first two horizons of Peru were the very early Pacaicasa materials with their choppers and lack of evidence of specialized hunting tools, characteristic of horizon 1 and the following culture, Ayacucho, again collectors of animals rather than hunters but now with semispecialized hunting tools, albeit bone and unifacial ones. The next horizons come from the Tehuacan data with the hunters of early Ajuereado with their semispecialized tools being representative of horizon 3—the specialized hunters of late Ajuereado being of horizon 4, the seasonal specialized plant gatherers or collectors of wild foods of El Riego being of horizon 5, the incipient agriculturalists of Coxcatlan being horizon 6, the base camp agriculturalists of Abejas being horizon 7, the agricultural hamlet people of Purron being horizon 8, and the agricultural villagers of Ajalpan representing the final horizon and final development in the problem of the origin of agriculture and concomitant village life. I have attempted to apply this scheme to the other major cultural areas. My comparable horizons and their generalized characteristics and dates for Meso-American, Andean, and Near Eastern areas are:

Horizon 1: Generalized hunters with unspecialized technology and huge interaction spheres
    Meso-America: Older than 25,000 B.C.
    Andes: Older than 14,000 B.C.
    Near East: Older than 100,000 B.C.
Horizon 2: Generalized hunters with semispecialized technology and huge interaction spheres
    Meso-America: 25,000 B.C. to 11,000 or 12,000 B.C.
    Andes: 14,000 B.C. to 11,000 B.C.
    Near East: 100,000 B.C. to 35,000 B.C.
Horizon 3: Specialized hunters with only semispecialized technology and large interaction spheres
    Meso-America: 11,000 B.C. to 8100 B.C.
    Andes: 11,000 B.C. to 9000 B.C.
    Near East: 35,000 B.C. to 20,000 to 16,000 B.C.
Horizon 4: Specialized hunters with specialized technology and specialized interaction sphere (highland herd, nonherd)
    Meso-America: 8100 B.C. to 7000 B.C.
    Andes: 9000 B.C. to 5800 B.C.
    Near East: 20,000 or 16,000 B.C. to 12,500 B.C.
Horizon 5: Specialized collectors, with a range from base camp groups (composite bands) to seasonal nomadic (patrilineal) bands
    Meso-America: 7000 B.C. to 5000 B.C.
    Andes: 5800 B.C. to 4450 B.C.
    Near East: 12,500 B.C. to 10,750 B.C.
Horizon 6: Preagricultural composite bands or hamlets to incipient agricultural seasonal macro-microbands
    Meso-America: 5000 B.C. to 3400 B.C.
    Andes: 4450 B.C. to 3100 B.C.
    Near East: 10,750 B.C. to 9500 B.C.
Horizon 7: Incipient agricultural hamlets (lineages) to agricultural base camp bands

Meso-America: 3400 B.C. to 2300 B.C.

Andes: 3100 B.C. to 1750 B.C.

Near East: 9500 B.C. to 8500 B.C.

Horizon 8: Incipient agricultural villages (chiefdoms) to agricultural hamlets (lineages)

Meso-America: 2300 B.C. to 1500 B.C.

Andes: 1750 B.C. to 1200 B.C.

Near East: 8500 B.C. to 7250 B.C.

Horizon 9: Pristine agricultural villages

Meso-America: 1500 B.C. to 900 B.C.

Andes: 1200 to 1000 B.C. to 700 B.C.

Near East: 7250 B.C. to 6750 B.C.

These two mechanisms of interpreting subareas or hypothetical spheres and hypothetical horizons will allow us to see the basic data in a comparable manner. Obviously the traditions and the phases or cultural systems of each horizon of each subarea are distinctive and complex, and their exact description must be sought in the basic descriptive site reports concerning them. In the following comparative data, I will only touch upon them and give the general basic date in terms of time (horizons) and space (areas). Then we can move on to using this comparative data to test hypotheses and establish generalizations.

THE COMPARABLE INTERACTION
SPHERES

Meso-America

However, let us delimit Meso-America as a whole in the period from 10,000 B.C. to 1000 B.C. The northern limits seem to have been West's dry lands (*Extratropical dry lands*): the Mesa del Norte (desert), including the steppe lands of the western margin, eastern Coahuila, and northern Nuevo Léon; Sonora and northern Sinaloa, Baja California, and Texas. To the south, West's various kinds of tropical divisions are south of its border, namely the mosquito coast, the Caribbean rain-forest area of Central America, the savanna of central Panama, the Azuero rain-forest area, and the rain forest of southwestern Costa Rica.

Obviously, the Gulf and Pacific oceans are the eastern and western limits. Although these may have been the boundaries from 5000 B.C. to about 1000 B.C., I am not sure they were in the earlier 5000 years (during the Pleistocene). Horizon 1 to 3 all were within a single larger interaction sphere, and there are hints—in terms of the desert culture complex—that the northern border of the Meso-American interaction sphere in the horizon, from 5000 B.C. to 1000 B.C., may have extended farther south into West's dry lands. Only time and many more soil and pollen studies can decide this matter.

Subarea 1: Dry Subtropical Lowlands
Environmental Characteristics   The first of the eight cultural areas within the Meso-American interaction sphere from at least 10,000 B.C. to 1000 B.C. is the xerophytic Tamaulipas zone east of the Sierra Madre Oriental. According to West's classification, it is the Tamaulipas subhumid lowlands (A4). In my system it is subarea 1 of the primitive agriculture interaction sphere and is called the *dry subtropical lowlands.* (See figure 6.1)

This area's best resources are marine life from along its coasts, although other important flora and fauna occur along its rivers and oases. There is great seasonality and game and plant foods abound in the wet season. These are concentrated in the dry season, thereby favoring a home-base camp type of settlement pattern where the early inhabitants could fan out in a radial manner to exploit a number of microzones or microenvironments, a catchment basin system. Whitetail deer, rabbits, peccary, and wild turkey were fairly abundant, as were acorns, seeds, and cactus foods.

Faunal studies suggest a more abundant fauna with horse and mammoth in the Pleistocene and less fauna in the drier postglacial optimum period from 5000 B.C. to 2500 B.C., but those conclusions must be checked by pollen and soil analysis.

Achaeological Horizons   The evidence for determining when the area was within the Meso-American developmental agriculture interaction sphere is far from perfect, but four regional sequences (all with gaps within them) existed between 10,000 B.C. and 1000 B.C. The most complete data come from the Sierra de Tamaulipas

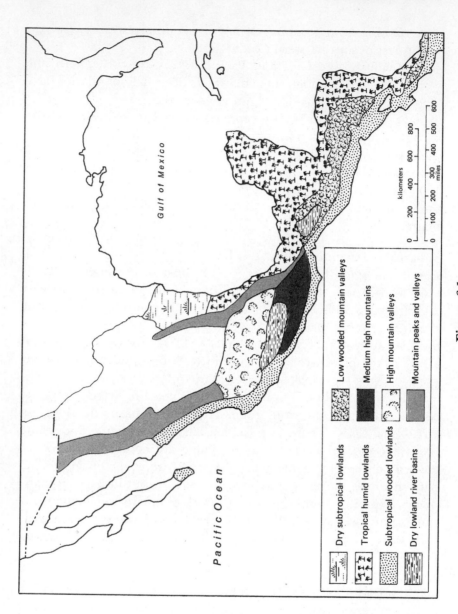

Figure 6.1

Ecological subareas of the Meso-American interaction sphere.

HORIZONS (Carbon 14 time)	CALENDAR (Sidereal) YEARS	SUB-AREA 1 Dry Sub-tropical Lowlands / Tamaulipas Subhumid Lowlands	SUB-AREA 2 Tropical Humid Lowlands Caribbean-Gulf Lowlands	SUB-AREA 3 Sub-tropical Wooded Lowlands / Pacific Lowlands	SUB-AREA 4 Dry Lowlands River Basins Balsas R. Grijalva R.	SUB-AREA 5 Low Wooded Mountain Valleys Guatemala	SUB-AREA 6 Medium High Mountain Valleys Mesa del Sur	SUB-AREA 7 Pueblo region	SUB-AREA 7 Valley of Mexico region	SUB-AREA 7 Hidalgo and Queretaro regions	SUB-AREA 8 Mountain Peaks and Valleys Northeast Sierra Madre
850 B.C. — Horizon 9 — 1500 B.C.	1000 B.C.	Ahasolo and/or	Ojite and/or Ponce; Pavon; San Lorenzo Chicharras Bajio Ojochi	Cuadros; Ocos	Cotorra	Arevalo	San Jose; Tierras Largas	Ajalpan	Ayotla; Nevada	La Mina	Mesa del Guaje
Horizon 8 — 2300 B.C.	2000 B.C.	Almagre	Santa Luisa	and/or La Barra; Pox Pottery				Purron			Guerra; Flacco
Horizon 7 — 3400 B.C.	3000 B.C. / 4000 B.C.	Repelo and/or La Perra	Palo Hueco	Isla del Chantuto			Coxcatlan- like	Abejas	Zopilco	San Nicolas	Ocampo
Horizon 6 — 5000 B.C.	5000 B.C.	Nogales	Palma Sola				Coxcatlan		Coxcatlan; Playa 2; Playa 1	Tecolote	La Calzada Unit 4
Horizon 5 — 7000 B.C.	6000 B.C. / 7000 B.C.				Santa Marta Complex	Guila Naquitz		El Riego		Hidalgo	Infiernillo
Horizon 4 — 8100 B.C.	8000 B.C.	Lerma				Guila Naquitz		Late Ajuereado		San Juan	La Calzada Unit 6
Horizon 3 — 11,000 B.C.	9000 B.C. / 10,000 B.C.				Santa Marta	Los Tapiales		Early Ajuereado	Tlapacoya 2; Iztapan		
Horizon 2	11,000 B.C. / 25,000 B.C.				Santa Marta ?			Valsequillo	Tlapacoya 1		
Horizon 1		Diablo	Richmond Hill						Tequixquiac		

Figure 6.2

Sequence by relevant horizons in the eight subareas in the Meso-American interaction sphere.

and are based upon stratified deposits from five excavated rock shelters. Evidence from the coast and the interior is based upon minor testing and seriation,[13] and the final one is based upon typology of the San Isidro site materials in Nuevo Leon.[14]

In terms of being part of the Meso-American interaction sphere, although the Diablo complex or tentative phase and earliest San Isidro remains may be part of horizon 1 before 25,000 years ago when perhaps all of the New World was a single culture area, the first well-defined remains are those of the early nomadic hunters of the Lerma phase of horizon 4, when much of the western Cordilleran was a single interaction sphere. After this there is a gap until horizons 6 and 7 (Nogales-La Perra phases and/or Repelo from roughly 6000 B.C. to 2500 B.C.) when corn, pumpkins, and perhaps gourds in La Perra indicate these seasonal micro-macrobands were interacting with other developing groups farther south. However, the Almagre and perhaps Abasolo phases with large macroband encampments hint of a more settled life which seems to be out of the Meso-American interaction sphere from 2500 B.C. to 1000 B.C. in horizons 8 and 9.

Subarea 2: Tropical Humid Lowlands

Environmental Characteristics   West calls the next subarea the Caribbean-Gulf lowland. I call it the *tropical humid lowlands.* Also included are his various subareas or regions: the Peten-Yucatán rain forest (11a), the southern Veracruz-Tabasco rain forest (11b), Las Tuxtlas (11c), the deciduous forest area of northern Veracruz (11d), and northern Yucatán (11e). Few microenvironmental studies of these various regions have been made. All have littoral resources, as well as riverine ones. The jungle, grassland, and scrub forest are back from the coast, and the rain forest is farther inland (often against the rising fronts of the Sierra Madre). There is a drenching rain season and a humid dry season, when foodstuffs from jungle fruit and seed abound, as does game, in addition to the marine and riverine resources. There are few wild relatives of plants that were domesticated, although wild manioc, avocado, zapotes, and perhaps cucurbits do occur in this tropical area.

Archaeological Horizons   That this area was always part of the Meso-American interaction sphere is an assumption, not a fact. The little data available come mainly from the northern Veracruz subarea. There are no data for horizons 1 to 4, and even the first complex (dubbed Palma Sola) dates only from about 5500 B.C., the last part of horizon 5 and the beginning of horizon 6. At this time there seems to have been a large coastal base camp at Palo Hueco where marine resources and game were exploited primarily by hunting and possibly by gathering forays made into the edge of the mountains seasonally (perhaps at the dry time). By the end of horizon 6 and in horizon 7 coastal hamlets, at least at the Palo Hueco site of central Veracruz, seem to have been developed.[15] However, these were seemingly without agriculture for there is no evidence of the use of grinding stones or metates. The obsidian

scraper types and rare projectile points do, however, show interaction with interior regions (that may have had agriculture or at
least domesticated plants).

The hamlet way of life continued in central Veracruz through
horizon 7 except for some pottery and metates carbon 14 dated at
about 1700 B.C. (horizon 8), perhaps when at last corn agriculture
spread to the cost. Horizon 9 is relatively poorly defined. During
this time the Olmec rose in southern Veracruz, and other less
ornate village agriculture complexes occurred in other regions or
subregions.

Here, unlike Oaxaca and Tehuacan, hamlets seem to have
arisen without agriculture, and the addition of agriculture perhaps to an already stable economy seems to have led to the rise of
cults with village or town centers. Again, this subarea, like Tamaulipas, favors a catchment type of early exploitation.

Subarea 3: Subtropical Wooded Lowlands

Environmental Characteristics   My subarea 3, *subtropical
wooded lowlands,* is almost the same as West's Pacific lowlands; it
includes the volcanic lowlands of Central America, the coastal
lowlands of southwest Mexico, and the coastal lowlands of Nayarit-Sinaloa. Although it has many resemblances to the Gulf
Coast area, particularly in the use of a radial type of early catchment exploitation, it has a narrower coastal plain with less scrubby
vegetation, few major rivers, and more bays and swampy regions.
Flannery has classified one region near Ocos into a series of
microenvironments (better called ecozones): subarea 1, beach sand
and low brush scrub with marine resources; subarea 2, marine
estuaries and laguna systems with clams, fish, and crocodiles; subarea 3, mangrove forest with crabs and fruit trees; subarea 4, a
riverine zone with more fish and some small animals; subarea 5,
salt flats; subarea 6, mixed tropical forest with many animals, as
well as fruit trees, including potential domesticates like zapote,
palm, and sapodilla; subarea 7, tropical savanna; and subarea 8,
densely forested regions on mountain slopes, which have the
densest fauna.[16] Exploitation of these zones parallel to the coast
seems to have been by working out radially across them from a
base camp, which could change with the season.

Achaeological Horizons   Our archaeological knowledge of how
this area fits into the Meso-American interaction sphere is poor.

We know almost nothing of the period from 10,000 B.C. to 4000
B.C. or 3000 B.C. Also, the data from 4000 B.C. to 3000 B.C., horizons
7 and 8, are based mainly on the Isla de Chantuto excavations on
the Chiapas coast [17] and from Puerto Marquez near Acapulco.[18]
The latter has very few preceramic artifacts associated with its
shell refuse of year-round hamlets and its one house and above it
only a few sherds of Pox pottery in the layer carbon dated from
2300 B.C. to 1500 B.C. The Chiapas coast material is almost as poor;
the lowest preceramic layers (roughly 3000 B.C. to 2000 B.C.) are
without grinding stones and maybe were base camps, while the
shell strata above have grinding stones and chipped tools, suggesting agricultural hamlets. There are few, if any, house remains or
evidence of any early pottery. Artifact types and obsidian do, however, come from the highlands, so interaction with the area took
place. The only reliable ceramic remains from these regions are in
horizon 9.

Subarea 4: Dry Lowland River Basins and/or Drainages
Environmental Characteristics   The remains from the next
general subarea, the *dry lowland river basins and/or drainages,* are
also meager. Included here are the Pacific drainages of the Rio
Balsas in Guerrero and the central depression of Chiapas that was
formed by the Grijalva River and its several large tributaries. Although both areas have small, dry, tropical, savanna-covered portions with a relatively long, dry season, much of the basin and its
flanks, as well as the river drainage areas, are tropical rain forest
with abundant game and fruits, including zapotes and avocados,
and little or no real dry season. Wild tepary, sieva, and common
beans have also been reported for this area, as well as in the lusher
Sierra subareas to the south.

Archaeological Horizons   Our archaeological knowledge of the
periods under discussion comes mainly from Santa Marta Cave in
Chiapas, and here the sequence is far from complete. The data
concern mainly horizons 5 and 6, roughly from 7000 B.C. to 3500
B.C.[19] More recent testing has uncovered materials in Santa Marta
Cave that might be of horizons 2 and 3, roughly from 8,000 to
25,000 years ago. These latter diggings yielding few artifacts contrast with the fine archaeological investigations by the New World
Archaeological Foundation, which have given us abundant data on
the Cotorra and La Barra phases for the final horizon 9, but again,

these horizons are of little help in testing hypotheses about changes
in agricultural systems that occurred previously.

Subarea 5: Low Wooded Mountain Valleys   Subarea 5, the *low
wooded mountain valleys,* is subtransitional from the major highland and lowland areas. (It was number 9 in West's classification,
the highlands of northern Central America.) It includes the lush
highlands of Guatemala, San Salvador, and southern and highland
Chiapas with their covering of rain forest and coniferous forest
and broad fertile valley bottoms with savanna or jungle.

Little attempt has been made to divide these valleys into
microenvironments, but I suspect that the environmental zones
are vertically layered, with different ones occurring at various elevations above the lush valley bottoms. Plants and animals abound,
and the wet and dry season differences are cloaked by the fact that
the climate is always fairly humid. Because of the great variation
in flora with many wild relatives of modern domesticates, as well
as a great range of races of many domesticates, many scientists
have thought of this as being a center of plant domestication and/
or agriculture. It is a tragedy that we have almost nothing from
the pertinent archaeological horizons from 10,000 B.C. to 1000 B.C.

Subarea 6: Medium High Mountain Valleys
Environmental Characteristics   West's Sierra and Mesa del Sur,
mainly in Oaxaca, is my subarea 6, the *medium high mountain
valleys.* Flannery's work in the valley of Oaxaca has defined four
microzones: the flood plain with bald cypress, willow, wild figs,
and much small game; the high alluvium, a grassier area with
mesquite and other woody legumes and many deer, rabbits, and
other small game; the piedmont, with more game, tree legumes,
prickly pear, organ cactus, agave, and, at higher elevations, oak;
and the high mountains with oak, pine, and manzanita forests, as
well as much game.[20] There is a very noticeable wet-dry season,
and one must exploit these stratified zones at different seasons of
the year. Here, there is no single catchment basin system, but two
to four of them with each season in a different zone—a seasonal
scheduled system. Wild corn, pumpkins, and runner beans may
have existed in one or more of these four ecozones in prehistoric
times, but no studies have been undertaken to determine ecological changes in the crucial period from 10,000 B.C. to 1000 B.C.

Archaeological Horizons[21]   The earliest complex with evidence of much plant collecting but little hunting and with projectile points like El Riego—variously referred to as Guila Naquitz or Naquitz—seems to be of horizon 5, about from 7000 B.C. to 5000 B.C., although some dates are older. After a considerable gap, two other zones, Coxcatlan and/or Abejas, including primitive domesticated corn materials, occurred between 3300 B.C. and 2800 B.C., carbon 14 time. There is another gap until 1500 B.C. when horizon 9 remains of the Tierras Largas and San Jose Mogote phases occurred, and settled agricultural villages and pottery appeared. Although the available materials are limited, they do display regional linkages indicating that Meso-America in all these horizons was indeed operating as an interaction sphere. The Naquitz materials in terms of overlapping chipped stone types link closely with Santa Marta of Chiapas although some point types are common with Tehuacan. The Coxcatlan materials are mere extensions of Coxcatlan of Tehuacan, while the ceramics of horizon 9 are most similar to those of Veracruz but also display affiliation with Ocos of the Guatemala coast and with Ajalpan of Tehuacan to the north. According to Jane Wheeler Pires-Ferreira, obsidian from different sources moved into the region at different times.[22] Obviously, more investigation is needed in this area particularly to determine the preceramic way of life, but also to determine the cultural interaction of all periods as well as the cultures of horizons 1, 2, 3, 5, 7, and 8.

Subarea 7: High Mountain Valleys   Next to this highland area and starting at about the same elevation is the Tehuacan region; rising above it is subarea 7, the *high mountain valleys* (West's mesa central). This is perhaps the best-known area for this crucial early period for Meso-America, although horizon 8, 2300 B.C. to 1500 B.C., is represented by but a single poorly defined pottery complex, Purron, from three small cave occupations in Tehuacan.[23]

     In addition to the fairly full sequence from Tehuacan, there are recovered materials from northern Puebla from horizons 2, 3, and 4, and, across the lake from these careful excavations are more poorly exhumed materials that have been classified into three stages equivalent to El Riego, Coxcatlan, and Abejas. These ill-defined materials probably represented occupations by these cultural groups.[24] Studies in this Puebla region of horizons 3 and 4, 9000 B.C. to 7000 B.C., give a clearer picture for the transition at the end of the Pleistocene than we have in Tehuacan. Unfortunately, the archaeology of the Valley of Mexico does not come up to these high standards. We have some very limited materials from Tlapacoya from horizon 2 and perhaps from horizon 3 [25] and some better-documented artifacts from the mammoth kill at Itzapan (horizon 4 times).[26] Nothing exists for horizon 5, and two poorly documented complexes, Playa 1 and 2, roughly of horizon 6, have been interpreted as year-round occupations, which they assuredly are not.[27] Above these remains are a series of zones having few artifacts (mainly nondiagnostic but including some ground stone types) that are called Zohapilco. There are no horizon 8 materials, although horizon 9 (1500 B.C. to 1000 B.C.) remains in the Nevada and Ayotla ceramic phases are numerous. This late florescence contrasts with the cave sequence we have from Queretaro and Hidalgo where in San Nicolas Cave we have abundant remains of horizons 3, 7, and 8, while in Hidalgo and Tecolote Cave only materials from horizons 4, 5, and 6 occur.[28] However, enough of this—for we have already dealt with Tehuacan remains from this area.

Subarea 8: Mountain Peaks and Valleys   Subarea 8 is the *mountain peaks and valleys* (West's highland extratropical appendages). One incomplete sequence is based mainly on excavations in three caves in Canyon Infiernillo in southwest Tamaulipas, which yielded abundant food remains, including a sequence of domesticated plants: pumpkins and gourds at about 6000 B.C., common beans and peppers at 4000 B.C., amaranth and corn at 2000 B.C., squash (cucurbita moschata), and teosinte at about 1500 B.C. (there are also remains of the first villages). The early part of our sequence (horizons 1, 2, 3, and 4) is missing from these caves, but the lower levels of the La Calzada Cave of Nuevo Leon to the north have remains of early hunters, perhaps horizons 3 and 4.[29] If those remains are comparable, then the only gap in the sequence is between about 7500 B.C. and 6000 B.C. Nevertheless from 9000 B.C. on, a sequence of food-gathering remains shows increasing domestication and of agriculture until about 1800 B.C. when sustenance came mainly from agriculture, which led to village life at about 1500 B.C. All the above evidence, plus the vari-

ous artifact types in this sequence, attest to the fact that the area
was within the Meso-American interaction sphere from 10,000 B.C.
to about 1500 B.C.

Studies of the environment for archaeological purposes are
almost nonexistent. It is my impression that the microenvirons
are layered at different elevations, with the top ones being near
the mountain peaks having a tundra vegetation. These in turn are
over larger zones of cloud (rain zones) and/or coniferous forests,
which in turn are above valley flank zones, often of thorn forests;
the well-watered valley bottoms have thick gallery forest. I know
of no studies of environmental changes during the last 12,000
years, so the whole ecological knowledge of this final area leaves
much to be desired.

Summary   Both the ecological and archaeological aspects of
the Meso-American interaction sphere from 10,000 B.C. to 1000
B.C. have been inadequately investigated. Nevertheless the data
available provide a basis for making comparisons with the other
areas.

The Andes

The interaction sphere of the Andean area is limited by the Pacific Ocean on the west and the more wooded lower mountains of
Ecuador on the north. The southern boundary is impossible to
determine because of inadequate archaeological work. So is the
eastern boundary, which was probably some part of the lowland
jungle or selva because many plants from 5000 B.C. to 1000 B.C.
diffuse into the Andean area. Our limited preceramic archaeology
in the selva makes any definite statements impossible. Certainly,
when manioc became a main staple of the selva subsistence system, this selva region was outside the Andean interaction sphere,
but this may have been a development too late for the periods
under consideration (9000 B.C. to 1000 B.C.), indicating that this
root crop development was a secondary development and not a
pristine one like those of the Andes.[30]

Subarea 1: Dry Subtropical Lowlands
Environmental Characteristics   This is the coastal desert zone
roughly from the Ecuador to the Chilean borders, an area much
longer than the comparable zone in Meso-America or coastal

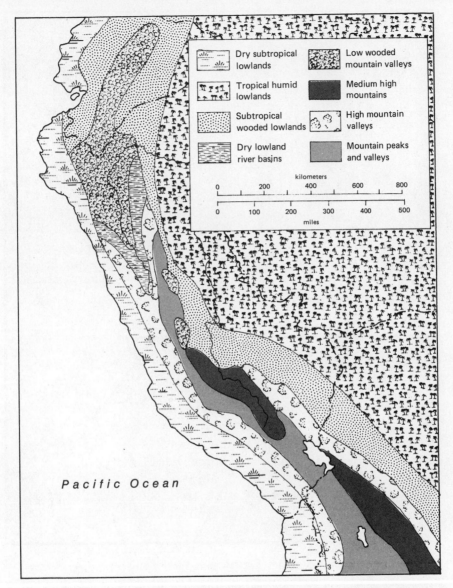

Figure 6.3

Ecological subareas of the Andean interaction sphere.

Levant in the Near East. Tosi has classified it as including seven of his desert zones: maleza desertica tropical, maleza desertica subtropical, maleza desertica montano bajo, desierto tropical, desierto subtropical, desierto montano bajo, and chaparral bajo montano.

Moseley and Patterson have classified the central Peruvian

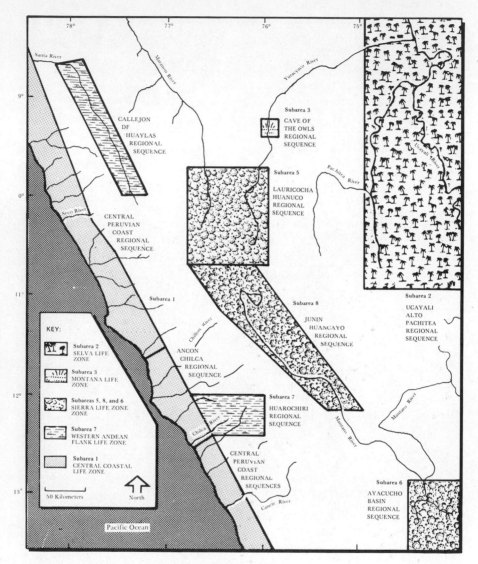

Figure 6.4

Life zones in the subareas of the central Peruvian inter-
action sphere where there are excavated sequences.

coast region into a number of microenvironments in terms of
human adaptations and natural resources.[31] These include the
rocky points and sandy beach locales where marine resources were
available in certain seasons, as well as deltaic, mid-river, and up-
river microzones on those watered and lusher strips that cut across

HORIZONS Carbon 14 time	CALENDAR (Sidereal) YEARS	SUB-AREA 1 Dry Sub-tropical Lowlands Peruvian Pacific Coast	SUB-AREA 2 Tropical Humid Lowlands Selva of R. Pachitea	SUB-AREA 3 Sub-tropical Wooded Lowlands Montana R. Huallaga	SUB-AREA 4	SUB-AREA 5 Low Wooded Mountain Valleys Huanuco Basin	SUB-AREA 6 Medium High Mountain Valleys Ayacucho Region	SUB-AREA 7 High Mountain Valleys Huarochiri Valley	SUB-AREA 7 Callejon de Huaylas	SUB-AREA 8 La Oroya Region	SUB-AREA 8 Lake Junin Region	SUB-AREA 8 Junin-Terma Region	SUB-AREA 8 Highland Huanuco
1000 B.C. Horizon 9 1200 B.C.	1200 B.C.	Curavacu	Pangotsi	Cave of the Owls		Kitosh	Wichqana		Initial Pottery		San Blas II	Telar-machay IV	Lauricocha IV
1200 B.C. Horizon 8 1750 B.C.	2000 B.C.	La Florida	Cobichaniqui			Wairajirca	Andamarka	Quiche	Initial Pottery		San Blas I	machay Level 4	
Horizon 7 3000 B.C. 3100 B.C.	3000 B.C.	Gaviota Conchas Playa Hermosa Pampa				Mitos	Cachi		Punta Callan	Tilarnioc Cave Levels 1-3	Pacha machay Levels 7-3		Telarmachay Level 5 and Acomachay Levels 2-4 and Cuchimachay Cave Levels 1-3
Horizon 6 4450 B.C.	4000 B.C. 5000 B.C.	Encanto Corbina					Chihua		Quishqui Punca	Tilarnioc Cave Level 4 and Panalagua Cave Levels 1-3	Pacha machay Levels 8-12	Cuchimachay Cave Level 6B	Lauricocha III
Horizon 5 5800 B.C.	6000 B.C.	Canario Arenal				Ambo	Piki	Tres Ventanas III	Guitarrero IIb - e	Tilarnioc Cave Level 5 and Panalagua Cave Levels 4-6	Pacha machay Lower Levels		
7000 B.C. 7100 B.C. Horizon 4	7000 B.C.	Pampilla					Jaywa	Tres Ventanas II	Lampras	Tilarnioc Cave Level 6			Lauricocha II
8000 B.C. Horizon 4 9000 B.C.	8000 B.C.	Conchitas					Puente	Tres Ventanas I	Guitarrero Ib - IIa	Panalagua Cave Level 7			Lauricocha I
9000 B.C.	9000 B.C.	Chivaterros I											
Horizon 3 11,000 B.C.	10,000 B.C. 11,000 B.C.						Huanta		Yungas Guitarrero Ia	Tilarnioc Cave Level 7			Huargo
Horizon 2	14,000 B.C.	Red Zone					Ayacurho						
Horizon 1							Pacaicasa						

Figure 6.5

Sequence by relevant horizons in the eight subareas in the central Peruvian interaction sphere.

the large sand dune desert sections and have some low hills in them (the loma), which turn green with the winter fogs. All of the latter have varying amounts of plant and animal resources, but only wild achiva seems to have had the potential for domestication. Preliminary studies suggest that the loma and desert were more hospitable during Pleistocene times. Perhaps there were lakes as well as grassland areas, with more game, such as horse, and some forms of giant sloth and mastodon.

Archaeological Horizons   Considerable archaeology has been undertaken in various regions of the coast, but there are few adequate site reports, and only the Lima region has even the semblance of a cultural sequence for the period under discussion. Just north of Lima a quarry site that has been exhumed, Chivaterros I (9500–8500 B.C.), our horizon 3, yielded remains that may be of early hunters of megafauna, such as sloth, mastodon, and the like. Above it were remains of Chivaterros II, here called Conchitas, dated at about 8500–7000 B.C. in horizon 4. There is some slim evidence that the inhabitants consumed marine shellfish year-round, exploited loma plant and animal resources during the wet season, and may have hunted in valley floors and riverine areas in the dry season. Both these first two complexes are inadequately defined, as is the Pampilla complex, 7000–6500 B.C., of the next horizon, although it seems similar to Conchitas. Arenal, 6000–5300 B.C., is similar (and equally ill defined) but the following Canario complex, 5300–4200 B.C., can definitely be placed in horizon 5, 5800–4450 B.C.[32] Similar sites extend from Paracas on the south coast to the Virú Valley on the north central coast, but little attempt has been made to describe them.

Subsistence seems to have been based on wild plants collected from the lomas during the wet season and valley floor resource areas during the dry season. Hunting, shellfish gathering, and fishing (possibly only in the Lurin Valley) occurred throughout the year.

The proximity of seasonal food resource areas played a major role in determining the location and permanency of settlements on the central coast. In the few localities where all of the resource areas are close to each other, permanent settlements arose. A clear example of this pattern is in the southwest corner of the Lurin Valley and in the Paloma quebrada of the Chilca Valley where the inhabitants exploited all of the seasonal and permanent food resources from a single location that they occupied continuously throughout the year. While some of the Lurin sites may have been base camps, the Paloma site was a hamlet with a number of oval pithouses.[33] Neither yielded any evidence of plant domestication or cultivation.

Two sites located in the lomas, one in the Lurin-Chilca interfluvial area and the other on the north side of the Lurin Valley, have yielded radiocarbon dates of about 5000 B.C.

When the season resource areas were too widely separated from each other to be conveniently exploited from a single locality, the populations lived in wet season camps along the rivers

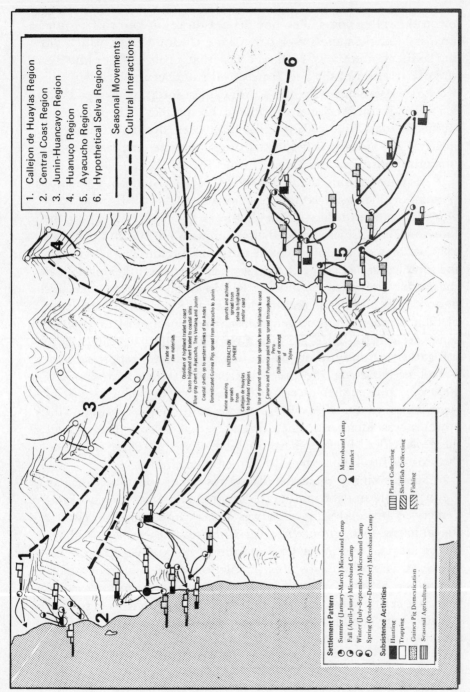

Figure 6.6

The central Peruvian interaction sphere in horizon 5 showing sedentary groups without agriculture on the coast and seasonal nomadic groups with agriculture in Ayacucho.

or on the valley floors. The one dry season camp known from the area is located in the lower part of the Chilca Valley, which has never been extensively farmed, a fact that probably accounts for the preservation of the site. It may well have been paired with the wet season settlement in the Lurin-Chilca interfluvial area. Wet season camps at Ancón were presumably paired with dry season camps in the Chillon Valley that have been destroyed either by nearly 4,000 years of intensive cultivation or the encroachment of modern industries from Lima.

More numerous than those sites, perhaps denoting a major population increase, are those of horizon 6, 4450–3100 B.C.[34] Included in this are the Corbina complex (4200–3750 B.C.) in the lomas north of Lima and the better represented Encanto complex (3750–2750 B.C.) extending from the Lima region well down into the south coast of Peru. Other slightly different complexes, such as the Lachay complex around the Rio Seco, also appear with this period of seemingly increasing population. Our firmest evidence of the cultural type, however, comes from Encanto of the central coast. Here subsistence was based on wild plants, hunting, shell-fish gathering, and fishing, which was much more important than it had been during the preceding period. After approximately 3000 B.C., two species of cultivated squash and one wild species were added to the diet of the Ancón-Chillon population. This however was incipient agriculture at its worst and probably all these plants had been domesticated elsewhere and later spread to the coast as little more than dietary supplements.

The proximity of seasonal food resources continued to play the major role in determining the location and permanency of settlements. Chilca Monument I was an Encanto village occupied continuously throughout the year because of the spacing of resource areas in the lower Chilca Valley.[35] Virtually all of the resource areas exploited by this population were contiguous with each other. Seasonal resource areas in the Ancón-Chillon region were not contiguous, and the population continued to reside in separate wet- and dry-season camps. Cultivated squash from an Encanto wet season camp, located in an area where agriculture could not have been practiced under any conditions, indicates that the population used the valley floor environments for gardening.

It seems likely that the growing reliance on fish, the continuing reliance on flour made from wild grass seeds, and the new

reliance on cultivated squashes during the later part of the Encanto phase apparently increased the nutritional level of some
central coastal groups, which ultimately set off a period of sus-
tained population growth at a time when the prevailing climatic
conditions were effectively reducing the size and extent of the
lomas.

Horizon 7, 3100–1750 B.C., on the central coast was the time
of the Pampa phase (2750–2400 B.C.), the Playa Hermosa phase
(2400–2200 B.C.), and the Conchas phase (2200–2000 B.C.). How
populations spaced themselves with respect to the resources they
were exploiting in order to maintain their self-sufficiency changed
at the beginning of the period. Previously many resources were
utilized on a calendar-round basis, with the population moving
from one resource area to the next as the resources of each became
seasonally available. The populations had to move when the resource areas were widely separated from each other or had to exploit areas in different directions from the same base camp or hamlet when the resources were contiguous with each other, as they
were in Chilca and Lurin.[36] During the earlier part of the period,
the location and permanency of settlements were governed by
other factors: the availability of marine products and the availability of arable land in the lower parts of the valley that could be
farmed during the dry season. Large year-round fishing villages
were established in the immediate vicinity of rich fishing grounds
and shellfish beds at Ancon and Ventanilla, which are located in
the coastal desert zone where agriculture cannot be practiced under any conditions. Small year-round hamlets were established in
areas of the Chillon Valley where single-crop farming could be
carried on. What had formerly been one population was now
divided into two distinct segments: a large coastal fishing group
and a small inland farming group. Both groups apparently remained in or near the same resource area throughout the year.
The fishermen sent marine protein foods into the valley and
received cultivated plant foods in return. The self-sufficiency of
the original population was maintained through this exchange
mechanism.

During horizon 7, settlement size was governed largely by
proximity to marine resource areas. Consequently the larger proportion of the population lived in coastal fishing villages and the
smaller proportion near agricultural lands in the low valley.

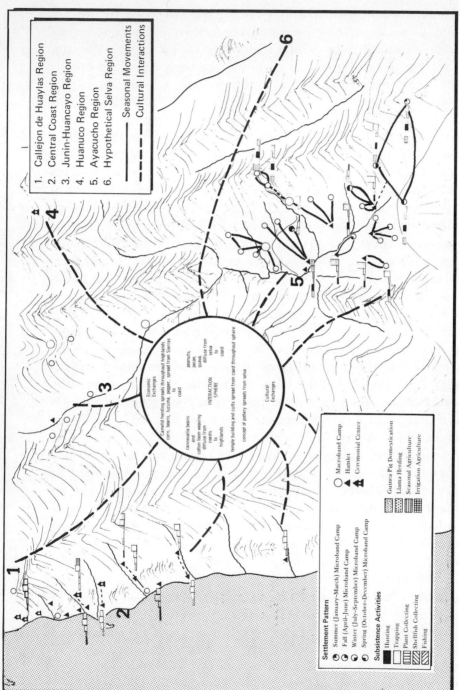

Figure 6.7

The central Peruvian interaction sphere in horizon 7 showing sedentary villages with redistribution centers in various river valleys that interact with the vertical economy system of Ayacucho.

The population of the Ancon-Chillon sector grew steadily during this period from an estimated fifty individuals around 3000 B.C. to more than 1,500 by the time of the following Gaviota phase at the end of the horizon. Similar rates of population growth probably occurred in both the Rimac and Lurin valleys, where substantial numbers of Gaviota phase settlements have been found.

Cultivated plant foods became increasingly more important during this period.[37] Canavalia, achira, paca, guava, chili peppers, corn, lima beans, lucuma, and sweet potatoes appeared. These plants were largely domesticated elsewhere and were then imported into the central coastal region.

Again there were numerous related complexes all up and down the coast, each one a little different from the other: Asia to the south at Lima, Huaca Prieta, Culebras and so on to the north.

In the final part of horizon 7 (2000–1750 B.C.) there was even greater differentiation in terms of individual valleys' cultural complexes and the construction of some fairly large structures, as well as huge towns, such as those at Rio Seco and La Florida classified as belonging to the Gaviota phase. At this time, being the center of an exchange network was crucial in determining settlement size. Consequently the largest sites were those that had a monopoly on marine products, a central position in the exchange network, or both. The major settlements in each valley exchange system— Chuquitanta, Rio Seco, Canto Grande, and Pachacamac—all have large public architecture.[38]

The existence of Gaviota phase farming hamlets in the middle parts of the Rimac and Lurin valleys has interesting implications concerning the agricultural technology of this coastal region. Given the gradients of the rivers and the amount of postglacial river cutting that has occurred, it is virtually impossible to farm anywhere in the middle elevations of these valleys without some form of water diversion system. The locations of the four middle valley settlements discovered so far suggest that short canals with or without diversion dams were used to divert water from the rivers to areas where arable land was available. The location of farming settlements in the lower parts of the Chillon, Rimac, and Lurin valleys does not suggest that water diversion systems were being used in the low valleys. However, whether there was irrigation or not, agriculture was a major subsistence activity. Cultivated plants became much more important dietary items after

1900 B.C., judging by the significant increase in both the quantity and variety of cultivated plants found in refuse deposits at coastal fishing settlements, the tremendous increase in the proportion of the total population that resided in the valley where farming could be practiced, the appearance of small hamlets in the middle parts of the river valleys where the prevailing environmental conditions favor the high productivity of certain crops, particularly coca, and the appearance of these middle valley crops in low valley and coastal settlements.

Perhaps more poorly known and described are the remains for our horizon 8, 1750–1200 B.C., and horizon 9, 1200–1000 B.C., when each region at the coast had it own distinctive ceramic complex. Pottery belonging to one of the brownware styles (1750–1400 B.C.) has been found throughout the region from the first half of the period. In the later half, the Colinas style (1400–1050 B.C.) occurred mainly in the northern sector, and the Curayacu style (1200–1050 B.C.) predominated in the southern sector. The stylistic difference between the two sectors in the later part of the period has important implications concerning the number of semi-independent exchange networks that were operating in the region as a whole. Therefore, it is again convenient to distinguish between the earlier and later parts of the period, using 1400 B.C. to 1200 B.C. as the dividing date for horizons 8 and 9.

The major settlements on the coastal plain during the preceding period were apparently abandoned and replaced by new ones featuring single, large pyramids. Judging by both the size of the pyramid and extent of the habitation area, the most important settlement in the entire region was La Florida, located about eleven kilometers from the ocean in the lower Rimac Valley and a few kilometers from the old exchange center at Canto Grande. It seems likely that the bulk of the population from both Chuquitanta and Canto Grande were incorporated into a single group center at La Florida during the early part of this period. There was a subsidiary population center with a pyramid at Mina Peridida in the lower Lurin Valley. In addition, there were numerous economically specialized hamlets located in the lower and middle parts of the Lurin and Rimac valleys, as well as at Ancon. Site locations, as well as the contents of habitation refuse deposits, have a number of implications concerning subsistence activities.

La Florida, the largest settlement in the region, is located in a

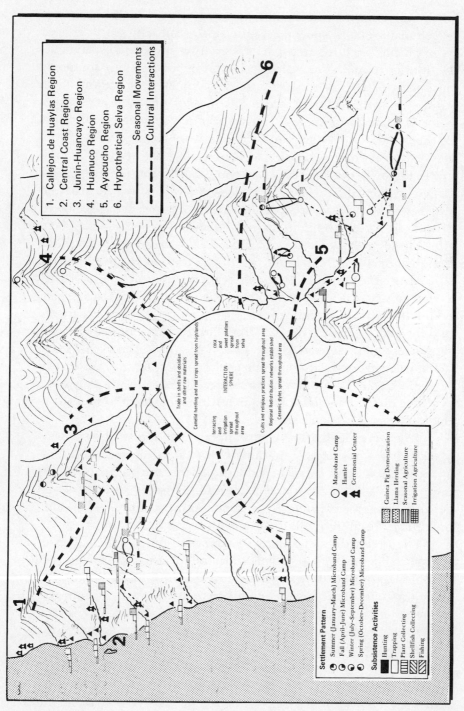

Figure 6.8

The central Peruvian interaction sphere showing the reconstructed settlement and subsistence patterns during horizon 9 on the central coast as well as in the Ayacucho Basin.

place where agriculture cannot be practiced without some sort of water management system because of the amount of postglacial river cutting in this part of the valley. It is highly likely that the La Florida population utilized a water-control system composed minimally of a single canal four to six kilometers in length, which would have roughly quadrupled the amount of arable land available. In addition to the small farming hamlets in the middle parts of the Rimac and Lurin valleys, there were small hamlets in localities in the lower Chillon and Rimac valleys where single crop riverbank or barranca agriculture could have been practiced. The largest segment of the low valley populations in the Rimac and Lurin valleys utilized water management systems; small segments of the low valley populations continued to farm along the riverbanks in the traditional way. Middle-sized segments of the populations continued to specialize in fishing and shellfish gathering.

All of the population segments were linked together by an exchange network. The major network on the central coast was dominated by La Florida and probably included hamlets in the middle parts of both the Chillon and Rimac valleys. Ceramic similarities between the Lurin Valley and those immediately to the north suggest that the exchange network of this valley was linked with the La Florida network. In other words, there is some evidence of the existence of a multivalley exchange system during the early part of this period.

The large population centers were abandoned about 1400–1200 B.C. and new ones were built in localities where even larger areas of arable land could be brought under cultivation with the use of simple water-control systems. Public architecture occurred at all of the larger settlements and at several of the smaller ones, including the fishing village at Ancon.

The major difference between the first and second halves of the period involved the number of independent exchange networks operating in the region. The distribution of ceramic styles after 1400 B.C. indicates that there were two exchange networks toward the end of the period, judging by the fact that Curayacu pottery has been found in the northern sector and that Colinas pottery occurs occasionally in the southern one.[39]

Subarea 2: Tropical Humid Lowlands   Turning now from this relatively well-investigated area of the Peruvian coast to the

next one, the *tropical humid lowlands,* is a distinct letdown because of the paucity of information available. Tosi has included
within this zone a number of subregions: bosque muy humedo
tropical, bosque humedo tropical, bosque seco tropical, bosque
muy humedo subtropical, bosque humedo subtropical, and bosque
pluvial subtropical. Unfortunately no attempts to define microenvironments have been made, and we know nothing about the
changes in environment from 10,000 B.C. to 1000 B.C. No archaeological complexes from horizons 1 to 7 have been dug, and Cobi-
chaniqui and early Tutishcainyo ceramic remains (perhaps of
horizon 8) indicate little of their agriculture systems, populations,
or settlement pattern systems, nor do horizon 9, Pangotsi, and late
Tutishcainyo complexes.[40] However, the presence of tropical
plants such as lucuma, peanuts, guava, sweet potatoes, and others
in the Peruvian culture complexes dating back to about 4000 B.C.
indicate intimate interaction with the other parts of the Andean
interaction sphere, as do the ceramic resemblances between the various regions or subareas in horizon 8. In spite of this there is little
we can say about the selva contribution to the process of plant
domestication.

Subarea 3: Subtropical Wooded Lowlands   Much the same
might be said of the work in the montano, which I have classified
as subarea 3, the *subtropical wooded lowlands.* Again, a host of
Tosi life zones are included in my single group: bosque muy
humedo montano bajo, bosque humedo montano bajo, bosque
pluvial montano bajo, bosque muy humedo montano, bosque
humedo montano, bosque pluvial montano, estepa montano, desierto montano, and maleza desertica montano.

Little ecological, geological, or archaeological investigation
has been undertaken in this area, so little can be said about it. In
fact, the only available archaeological materials from it date from
our final period, 2000–1000 B.C. These are a few Kotosh-type
sherds from the Cave of the Owls near Tinta Maria on the Hual-
laga River, a southern tributary of the Amazon.[41]

Subarea 4: Dry Lowland River Basins and/or Drainages   The
picture is equally bleak for subarea 4, the *dry lowland river basins
and/or drainages* on the eastern slopes of the Andes. Tosi's bosque
espinoso tropical, bosque muy seco tropical, and bosque seco sub-

tropical zones fall in this subarea. There are a number of promising archaeological areas—such as Baqua in northernmost lowland Peru, much of the northern flanks of the Maranon River, the flanks of the Apurimac near Abancay, and the basin just below Tarma in central Peru—but, as yet, no excavations have been undertaken in any of these regions.

Subarea 5: Low Wooded Mountain Valleys

Environmental Characteristics   Subarea 5 is the *low wooded mountain valleys* (1,000 to 2,000 meters in elevation), which includes Tosi's bosque seco subtropical, estepa espinosa montano bajo, chaparral alto montano bajo, and often his bosque espinosa subtropical. Itzumi has classified its microenvironments or eco-zones into three or four subtypes, recognizing that one of them is the high mountains surrounding the valley to the west where temperate forests occur.[42] Below it is an alpine steppe zone. Another encompasses the mountains to the east, which are covered with tropical cloud forest ceja vegetation. The valley itself contains a zone of cactus and huarango sort of thorn forest on the lower slopes and surfaces of the mountains, a badly disturbed sparse forest or warm savanna on the valley bottoms that includes such potential domesticates as guava, sapindus, tara, chirimoya, and possibly sweet potatoes, and along the river itself the deciduous forest region, a third or fourth zone. Unfortunately Itzumi's brief history of vegetational changes covers only the time of the Kotosh occupation and mainly after our main period of discussion.

Archaeological Horizons   Although some surface materials from Ambo are perhaps of horizon 5 times, most of the well-documented material from Kotosh is mainly of horizons 8 and 9, after the main part of the period under discussion. Here the earliest materials of the preceramic Kotosh Mito culture occurred from about 2000 B.C. to 1800 B.C. (carbon 14 time) and come from a ceremonial center practicing agriculture and constructing ornate temples like those of the Manos Cruzados type. The next two periods, both with beautiful incised pottery, Kotosh Waira-jirca and Kotosh-Kotosh culture, saw the augmentation of this relatively modest ceremonial center into a large one.

Subarea 6: Medium High Mountain Valleys

Environmental Characteristics   The most relevant data come from subarea 6, the *medium high mountain valleys* in Peru, between 2,000 and 3,000 meters. It includes Tosi's bosque seco montano bajo, bosque espinosa subtropical, and estepe espinosa montano bajo. These valleys are surrounded by a high forest zone situated below the low and high alpine tundra areas. Ayacucho is a prime example of a region within this kind of area. It typically has a series of vertically layered ecological zones—like Tehuacan in Mexico—that often were exploited seasonally by moving in a well-scheduled annual cycle, for wild food became available in each of the very different seasons. Roughly the major zones were the following:

1. The high puna: with mainly wild camelids, few deer, few edible plant foods; too high for any kind of agriculture (over 4,200 meters); subject to fog and snow in the wet season but good hunting or herding in the dry season.

2. The low puna: with wild camelids and deer; some edible plants and potato agriculture possible in the dry season; 4,200 to 3,600 meters above sea level.

3. The humid woodland: good deer hunting, some camelids; many edible plants in the wet season and potato agriculture possible; 3,600 to 3,200 meters above sea level.

4. The thorn forest: many deer and other animals in the wet season as well as edible plants and agriculture of seed plants; 3,200 to 2,800 meters above sea level.

5. The thorn forest riverine: some deer and small mammals all year round as well as wild plants and irrigation agriculture and fruit growing; more food available in the wet season; about 2,800 to 2,400 meters above sea level.

6. Xerophytic zone: livable only in the wet season, and even then the animals, plants, and possibilities of agriculture are limited; below 2,500 meters.

Now let us briefly discuss how the zones were exploited through our 25,000 years of cultural history.

Archaeological Horizons   Although final reports are not completed, there is a long sequence with many sites and components (occupations) belonging to the relevant period. In addition, a Pacaicasa complex dating from 20,000–13,500 B.C. and belonging to horizon 1 has been described, as have some of the tools from horizon 2, the Ayacucho phase (13,500–11,500 B.C.).[43] The first relevant archaeological complex, Huanta, is poorly represented by a piece of a bifacial crude leaf point, a prismatic blade, four worked flakes, and a denticulated pebble scraper plane in association with a medapoidal of an extinct horse, three camelid bones, and two rodent bones. Comparative materials with similar scraper planes from level 7 of Uchumachay (Tilarnioc) Cave from near Junín and remains from levels 7–9 of Huargo Cave in the mountains above Huanuco with a carbon 14 date of 11,510 B.C. ± 700 years suggest that the Huanta culture, existing from 11,500 B.C. to 9000 B.C., probably consisted of nomadic hunters of herd animals, such as horses, maybe extinct deer, as well as modern camelids, deer, and rodents (the last three are nonherd types).[44] The more reliable part of the sequence, however, does not start until after these horizon 3 remains. Two phases of Ayacucho, Puente, and Jaywa seem to belong to horizon 4 in the Andes from 9000 B.C. to 5800 B.C.

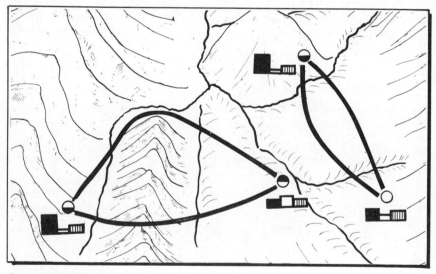

Settlement Pattern

◑ Spring–Summer (October–March) Microband Camp
◐ Fall–Winter (April–September) Microband Camp

Subsistence Activities

█ Hunting   ☐ Trapping   ⦀ Plant Collecting

Figure 6.9

An isometric view from the south of the southern part of the Ayacucho Basin showing the reconstructed settlement and subsistence patterns during horizons 3 and early 4 (10,000 B.C. to 5800 B.C.).

Components containing Puente phase (9000–7100 B.C.) arti-facts have been excavated and found on the surface in three of the present-day environment zones of the area. Soil profiles and pollen studies suggest that one of the present environmental zones—the thorn forest—was diminished in size by wetter conditions and that much of its area was covered by humid forests. Mammal bones found in these assemblages indicate that the riverine thorn forests were occupied during the wet season (October–March) and that the much expanded humid woodland environment zone was occupied during the dry season (April–September). The main ac-tivity of the dry season camp was hunting (mainly deer and some camelids), although there was also some trapping and plant collec-ing. This contrasts with the activities being carried out at the ex-cavated wet season camps, which contained proportionately fewer deer and camelids and more cavia and other small mammals that could probably be trapped. Although the evidence is not conclu-sive, it strongly suggests that there was some kind of seasonally scheduled subsistence system in the area. The uniformly small size of the six excavated components indicates that the base group was a microband composed of not more than a couple of families.[45]

The Jaywa phase (7100–5800 B.C. radiocarbon time) is repre-sented by many more ecofacts and artifacts from twelve excavated components and one surface site.[46] Jaywa sites occur in five of the six environmental zones of the region. A site excavated in the humid woodlands subzone contained five living floors that repre-sent dry season microband camps, judging by the large quantities of dry season mammal bone and projectile points. Furthermore, there were achiote seeds on one of the floors, and two of the three human feces recovered contained the stem of a berry, a grass seed, and monocot and dicot plant fibers, in addition to meat debris. Thus, the dry season hunters of the humid woodlands were also collecting some plant foods. Two sites in the low puna seem to have had similar subsistence patterns. One excavated site, Aya-machay, then in a wetter thorn scrub, contained bones and seeds and probably represents a microband occupation of hunters and plant collectors during the latter part of the dry season (August–September). A slightly later floor at the same site, about 5600 B.C., contained very early Piki phase artifacts and yielded the rind of a gourd. One site in the riverine thorn forest zone was composed of a series of living floors representing microband occupations dur-

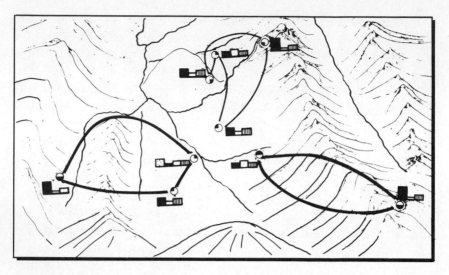

Settlement Pattern

- ◑ Summer (January–March) Microband Camp
- ◐ Fall (April–June) Microband Camp
- ◓ Winter (July–September) Microband Camp
- ◒ Spring (October–December) Microband Camp

Subsistence Activities

■ Hunting   ▨ Guinea Pig Domestication
□ Trapping   ⦀ Plant Collecting

Figure 6.10

An isometric view from the south of the southern part of the Ayacucho Basin showing the reconstructed settlement and subsistence patterns during late horizon 4 (7000 B.C. to 5800 B.C.).

ing the wet season (October–March). Each floor was covered with literally hundreds of bones of cavia, some of which may have been tamed. There also were a few small mammal bones, as well as a few deer and camelid bones. The kinds of bones recovered suggest that trapping was more important than hunting. Some charred seeds and a grinding stone found indicate that plant collecting was also more important than hunting during this season. One microband and at least two macroband camps were found in the area of the present dry thorn scrub, which was then a woodland zone. The presence of grinding stones in them suggests that they were also wet season occupations.

Evidence indicates that the populations of this region moved from one microenvironment to another as the seasonal food resources of each zone became available. The inhabitants exploited these resources with different subsistence techniques, and their diet varied somewhat from one season to the next. It is clear that they were not only experimenting with and perfecting their techniques for acquiring both plant and animal foods but were also gaining a much greater knowledge of their ecosystem as a whole.

The big change in their subsistence and settlement patterns came in horizon 5; the development is extremely well represented by the Piki phase. Many artifacts and ecofacts belonging to the Piki complex (5800–4550 B.C., radiocarbon time) were recovered from eighteen surface sites and seven excavated caves, which yielded twenty-four living floors.[47] These sites are located in all of the environmental zones of the region. Furthermore, five excavated components containing early Chihua complex (4550–4200 B.C.) artifacts are also relevant to this discussion. All of the excavated Piki and Chihua components contained abundant faunal remains, and, in addition, there were nine preserved human feces and several identifiable plant remains.

Dry season camps were represented at two excavated sites in the low puna, one in the humid woodlands and another in the riverine thorn scrub, where the inhabitants supplemented their predominantly meat protein diets with plant foods presumably collected in much the same way as they were in the preceding period. However, a series of seven wet season (November–March) living floors excavated in Pikimachay Cave, located in the slightly wetter dry thorn scrub zone, represented a sequence of microband occupations and yielded a very different subsistence pattern. There were few bones of either large or small mammals in these layers, but the presence of wild seeds, gourd remains, and the seeds of domesticated quinoa and squash suggest a wet season subsistence pattern based mainly on plant collecting and agriculture, incipient as it may have been, where hunting and trapping were of little importance.

Two microband camps, one in a canyon in the present-day dry thorn forest (pollen indicates it was then woodland) and another in a cave in the lower part of the humid woodlands, contained relatively few bones, some grinding stones, and some seeds; the inhabitants of these localities may have had a similar incipient agricultural subsistence pattern as did those of Pikimachay Cave. One of these also contained the remains of a tree gourd.

A third subsistence system is represented in a series of eighteen microband living floors excavated at Puente Cave in the riverine thorn scrub. Twelve floors showed clear evidence of wet season occupation; all of them contained a few camelid or deer bones and hundreds of small mammal bones, including those of seemingly tamed guinea pig. Many of them also yielded grinding stones, pebble rocker manos, majana for digging sticks, and unidentified charred seeds. This subsistence system was apparently composed of trapping and guinea pig penning, some plant collecting and/or incipient agriculture, and little, if any, hunting.

During this period, there was a year-round cycle in which populations shifted their camps from one microenvironment to another as the seasonal resources of each became available. The subsistence activities practiced during each season and in each microenvironment were different. Furthermore, there was a continually increasing tendency for wet season camps to become larger in size and longer in duration as storable domesticated plants and guinea pigs played continually growing roles in consumption patterns.

Horizon 6, 4450–3100 B.C., in terms of the beginning of the use of many domesticates and cultivars in Ayacucho is of key importance. It is represented by the new Chihua phase. Six excavated and twenty-seven surface sites with artifacts belonging to the middle and late Chihua complex (4200–3100 B.C.) are germane to the discussion of this horizon.[48] Three components excavated in the low puna environmental zone indicate that the older system of microband dry season camps where hunting was important continued. However, a human feces, containing a possible potato eye, and a hoe fragment suggest that the inhabitants of these localities were supplementing their diets with root crop agricultural produce grown during the dry season. One site in the high puna was found in survey. An excavated living floor from the humid woodlands yielded a hoe, grinding stones, and a few large mammal bones suggesting that the subsistence patterns of this environmental zone were much the same as the ones described above. The hoes hint at potato cultivation.

Information from the dry thorn scrub environmental zone shows different subsistence patterns. Here, there is evidence of po-

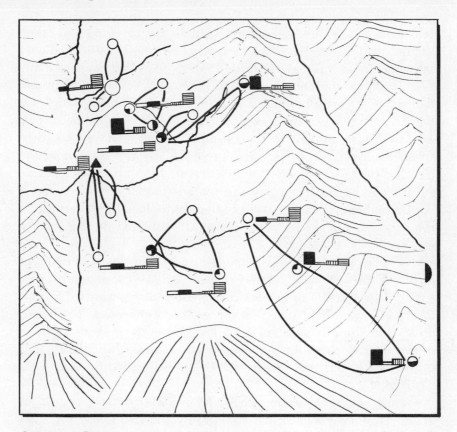

Settlement Pattern

◐ Summer (January–March) Microband Camp   ○ Macroband Camp

◑ Fall (April–June) Microband Camp   ▲ Hamlet

◒ Winter (July–September) Microband Camp

◓ Spring (October–December) Microband Camp

Subsistence Activities

▮ Hunting   ▦ Guinea Pig Domestication

▯ Trapping   ▨ Llama Herding

▥ Plant Collecting   ▤ Seasonal Agriculture

Figure 6.11

An isometric view from the south of the Ayacucho Basin showing the reconstructed settlement and subsistence patterns during horizon 6 (4200 B.C. to 2500 B.C.).

tato growing, domesticated corn, squash, gourd, common beans, lucuma, quinoa, and perhaps coca, all of which are associated with the remains of a few domesticated guinea pigs, a few large mammal bones, and wild plants. The sites in these microenvironmental zones are mainly wet season camps, a few of which extended well into the dry season; furthermore, a few of the surface sites are large enough to be considered macroband camps. Still another subsistence pattern is represented at sites located in the riverine thorn scrub zone. Small excavated floors produced some guinea pig remains, a few large mammal bones, and relatively large numbers of scraper planes, digging tools, and seed-grinding implements. These sites were apparently occupied during various seasons.

The evidence suggests that the most important settlement unit was the base camp in the riverine or dry thorn scrub zones with an agricultural or horticultural system that permitted groups to grow limited food surpluses during the wet season. These surpluses were not large enough to last the entire year, so groups supplemented them by hunting in the humid woodlands and upper and lower puna zones and by collecting in the dry thorn scrub zone.

Sites belonging to the early and middle parts of the Cachi phase (3100–1750 B.C. carbon 14 date) indicate a slightly drier period.[49] The population seems to have increased from the preceding period (thirty-three to fifty sites), and two new settlement-subsistence systems emerged. The major system, which occurred in the puna and the adjacent humid scrub forest, was based on a seasonal subsistence system involving camelid herding and potato farming in these zones. Some of the most ancient corrals seem to belong to this period. Mammal bones and artifacts from excavated components indicate that groups went to the high puna during the dry season to herd tamed guanaco and hunt and then moved to the low puna or humid woodlands during the wet season to grow potatoes. There was a corresponding deemphasis of herding and hunting activities. This life-style was linked—probably through kinship and ritual ties that served economic functions—to the major settlement-subsistence system (thirty-eight components), which took place at lower elevations, where camelid bones are found in excavation only occasionally.

Of particular importance in the lower settlement-subsistence system were seven or eight sites with architectural features, including three with agriculture terraces. These were probably hamlets that were occupied continuously throughout the year. The other lower elevation sites, including the twelve excavated components from caves, seem to be seasonal camps occupied sporadically by groups going out from the hamlets to plant, harvest, collect, hunt, and trap. Foodstuffs from the cave components include corn, squash, beans, gourd, tara, and lucuma, and possibly pepper, quinoa, and achira, as well as domesticated guinea pig, camelid, deer, and small mammals.

The minor settlement-subsistence system involved seasonal residence in different high-altitude localities and subsistence activities based on herding and root-crop farming. The major settlement-subsistence system involved permanent residence with occasional forays away from the hamlet and subsistence activities focused primarily around agriculture. The two systems were linked together by an exchange network—a vertical economy. Basically this pattern has persisted to the present day in the Ayacucho-Huanta region.

Horizon 8 (1750–1200 B.C.) is extremely poorly represented by but four components of the last part of the Cachi phase—two being camps and two being hamlets—and a single component in the lower layers of the Chupas site, which may have been a hamlet or ceremonial center that had Andomarka type pottery. Probably the subsistence system and settlement was not too different from that of the Cachi phase.

The same might be said of the next phase, Wichqana, in horizon 9. This phase is mainly defined by pottery types, but there are some other data, mainly from survey.

Information from two excavated components and a mountain top surface collection suggests that the high-elevation, seminomadic seasonal settlement pattern and the herding and potato farming subsistence system remained relatively unchanged. However, data from sites located at lower elevations indicate there was a new development in the settlement patterns in this part of the region. First, there are a number of architectural features made with boulder-type masonry; one is a truncated pyramid that may have had a ceremonial function. Second, the thirty-six lower elevation sites cluster in five geographically distinct localities; furthermore, in four, there is a single site with a pyramid and other ceremonial features, which served as a center for a series of other kinds of sites, including hamlets along waterways both with and without terrace features, open camps, and cave occupations. The clusters of sites around one of these pyramid centers were tied to it by kinship and ceremonial and economic arrangements. The larger proportion of llama bones in these pyramid centers suggests that they were not only the nuclear centers for farming communities but were also intermediaries between the lower elevation agricultural groups and the high elevation herds and root farmers.

Subarea 7: High Mountain Valleys

Environmental Characteristics   Subarea 7, the *high mountain valleys,* is in the Andes from 3,000 to 4,000 meters. However, at about 3,000 meters there is a distinct break in the vegetation, with tree growth confined to the river flanks, scrubs, and grassland in the flanks of the valleys with tundra-covered mountains sticking up from these bottom lands. In fact, in Tosi's life zones all would have large tundra components in either paramo muy humedo subalpino y tundra pluvial alpino, maleza desertica subalpino y tundra humeda alpino, or paramo humedo subalpino y tundra muy humido alpino.

The microenvironments, like those in subarea 6, are of the layered type, and there are great seasonal extremes.

Archaeological Horizons   Although some sequences do exist far above Huancayo in central Peru and at Toquepala Cave high in southern Peru, the best ones come from the west flanks of the Andes, particularly in the upper reaches of the Chilca Valley [50] and various sites and surveys in the Callejon de Huaylas in north central Peru.[51] Here the earliest remains come from the possibly mixed lowest levels at Guitarrero Cave in the latter region, but the few artifacts tell little about their subsistence system, although the date (10,610 B.C.) shows them to be of horizon 3; perhaps the people were hunters of extinct animals. Horizon 4 remains occur not only in zones Ib and IIa at Guitarrero but also in the lowest and middle levels of Tres Ventanas Cave.[52] Projectile points and animal bones indicate that populations in both were heavily involved in hunting, and the jicama roots reported indicate the Tres Ventanas people also collected plants. Marine shells in the latter deposits indicate interaction with coastal areas. For horizon 5

(5800–4450 B.C.) there are abundant materials from the upper levels of Tres Ventanas Cave, and there are good indications of seasonal hunting and gathering. However, more germane are the materials from zones IIc, IId, and IIe at Guitarrero Cave, with evidence of similar subsistence patterns, plus remains of domesticated common and lima beans. Since the only wild relatives of beans appear in the montane or low tropical valleys on the east slope of the Andes (like Kotosh), they were probably first domesticated there and then spread westward at this early time into the highlands. The rest of the horizons (6–9) are very poorly delimited for this region, but sites with initial period pottery from 1750 B.C. to 1000 B.C., in what seems to be sedentary agriculture villages, occur in the Callejon de Huaylas drainage of central Peru.

Subarea 8: Mountain Peaks and (Highest) Valleys

Environmental Characteristics   The final Andean subarea (8), the *mountain peaks and highest valleys,* occurs in Peru above 4,000 meters. Surprisingly enough, there is a considerable amount of data from this high region. Tosi would classify most of this area in his formacion nival, tundra pluvial alpino, and tundra humedo alpino. In terms of microenvironments there are the high puna, low puna, and small bushes and trees along the stream beds of shores or lakes. All areas are uncomfortable, whether it is snowing in the wet season or just foggy drizzle in the dry season.

Archaeological Horizons   Recently six stratified caves have been excavated in the Junin region: Uchcumachay, Cuchimachay, Panalagua, Pachamachay, Acomachay, and Telarmachay. Above Huanuco, Lauricocha and Huargo caves have been dug.[53] On this basis there is a fine sequence and the faunal material has been studied.

The earliest artifact complex, Hurpac, is of horizon 3 and is represented by remains from level 7 of Uchcumachay and from levels 7–9 of Huargo Cave. The inhabitants seem to have been nomadic microband horse herd hunters. They also stalked extinct and modern deer and perhaps trapped or collected small mammals and birds. There is no information as to whether they collected plants.

The next culture, Panalagua, is known only from level 7 at the cave of that name. There is evidence that they hunted mainly modern deer and some kinds of camelids. The projectile points

are much like those of Puente in Ayacucho and horizon 1 of Tres
Ventanas and Lauricocha. Like Jaywa are the Junin complex materials from level 6 at Uchcumachay and Lauricocha II. These
people killed about as many camelids as they did deer. They also
seem to have collected more plant remains seasonally.

The next period, Pachamachay, is represented by artifacts
from the lowest level of the cave of that name and level 5 of
Uchcumachay, as well as levels 4 to 6 of Panalagua and Lauricocha
II. More camelids than deer were then being killed, domesticated
dogs were utilized, and many wild plants seem to have been collected, perhaps seasonally. Pollen hints that quinoa may have been
domesticated and planted. The Callavalluari complex follows,
based on materials from level 4 of Uchcumachay, levels 1–3 of
Panalagua, and levels 8–12 of Pachamachay and Lauricocha III.
Camelid bones far outnumber those of deer, and there are indications, in terms of large numbers of juveniles, that there was at
least herding of camelids, but these were not necessarily of the
domesticated varieties. Also, plant remains suggest the use of both
wild and domesticated plants, and hoes may indicate that wild
potatoes were being grown.

The final preceramic complex of horizon 7, which perhaps
should be called Cuchimachay, is represented by upper levels from
that cave, as well as levels in Telarmachay, Acomachay, and Pachamachay. Herding of camelids (perhaps llama) was common, but
hunting and trapping continued, and plant collecting and planting may have occurred seasonally. Perhaps there was a seasonal
movement cycle like that of Cachi in Ayacucho.

The final representative of horizons 8 and 9 occurred at the
San Blas stratified open site near Junín. Though detailed reports
are not available, the lower levels seem to have been of agriculture
and herding people living in a hamlet with pottery like those of
Kotosh Waira-jirca, while the upper layers are of people with a
similar subsistence pattern and Kotosh-Kotosh pottery and seem
connected with some sort of ceremonial center.

Summary

The data for the Andes indicate that the area certainly was
functioning as a nonstatic interaction sphere for the period from
10,000 B.C. to 1000 B.C.[54] Our evidence of an interaction sphere is

far poorer for Meso-America because of a lack of data from early lowland materials, but it will improve with more research.

As far as the archaeology is concerned, both areas are relatively poor in many of the crucial periods under discussion, although the Meso-American highland data provide somewhat more germane plant data than do the Andean comparable regions. However, in the coastal Peruvian sites of these horizons, there are extremely good, important plant remains pertinent to agricultural studies.

The Near East

Subarea 1: Dry Subtropical Lowlands   The first region of this Asia Minor center of domestication is the Levant Mediterranean dry coast; it is subarea 1, the *dry subtropical lowlands*. Vita-Finzi and Higgs's *Site Catchment Analysis* indicates that the ecozones that occur are a marine sand-dune shore strip, a seasonal marshland, a dry grass steppe area as the land rises, the Jordanian rift, and, farther inland, a mixed forest area in the higher levels that fronts to the east on the desert, which is everywhere.[55] According to Vita-Finzi and Higgs's analysis, the exploitation of these microenvironments was probably done in a radial manner from a base camp in the period under discussion roughly 20,000 to 8,750 years ago. This system would be much like that of the Peruvian coast in horizons 4 to 8. These Near East environs include quite a number of plants potentially domesticable, such as emmer, wild bread wheat, wild two-rowed barley, and wild horse beans, as well as a potential domesticable animal—wild goats.

Archaeological Horizons   A tremendous amount of archaeology has been done in this region, but unfortunately most of it pertains to our later horizons, although, of course, there are lower Paleolithic materials of horizon 1. Mousterian materials, roughly horizon 2, are also known. Perhaps the earliest information about our period is the Kebaran culture, found in various caves, which seems to date from about 16,000 B.C. to 10,500 B.C.[56] These people were probably base camp hunters and gatherers during a period when the environment was lusher than at present.

Materials from horizon 7 (9500–8500 B.C.) come from the Ain Mallaha site near Eynan, Syria, Jericho in Jordan, and various other Natufian sites from Israel.[57] Uncovered at some of these

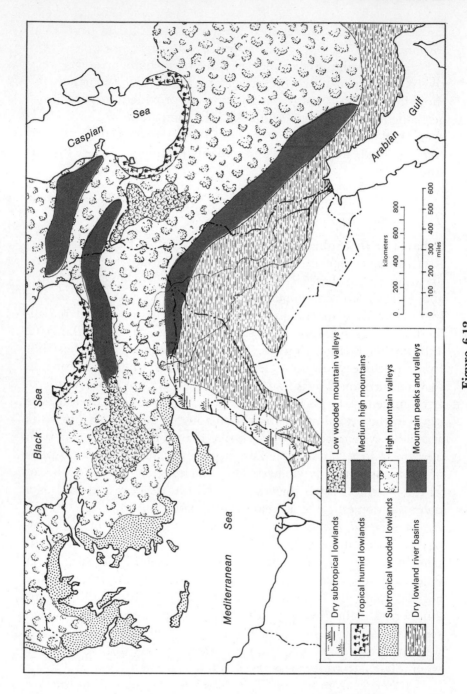

Figure 6.12

Ecological subareas of the Near Eastern interaction sphere.

HORIZONS Carbon 14 time	CALENDAR (Sidereal) YEARS	SUB-AREA 1 Dry Sub-tropical Lowlands The Levant — Coastal Plain	Hills	Central Rift	SUB-AREA 2 Tropical Humid Lowlands Caspian Sea Coast	SUB-AREA 3 Sub-tropical Wooded Turkey Greece Coasts	SUB-AREA 4 Dry Lowland River Drainage Tigris Euphrates	SUB-AREA 5 Low Wooded Mountain Valleys Central Turkey	SUB-AREA 6 Medium High Mountain Valleys East	West	SUB-AREA 7 High Mountain Valleys Northern Iraq	Central Western Iran	South Iranian Plateau	SUB-AREA 8 High Coniferous Forests
6750 B.C. Horizon 9 7250 B.C.	8000 B.C.	Megiddo	Ramad	Beida Jericho PPNB		Argissa	Bus Mordeh	Hacilar	Cayonu	M'Lefaat	Jarmo	Tepe Guran	Upper Ganj Dareh	
Horizon 8 8500 B.C.	8500 B.C.	Azor	Harifian	Jericho PPNA	Belt Cave Mesolithic	Franchthi Lower Mesolithic	Murey-bit						Asiab	
Horizon 7 9000 B.C. 9500 B.C.	9000 B.C.	Late Natufian El-Wad	Hayanim, Natufian Ain Mallaha			Beldibi				Shanidar Layer B1 Zawi Chemi	Karim Shahir		Lower Ganj Dareh	
Horizon 6 10,750 B.C.	10,000 B.C.	Early Natufian Kebara Negev	Kebaran	Jericho Natufian		Belbasi			Soqut Tarlosi	Shanidar Layer B2	Zarzi	Upper Pa Sangar		
Horizon 5 12,500 B.C.	11,000 B.C. 12,000 B.C.	Kebaran A		Kebaran A	Ali Tappeh	Upper Kastritsa					Palegawa	Lower Pa Sangar		
Horizon 4 16,000 B.C.	13,000 B.C. 14,000 B.C. 15,000 B.C. 16,000 B.C.	Kebaran		Kebaran Kebaran		Lower Kastritsa Franchthi Upper Paleolithic						Yafteh Cave	Upper Ghar-i Khar	
Horizon 3 35,000 B.C.	30,000 B.C.	Levantine Aurignacian				Aspro-chaliko				Shanidar Layer C Baradostian			Middle Ghar-i Khar	
Horizon 2	100,000 B.C.	Mousterian				Mousterian				Shanidar Layer D	Telephone Pole	Bisitun	Lower Ghar-i Khar	
Horizon 1		Tayacian												

Figure 6.13

Sequence by relevant horizons in the eight subareas in the Near Eastern interaction sphere.

sites were small oval houses, storage pits, grinding stones, and microliths but no domesticated plant or animal remains, although wild wheat and barley seeds are reported for Nahal Oren. Evidently these sedentary people—like those at Canario in Peru and perhaps Palma Sola on the Veracruz coast—were extremely successful wild plant collectors who did some hunting.

The subsistence portion remains roughly similar for horizon 8 (8500–7250 B.C.), which is represented by the earliest materials from Jericho PPNA and Beidha in Palestine. The tools are somewhat the same, although there are also many sickles. In addition there are ceremonial structures among the numerous round houses. A few grains of domesticated emmer, two-rowed barley, and wild goats have been found at both, but there is still little evidence of horticulture or agriculture. Harifian may also be of this horizon, although it has no evidence of horticulture. Horticulture appears in horizon 9 (7250–6750 B.C.), perhaps best represented in the prepottery PPNB neolithic levels at Jericho, which show evidence of domesticated einkorn, emmer, hulled two-rowed barley, peas, lentil, and vetch, as well as domesticated dogs, sheep, and goats. From many standpoints this whole sequence is comparable to that of the Peruvian coast, a similar environmental area within a pristine agriculture interaction sphere and one day the Tamaulipas and Veracruz coastal sequence may turn out to be comparable.

Subarea 2: Tropical Humid Lowlands   Unfortunately the archaeology of this and other areas is not so well known. From the lush wooded coastal environs of the Black Sea and Caspian Sea, subarea 2, the *tropical humid lowlands,* only two sites, Belt Cave and Ali Tappeh have yielded mesolithic materials, the former roughly between 7000 B.C and 6000 B.C. and the latter between 11,000 B.C. and 9000 B.C. There is no evidence of plant or animal domestication, just artifacts reflecting seasonal hunting and plant collecting (perhaps from a base camp).[58] Neolithic remains do appear above the mesolithic ones in Belt Cave, showing the use of pottery, agriculture, and domesticated animals, but this date (about 6000 B.C.) is after the period of our concern.

Subarea 3: Subtropical Wooded Lowlands   The lush Mediterranean coast of Turkey and Greece, which I have classified as subarea 3, the *subtropical wooded lowlands,* in spite of the fact that few paleoecological studies have been made of it, has yielded a long sequence of archaeological materials.

Not only has Franchthi Cave yielded a sequence of six phases extending from 20,000 B.C. to 3000 B.C.,[59] but early remains from Kastritsa Cave are between 12,000 and 14,000 years old, and a number of horizon 9 villages that have been dug show evidence of agriculture.[60] These later Aegean aceramic complexes such as at Sesklo, Knossos, and Argissa have substantial villages with evidence of farming emmer, bread wheat, hulled two-rowed and six-rowed barley, as well as peas, lentils, and vetch. Details about the development of agriculture have not yet been published, but it would appear that agriculture, with the above plants, came in suddenly in horizon 9 to be incorporated in successful collector subsistence systems that earlier had allowed for a sedentary way of life.

Subarea 4: Dry Lowland River Basins and/or Drainages
Environmental Characteristics   Although the development of agriculture seems similar for the grassland or steppe area flanking the Tigris and Euphrates, for our subarea 4, *dry lowland river basins and/or drainages,* the archaeological and ecological studies are very different. First of all, Hole and Flannery have undertaken detailed ecological studies of the Deh Luran plain of southern Iran.[61] They see a series of zones paralleling the Euphrates: (1) the river terraces with wild goats, joint fir and milk vetch; (2) the rocky hillsides with jujube trees, wild caper, and foxes; (3) salt rivers and saline plains with wild boar, deer, and cat, seablite and seaworts, as well as licorice, poplar, and tamarisk trees, and various chenopod plants; (4) shallow marshes with riverine foods, ducks, geese, cranes, and reeds and sea club-rushes; (5) open plains with sandy soils with such animals as onagers, gazelles, aurochs, red foxes, and gerbils as well as plants like spiny milk vetch, wild alfalfa, grasses, *prosopis,* and jujube trees; (6) rocky hillsides with more trees, grasses, birds, foxes, and jackals; and, finally, (7) the first mountain, area 8, with oak, pistachios, almonds, goats, deer, and partridges. However, in spite of the variety of life zones with different kinds of food, all can be exploited from a single base, often in ecozone 6, the open plains. Thus in terms of man's exploitation of the environment, this subarea is like the previous three.

Archaeological Horizons   Unfortunately most of the archaeological remains pertain to horizons 8 and 9, after the basic origins of agriculture in the Near East. Perhaps the most significant remains come from the Mureybit site in the upper reaches on the Euphrates, where in its lower layers, at horizon 8 have been found round houses and a hunting and gathering subsistence pattern. The upper layer yielded a square-housed village with barley, vetch, and einkorn wheat as part of their subsistence.[62] Also at this horizon are the Bus Mordeh village remains from the Ali Kosh site at the lower Tigris, which yielded domesticated einkorn, emmer, naked two-rowed barley, sheep, and goats.[63] Wild goats, vetch, and einkorn may have been found nearby in its steppes.

Subarea 5: Low Wooded Mountain Valleys   The lush central basins of central Turkey belong to this subarea, but little archaeological or ecological data are available. Of horizon 9, aceramic Hacilar materials in Turkey have yielded substantial remains of a large village using wild einkorn, domesticated emmer, naked six-rowed barley, peas, lentils, and vetches. Of more recent times is the Catal Hüyük site, a large ceremonial center with evidence of domesticated cattle, emmer, bread wheat, six-rowed barley, peas, and vetch but both occur long after agriculture began in the Near East. In fact, all the lowland sequences of the Near East, with their Natufian-like affinities, seem to see sedentary groups receiving agriculture developed somewhere else, not inventing it. This is much like the picture we saw in both lowland Meso-America as well as in the Andean area. Now let us consider some of the areas where plant cultivation, domestication, and agriculture began, which, like the Andes and Meso-America, are in the harsher highland subarea with more ecological diversity.

Subarea 6: Medium High Mountain Valleys
Environmental Characteristics   This large zone, with much of the mountainous zones between 1,000 and 2,500 meters is covered with deciduous and mixed forest in Iran, Iraq, Turkey, and Greece. Unfortunately only two areas, Shanidar Cave and Lake Zeribar in Iraq and Cayönü in southwest Turkey, have yielded relevant data. Preliminary ecological studies of the Shanidar Cave region suggest that this subarea, like similar ones in Meso-America and the Andes, had at least a series of layered ecozones: a riverine gallery forest ecozone; then a grassland steppe on the terraces in the valley bottoms, which gave way to a grassland-mixed forest zone on the flanks of the valleys, followed by a deciduous mixed forest on the mountain slopes with the tops of the mountains having mixed or coniferous forests.

Pollen studies show that these forest zones invaded the region about 15,000 years ago, but a closer scrutiny of them reveals some pertinent information concerning the beginning of agriculture.[64] These pollen cores show that not only did the forest become permanent after 12,800 B.C. but that between 12,500 B.C. and 11,000 B.C. (horizon 5) the weedy plant plantago pollen became prominent. Since plantago grows mainly in areas cleared for cultivation, I believe that this may be interpreted as indicating cultivation began at this time in subarea 6. Further, in part of the pollen profile of horizon 6, 10,750 B.C. to 9500 B.C., not only did the propagation of this weedy plant increase, but pollen of grasses and cerealia increased also. This I interpret as meaning that the inhabitants were planting grasses or cerealia—perhaps wheat, barley, einkorn or the like. Further, in these pollen profiles, as well as those from Zawi Chemi, the size of the cerealia pollen increased, indicating selection by man and the planting of domesticates, not cultivars.[65] Thus I believe that full-time agriculture was occurring by horizon 7, 9500 B.C. to 8500 B.C., in subarea 6.

Archaeological Horizons The archaeology of these crucial periods tends to confirm these opinions, although no data are available from the very important horizon 5. The earliest confirmation comes from Shanidar layer B2 of horizon 6, where there were many storage pits, mortars, and querns like those later used with domesticates.[66] Further, both Shanidar layer B1 and the nearby Zawi Chemi pithouse [67] see not only an increase in these features, but the larger pollen of increasing amounts of cereals. Thus I think agriculture was being practiced in horizon 7 (9500 B.C. to 8500 B.C.) in the highland areas of the Near East. As in Peru and Mexico, it occurred before, not after, village life. Village life in subarea 6 may be represented at the M'Lefaat site, but the evidence, as well as the dating, is not very secure. Horizon 9, however, represented by the Cayönü site of southwest Turkey, does give evidence of hamlets, as well as evidence of agriculture because grapes, emmer, einkorn, wheat, and rye were found along with bones of pigs, sheep, goats, and cattle.[68] The evidence is far from perfect, but it is convincing to me, and I believe more will be forthcoming.

Subarea 7: High Mountain Valleys The *high mountain valleys,* subarea 7, occurred along the flanks of the mountains north of the Tigris and Euphrates in the oak-pistachio forest zone. Braidwood's work has provided a somewhat longer sequence, with the Palegawra Cave remains of seasonal wild ass hunters and plant collectors and those of domesticated dogs from horizon 5 (12,500–

10,750 B.C.).[69] These seem to be followed by Zarzi and Karim Shahir type of remains. There are also stone house structures and evidence of some hunting and plant collecting and possibly plant domestication. From horizon 7 (9500–8500 B.C.) [70] are remains from the village site at Ganj-i-Dareh in the Zagros Mountains of Iran, where there is evidence of possible domestication of sheep in the earlier base camp levels and maybe agriculture in the overlying village remains of horizon 8.[71]

The Asiab site may be an extension of the latter in horizon 8 (8500–7250 B.C.). True villages occur in Jarmo horizon 9, with einkorn, emmer, peas, lentils, and goats being grown.[72]

This hilly flank zone is the homeland of many domesticates, including emmer, einkorn, wheat, barley, and oats, as well as sheep and goats. Pollen studies hint that a major change occurred at about 13,000 B.C. when the present woodlands invaded a grassland. At this time there was probably a sudden drop in numbers of onagers (wild ass) after Palegawa times. Thus, there was probably a change in biomass (herd animals) like that in Ajuereado times in Meso-America or like Puente-Jaywa in Peru.

Subarea 8: Mountain Peaks and Valleys   The final subarea of the Near East, the home of the coniferous forest, has had little or no archaeological investigations.

GENERALIZATIONS

General Statements

Now that we have considered the comparable data from the three relevant areas described as to the crucial horizons that might have been involved with the development of village agriculture, let us move on to the highest stage of our study: making generalizations about why this happened—laws of human behavior, if you will. These possible scientific formulations can be of two sorts: general or universal ones and rather specific or multilinear ones whereby specific hypotheses are tested and/or modified by the comparative data. Let us start with the more general ones, which can be divided into two parts: those that deal with space and those that deal with time.

Spatial Aspects When one compares the various areas and their subareas with each other in relationship to the problem of the origin of village agriculture, a number of features—necessary conditions for this to occur—become apparent:

1. All have major environmental subareas or areas involved with the problem of the origin of agriculture that have easy communication with each other, thus allowing the subareas or areas to form an interaction sphere.
2. The areas, subareas, or spheres they have in common fall into two general dichotomies: highland ones with fewer wild foods readily available and a tendency for the microenvironment to be stratified (the mountain peaks and highest valleys, the high mountain valleys, and the medium high mountain valleys and sometimes the low wooded mountain valleys) which gradually merge into lowland ones that in terms of food resources are lusher or richer and whose microenvironments are arranged so that one must exploit them in a radial manner (the dry subtropical lowlands, tropical humid lowlands, subtropical wooded lowlands, dry lowland river basins, and sometimes the low wooded mountain valleys).
3. There are considerable seasonal differences among subareas, which means that certain foods must be obtained in different microenvironments in different seasons.
4. All are in warm temperate to tropical climatic or temperature zones.
5. There has been only one major environmental change: at the end of the Pleistocene, grassland shrunk, and some animals became extinct or reduced in number so the overall biomass was reduced.
6. They have about the same number of plants and animals that potentially may be domesticated (this list, even if not complete, seems worthwhile because some scientists have assumed that the kinds and number of plants domesticated in each of our major areas are radically different):

Meso-American Sphere [73]

Maize	Amaranth
Common beans	Chile pepper
Runner beans	Avocado
Tepary beans	Black zapote

Sieva beans	White zapote
Gourds	Agave
Pumpkins	Opuntia
Squash (cucurbita mixta)	Turkey
Squash (cucurbita moschata)	

Andean Sphere [74]

Corn	Peanuts
Common beans	Avocado
Lima beans	Lucuma
Gourds	Guava
Squash (cucurbita maxima)	Sweet potato
Squash (cucurbita andina)	White potato
Squash (cucurbita ficifolia)	Guinea pig
Quinoa	Llama
Chile peppers	Alpaca

Near East Sphere [75]

Einkorn	Broom corn
Emmer	Rye
Bread wheat	Peas
Club wheat	Lentils
Spelt wheat	Vetch
Naked two-rowed barley	Goat
Hulled two-rowed barley	Sheep
Naked six-rowed barley	Pig
Hulled six-rowed barley	Cattle

These six major characteristics are rarely duplicated in other portions of the world.

Temporal Aspects   Although the six characteristics may be prerequisite or necessary conditions for pristine village agriculture to develop, they are not the triggering cause or sufficient conditions. The real triggering causes are other cultural phenomena (although some environmental ones may have occurred). Therefore, to understand why agriculture began, we must have the cultural data. This means twenty-four sequences of horizons for each of the eight subareas for these pristine agriculture interaction spheres. Obviously we are a long way from having such data. In fact, we are a long way from having enough solid data to understand why domestication and agriculture initially began in any of them. Horizons 3 and 4 are very poorly known for the Near East, only barely understood for Tehuacan, and for the Andes only three highland and one lowland area have some small amount of data that pertain. For horizon 5 the same amount of inadequate data are available for the Andes.

In Mexico, however, subareas 4 and 5 have yielded fairly good information pertaining to the ancient subsistences. For horizon 6, when domesticated plants spread over large parts of each sphere, there are some data from four or five Andean areas, limited materials from six regions of Mexico, and even more limited and debatable data from two areas of the Near East. Knowledge of the last three horizons does improve. There is information about the culture of six regions of Meso-America, five regions of the Andes, and limited data from two highland and two lowland areas of the Near East for horizon 7. In fact, it is only with horizons 8 and 9 that the interaction spheres approach having enough data to reach any conclusions, and at that time most of the major developments had taken place. Unfortunately in Meso-America much more data are needed for horizon 8.

Cultures representing the shift from horizon 3 to 4 or 4 to 5 occur in few regions of any of three interaction spheres. In fact the best example of the horizon 3 to 4 shift is from Tehuacan (the development from the early to late subphases of Ajuereado), and this is far from adequate. The second shift from horizon 4 (late Ajuereado) to horizon 5 (El Riego) is better documented and crucial to our first hypothesis about cultural changes. In a vague way it seems similar to the changes in middle (Jaywa to Piki phases) high (Guitarrero to Quishqui Punca complexes) and the very high regions (Junín to Pachamachay phases) in the Andes, but these data are too inadequate to allow for valid comparisons and there is absolutely nothing comparable from horizons 3 and 4 from the Near East. The Palegawa and Zarzi materials from the medium highland zones are most inadequate. Thus, at present, there is no way to test our hypothesis adequately without having more data derived from intensive investigation on these time periods in many areas of the three spheres. The Tehuacan process of change does seem different from that at the lowland region of Peru from Chivaterros to Pampilla, but even here the sequential archaeological data are poor.

We must modify our Tehuacan-derived hypotheses by some

sort of additional necessary condition statement to the effect that
the process we described is confined to special highland zones with
stratified microenvirons and limited resources. It might also be
added that further archaeological studies of various hunting complexes and even social anthropological synchronic studies are
needed to define both our Ajuereado culture type as well as that of
El Riego.

Although our data are woefully inadequate for many horizons
and for many subareas, there are similar developments in each of
the relevant major culture areas, although they are of a dichotomous nature. In Meso-America there was a highland development
from specialized nomadic microband hunters (late Ajuereado,
horizon 4) to seasonal micro-macroband collectors (El Riego, horizon 5) to seasonal macroband collectors with horticulture (Coxcatlan, horizon 6) to central-based bands with agriculture (Abejas,
horizon 7) to hamlets with agriculture (Purron, horizon 8) to
villages with agriculture (Ajalpan, horizon 9). This might be
called the Tehuacan tradition of development, which closely
paralleled the Ayacucho development that occurred in highland
Peru, which saw a similar development from Puente-Jaywa at
horizon 4 to Piki of horizon 5 to Chihua of horizon 6 to Cachi of
horizon 7 to Andamarka of horizon 8, ending up with village agriculture represented by Wichqana in horizon 9. Although the data
are far from complete, particularly as to the beginning of horizon
4, which is absent, the development in the highlands of the Near
East—one that might be called Zarzian—seemed to be going
through the same sort of development. Palegawra might represent
seasonal macroband collectors of horizon 5, who developed into
Zarzi horticultural seasonal macro-microbands with horizon 6,
who became central-based agricultural bands of horizon 7 as Zawi
Chemi people, who became hamlet agriculturalists of horizon 8,
perhaps represented by the remains of Asiab, with the Jarmo material of horizon 9 as well as others representing the ultimate development of village agriculture.

These three highland developments and traditions—Tehuacan, Ayacucho, and Zarzi—would have been interconnected
with, but having different development from, the lowland subareas. Here we would see specialized nomadic hunters of horizon
4 (Lerma in Mexico, Conchitas of Peru, and early Kebaran of the
Levant) develop into highly specialized collectors living in base

camps or hamlets, perhaps as composite bands, in horizon 5 (early Palma Sola in Veracruz of Mexico, Arenal in Canario of coastal Peru, and late Kebaran A of the Levant), who in turn became in horizon 6 collectors or incipient cultivators living in hamlets (Palo Hueco of Meso-America, Encanto of coastal Peru, and early Natufian of the Levant); these developed in horizon 7 into hamlets with little or no incipient agriculture (La Perra or Repelo of Mexico, Gaviota of coastal Peru, and late Natufian of the Levant), who in horizon 8 became villagers with incipient agriculture (Almagre of Tamaulipas, La Florida of Peru, and Jericho PPNA of the Levant) ending up in horizon 9 as village agriculturalists represented by the Olmec of Mexico, Curayaca of coastal Peru, and Jericho of the Levant. Those three developments might be called Palo Hueco for Meso-America, Chilca for the Andean area, and Natufian for the Near East.

Thus our comparisons have showed that two parallel (one highland and the other lowland) developments of village agriculture occurred in each of the major areas. What is more, during any single time horizon, the dichotomous developments interacted with each other. Thus we have a vague outline of how village agriculture developed generally.

Specific Statements: Testing the Tehuacan Hypothesis

From Horizon 4 to Horizon 5 Cultural Systems   Now let us restate our Tehuacan hypothesis in light of our comparative data giving rather definite data about why various developments leading to village agriculture in pristine centers took place.

If a cultural type like that at Ajuereado (microband) has the following necessary conditions:

1. an existence in an area of considerable ecological diversity that yields food in different microenvironments at different seasons of the year, and this
2. environment has layered microenvironments with relatively limited food resources, but
3. with a number of plants or animals that could be cultivated or domesticated, and has
4. a gradually increasing population,

then if the following sufficient conditions occur:

1.   an ecosystem change that reduces the faunal subsystem (bio-
      mass) to such an extent that extensive hunting or animal col-
      lecting or a single subsistence option is no longer tenable in
      terms of energy output and input, and this coincides with
2.   the development of a series of seasonally adaptive options, in-
      cluding the necessary ecosystem knowledge,

then a cultural type like the El Riego micro-macrobands with a
seasonally scheduled subsistence system type will evolve.

The rather different Peruvian coastal data at this time period
suggest that other hypotheses can be set up about other kinds of
developments to another type featuring intensive collecting by
macrobands at base camps in another kind of environment. Perhaps the difference in the evolutions is that there are two different
kinds of necessary conditions: domesticated plants (the opposite of
number 3 for the highland zone) and a lowland environment that
is best used by radially exploiting a lusher sort of catchment basin
region. Thus, there may be a whole series of other testable hypotheses growing out of our using comparative data, but as of
now, the comparable data are so inadequate that there is little
point in more speculation.

From Horizon 5 to Horizon 6 Cultural Systems   Let us consider our second Tehuacan hypothesis for the change from horizon 5 to 6 (El Riego to Coxcatlan). Although the data are not so
full, the same sort of process seems to have been happening in
two of the three other Meso-American highland areas: the low
highland of the Mesa del Sur at Oaxaca with its sequence from
Naquitz to Coxcatlan and the very high highlands with the Infiernillo to Ocampo development in Tamaulipas. Further, there
are hints that what was happening in the Meso-American highlands was different from the process at lower elevations. Different
developments in the highlands and lowlands is further brought
out by our Andean data; the coastal development from Canario to
Encanto bore little similarity to those highland subareas such as
Ayacucho with its development from Piki to Chihua, or subarea 7,
Callejon de Huaylas development with Quishqui to Punta Callan

development, or that in Junín (subarea 8), with Pachamachay overlying into San Blas. Unfortunately, plant remains are too few in the Andes to reconstruct the changing subsistence systems adequately. Also, seemingly similar to the Andean and Meso-American evolution was the development in the highlands of the Near East but it is represented by a single sequence, the controversial one from Zarzi to Shanidar, layer B1 in the high valley of Iraq. The original Tehuacan hypothesis about the changes in light of these comparative data must be modified:

If the newly developed El Riego type, a cultural system with a micro-macroband settlement pattern and a seasonally scheduled subsistence, occurs in an ecosystem with the following necessary conditions:

1. plants and animals that can be domesticated or cultivated, and
2. great ecological highland harsh diversity including marked seasonality, and
3. the area has easy communications and interaction with other areas of great ecological diversity or lush ecological uniformity, and

if the following sufficient conditions occur:

1. the population of that system increases to a point where the equilibrium in terms of energy flow between the ecosystem and subsistence is upset, occurring at about the same time that
2. horticulture gradually comes into being (and perhaps tamed animals) as a result of a scheduled subsistence system,

then this system will evolve into one that has a macro-microband settlement pattern subsystem with a seasonally scheduled subsistence system with horticulture (or tamed animals): the Coxcatlan, Chihua, or Shanidar type of system.

This hypothesis, however, does not account for all of the changes that were happening from horizon 5 to horizon 6 in lowland zones, and our Peruvian coast data suggest a corollary:

Perhaps if a cultural type (like Canario and/or Kebaran) with intensive food collectors living in lowland base camps has the following necessary conditions:

1.   an environment with great ecological diversity that may be exploited by radially working out from a center or base camp and if
2.   all microenvironments have food resources that can easily be collected from a single base, and if
3.   the area has easy communication and interaction with other lush or harsh areas of great ecological diversity with or without domesticated plants, and

if the following sufficient conditions occur:

1.   increasing population because of great sedentarism and a stable, collected food supply

then a cultural system (like Encanto of Peru or Natufian of the Near East or Palma Sola of Veracruz, Mexico) with sedentary hamlets based on collecting wild food stuffs with little use of domesticates may develop.

Here is a new hypothesis to test. It may be that other sequences not in a pristine agricultural interaction sphere may be used to test it, such as the desert culture of Arizona. In fact, it may lead to a host of other hypotheses about the changes among bands.

From Horizon 6 to Horizon 7   Now let us turn to the hypotheses about why the Coxcatlan type evolved into the Abejas type: the shift from horizon 6 to 7 in the harsh high valleys of the mountain areas of meso-America. The only other Meso-American highland sequence comes from the highest valleys of the high mountains in Tamaulipas with the shift from Ocampo to Flacco while in the Andes the Ayacucho Valley's shift from Chihua to Cachi, the medium high valley development from Quishqui Puncu to Punta Callan, and the very high Junín development from Callavalluari to Telarmachay may be vaguely comparable, as would be the shift from the Shanidar B2 complex to the Zawi Chemi and Shanidar B1 complex in the high mountain area of Iraq in the Near East. In fact, all these data indicate that our Tehuacan hypotheses are at least probable after they have been modified as follows:

If a cultural type like Coxcatlan, Chihua, Quishqui Puncu, Callavalluari, and Shanidar B2 has the following necessary conditions:

1.   horticulture and cultivated or tamed plants and animals,
2.   increasing population,
3.   accessibility to other highland zones where horticulture has developed, and is
4.   in areas with great ecosystem diversity that is usually layered,

then the following sufficient conditions:

1.   interstimulating interaction involving the exchange of various aspects of cultures and/or domesticates, plus
2.   a shift from storage of wild plants to growing plants for storage

will lead to a culture type like Abejas, Cachi, Telarmachay, and Shanidar B1, which have a central-based band type of settlement or hamlet bases with a seasonally scheduled subsistence system, which includes both horticulture and agriculture.

Obviously the developments on the coast as well as on the lower elevation areas are very different and must be explained with other hypotheses.

Other Conditions Changing Later Horizons

And now we come to my final set of hypotheses about cultural change based upon Tehuacan data. In light of the new comparative data it is obvious there should be two sets of hypotheses, not one. Other Meso-American sequences like that of Tehuacan in horizons 7, 8, and 9 do not exist, while the Ayacucho and Junín data are only vaguely comparable as is the Karim Shahir to Jarmo and Shanidar to Cayönü sequences of the Near East. Part of this lack of similarity is, of course, the fact that these final developments in Peru and Iraq include herding as a major aspect of their subsistence. In fact, there is little to confirm the final Tehuacan hypothesis from this final set of comparisons and a suggestion that when more data become available (even from Tehuacan) that this hypothesis should be restated. Other hypotheses will also be needed to explain why other developments happened in other highland and lowland areas in this general time period.

CONCLUSION

Thus we close this volume on a discouraging note in terms of deriving generalizations and furthering archaeology as a science. But, at least, we have started by attempting to test hypotheses by the comparative method and we have been able to discern some of the problems involved in this attempt. Obviously, determining how comparable the areas, subareas, or regions are represents a problem that cries for more sophisticated environmental and ecological investigations. An even more important problem is that of defining the cultural types that evolved. Perhaps a solution to this latter problem lies in the field of systemics—that is, making our compared archaeological phases, entities, or events into various kinds of cultural systems and then classifying similar systems into cultural types. We tried this in the last few pages but it is only a very preliminary effort. In order to solve still another problem, some sort of conceptual framework for classifying the processes and conditions that bring about the change of one system into another is needed. Classifying the conditions as to whether they are necessary or sufficient is just not enough, because there may be various classes of necessary and/or sufficient conditions. These sorts of problems, concerning our highest level of making generalizations or scientific laws, need solutions and certainly are worthy of discussion, study, and considerable thought.

However, just as crucial to making archaeology a science—that is, arriving at generalizations based upon tested hypotheses—is the problem of deriving hypotheses to test. In terms of our strategy, deriving hypotheses of systematic change, was the next to last step and went under the general title of analysis. Only occasionally do archaeologists attempt to establish hypotheses about why cultures change, and about the cause of change or the conditions that bring about one event changing into another. Not only is this a rare practice, but also the methods, when stated, seem as numerous and varied as the archaeologists who attempt them. Isn't it about time we give some thought to how this can best be done?

That is, can't we establish some methods for deriving hypotheses about cultural change from archaeological data?

While this is where the field as a whole seems to be going, for now we are beginning to synthesize our ever increasing archaeological data into series of cultural-historical integrations. We have very complete descriptions of the sequence for a 10,000-year period for areas such as the U.S. Southwest. Other areas and regions are approaching this ideal as well. Further, general books are being written that describe the cultural sequence for wide areas of the New World—in fact, we even have one or two describing this for both North and South America. But, are we doing it right? As I pointed out earlier, I have considerable doubts that we are since many of our cultural-historical integrations do not seem amenable to the kind of analysis needed for deriving hypotheses about cultural change or for testing these hypotheses to make generalizations.

I am now investigating the possibility of setting up culture phases as energy flow systems with the various activities of the cultural phases linked to each other by energy input and output (calculated in terms of calories—heat—expended or consumed in each activity) in order to devise a structure or model that might be a direct reflection of a particular cultural phase or system. This investigation is based on the assumption that during the life span of any system, changes in the energy input and output, which bring about positive feedback between two or more of the activities that in turn bring about a change in the whole system, might be considered causes or conditions of the systemic change. A sequence of such an energy flow system might be a cultural-historical integration amenable to analysis to derive hypotheses about cultural change. Here might be a method for deriving hypotheses about why a system changes into another. However, my research in this realm is in its infancy and far too preliminary to describe here. Nevertheless, the more I reflect on chapter 3, which discusses theory and this third stage of deriving testable hypotheses and generalizations, the more I am convinced that the title of K. C. Chang's book, *Rethinking Archaeology,* is just what we should be doing.[76]

So far I have noted where most of our field of archaeology is going, not where it is at. In my opinion, for the last ten to fifteen years most of us, directly or indirectly, have been involved in describing or reconstructing cultural contexts. In fact many of the New Archaeologists, following Lew Binford's lead, spend most of their efforts doing just this, although they pay lip service to going to higher levels and making generalizations.[77] Reconstruction of cultural contexts, first emphasized by Walt Taylor some thirty years ago,[78] has now come into its own and the techniques are much improved. Archaeologists are defining activity areas by computerized statistical techniques, making microscopic studies of edge wear on artifacts, and collecting ethnographic data that may be analogous to archaeological data, and even ethnologists, such as John Yellen, are presenting their data so that archaeologists can use it in their contextual interpretations.[79] In chapters 4 and 5 I have recounted our endeavors in this line in Tehuacan. Reconstructing past events with deductive tricks that even Sherlock Holmes would admire is exciting and if you accept Jim Deetz's *Invitation to Archaeology* you too are likely to become involved in this kind of study.[80]

Of course, you could well be involved in defining sequences or describing chronologies, the other aspect of the descriptive second stage of our studies. American archaeologists have been doing this relatively well for the last forty or fifty years and with more and more dating techniques they get better and better at it. I have outlined our work in this realm for Tehuacan and Ayacucho, but lest someone get the idea that there are no new chronologies to build or sequences to discover, let me point out that in my studies on the origin of agriculture more than half of the pertinent subareas did not have adequate cultural chronologies. There is still lots to do in defining cultural chronologies and you can learn to do it with ever improving techniques.

This is equally true of the most basic stage of our incipient science—data collection. I hope my data concerning the origin of agriculture has enhanced your general knowledge. We now have examples of how good interdisciplinary studies have been done and we can learn how to do them. The same might be said of learning excavation techniques. There is no excuse for not doing skilled and scientific digging. In fact, it is criminal if one does not dig well because archaeological remains are a nonrenewable resource—once you destroy the information by bad digging it cannot be replaced or duplicated. Besides, digging like surveying is healthy and enjoyable to most people, so do it well.

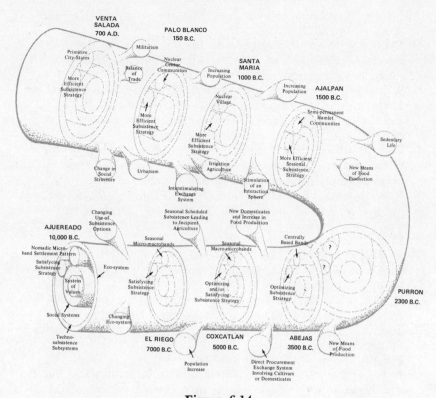

Figure 6.14

A systemic model of cultural change in prehistoric Tehuacan.

Yes, in a relatively brief span of time American archaeology has come a long way and I have tried to record some of its progress and note where I am, if not the field as a whole. Although my critics may disagree with much that I have written, few, if any, would not agree that our field is moving ahead rapidly and that it is a fascinating one. Thus I close hoping that I have piqued your interest in archaeology and hoping that I have stimulated you to join us—the best is yet to come!

REFERENCES

1. ROBERT C. WEST, "The Natural Regions of Middle America," in R. C. West, ed., *Handbook of Middle American Indians,* vol. 1:

Natural Environment and Early Cultures (Austin: University of Texas Press, 1964).

2. R. S. MacNeish, *Preliminary Archaeological Investigations in the Sierra de Tamaulipas, Mexico* (Philadelphia: American Philosophical Society, 1958).

3. S. Jeffrey Wilkerson, "An Archaeological Sequence from Santa Luisa," unpublished manuscript (Veracruz, Mexico, 1972).

4. Barbara Voorhies, "The Paleoecology of the Preceramic of Coastal Chiapas" (Ph.D. diss., Yale University, 1974).

5. R. S. MacNeish and F. Peterson, *The Santa Marta Rock Shelter, Ocozocoautla, Chiapas, Mexico,* Papers of the New World Archaeological Foundation, no. 14 (Provo, Utah).

6. Ruth Gruhn and A. L. Bryan, "Los Tapielos: A Paleoindian Campsite in the Guatemalan Highlands," *Proceedings of the American Philosophical Society,* vol. 121, no. 3 (Philadelphia, 1977).

7. K. Flannery et al., "Preliminary Archaeological Investigations in the Valley of Oaxaca, Mexico, 1966–1969," unpublished manuscript.

8. R. S. MacNeish, *An Early Archaeological Site Near Panuco, Veracruz* (Philadelphia: American Philosophical Society, 1954).

9. Joseph A. Tosi, *Zonas de Vida Natural en El Peru,* Instituto Interamericano de Ciencias Agricolas de la OEA Zona Andina, Boletin Tecnico, no. 5 (Lima, 1960).

10. R. S. MacNeish, T. C. Patterson, and D. L. Browman, *The Central Peruvian Prehistoric Interaction Sphere,* Papers of the R. S. Peabody Foundation for Archaeology, vol. 7 (Andover, Mass., 1975).

11. Karl W. Butzer, *Environment and Archaeology: An Ecological Approach to Prehistory* (Chicago: Aldine-Atherton, 1971).

12. F. Hole, K. V. Flannery, and James A. Neely, *Prehistory and Human Ecology of the Deh Luran Plain: An Early Village Sequence from Khuzistan, Iran* (Ann Arbor: University of Michigan Press, 1969).

13. MacNeish, *Preliminary Archaeological Investigations.*

14. Jeremiah F. Epstein, *The San Isidro Site: An Early Man Campsite in Nuevo Leon, Mexico,* University of Texas at Austin Anthropology Series, no. 7 (Austin: University of Texas Press, 1969).

15. Wilkerson, "An Archaeological Sequence."

16. M. D. Coe and K. V. Flannery, *Early Cultures and Human Ecology in South Coastal Guatemala* (Washington, D.C.: Smithsonian Press, 1967).

17. Voorhies, "Paleoecology."

18. C. F. Brush, "Pox Pottery: Earliest Identified Mexican Ceramic," *Science* 149: 194–195.

19. MacNeish and Peterson, *The Santa Marta Rock Shelter.*

20. K. Flannery, A. Kirkby, M. Kirkby, and A. Williams, "Farming

Systems and Political Growth in Ancient Oaxaca," *Science* 158 (1967).

21. FLANNERY et al., "Preliminary Archaeological Investigations."

22. JANE WHEELER PIRES-FERREIRA, EDGARDO PIRES-FERREIRA, and PETER KAULICKE, "Preceramic Animal Utilization in the Central Peruvian Andes," *Science* 194 (1976).

23. R. S. MACNEISH, "Ancient Mesoamerican Civilization," *Science* 143, no. 3606 (1964).

24. CYNTHIA IRWIN-WILLIAMS, "Associations of Early Man with Horse, Camel, and Mastodon at Hueyatlaco, Valsequillo (Puebla, Mexico)," in P. S. Martin and H. E. Wright, Jr., eds., *Pleistocene Extinctions: The Search for a Cause* (New Haven: Yale University Press, 1967).

25. LORENA MIRAMBELL, *Excavaciones en sitios Pleistocenicos y Postpleistocenicos en Tlapacoya, Estado de Mexico*, Boletin INAH 4 (Mexico, 1973).

26. LUIS AVELEYRA, *El Segundo Mamut Fosil de Santa Isabel Iztapan, Mexico y Artefactos Asociados Direccion de Prehistoria*, INAH 1 (Mexico, 1955).

27. CHRISTINE NEIDERBERGER, *Zohapilco* (Mexico: Instituto Nacional de Antropologia e Historia, 1976).

28. R. S. MACNEISH, A. NELKEN-TERNER, and A. GARCIA COOK, *Second Annual Report of the Ayacucho Archaeological-Botanical Project* (Andover, Ma.: R. S. Peabody Foundation, 1970).

29. P. C. MANGELSDORF, R. S. MACNEISH, and W. C. GALINAT, "Prehistoric Maize, Teosinte, and Tripsacum from Tamaulipas, Mexico," *Botanical Museum Leaflets, Harvard University* 22, no. 2 (1967); T. W. Whitaker, H. C. Cutler, and R. S. MacNeish, "Cucurbit Materials from Three Caves near Ocampo, Tamaulipas," *American Antiquity* 22, no. 4 (1957); L. Kaplan and R. S. MacNeish, "Prehistoric Bean Remains from Caves in the Ocampo Region of Tamaulipas, Mexico," *Botanical Museum Leaflets, Harvard University* 19, no. 2 (1960).

30. D. W. LATHRAP, *Upper Amazon* (London: Thames and Hudson, 1970).

31. THOMAS PATTERSON, "Central Peru: Its Population and Economy," *Archaeology* 24, no. 4 (1971).

32. MACNEISH, PATTERSON, and BROWMAN, *The Central Peruvian Prehistoric Interaction Sphere*.

33. F. ENGEL, "Exploration of the Chilca Canyon," *Peru* 11, no. 1 (1970).

34. T. C. PATTERSON, "Central Peru."

35. F. ENGEL, "Exploration of the Chilca Canyon," *Peru* 11, no. 1 (1970).

36. PATTERSON, "Central Peru."

37. MACNEISH, PATTERSON, and BROWMAN, *The Central Peruvian Prehistoric Interaction Sphere*.

38. F. ENGEL, "Exploration of the Chilca Canyon," *Peru* 11, no. 1 (1970).
39. PATTERSON, "Central Peru."
40. D. W. LATHRAP, *Upper Amazon* (London: Thames and Hudson, 1970).
41. Ibid.
42. SEIICHI IZUMI and TOSHIHIKO SONO, *Excavations at Kotosh, Peru, 1960* (Tokyo: Kadokawa Publishing Co., 1963).
43. MACNEISH, NELKEN-TERNER, and COOK, *Second Annual Report.*
44. PIRES-FERREIRA, PIRES-FERREIRA, and KAULICKE, "Preceramic Animal Utilization."
45. MACNEISH, PATTERSON, and BROWMAN, *Central Peruvian Prehistoric Interaction Sphere.*
46. Ibid.
47. MACNEISH, NELKEN-TERNER, and COOK, *Second Annual Report.*
48. MACNEISH, PATTERSON, and BROWMAN, *Central Peruvian Prehistoric Interaction Sphere.*
49. Ibid.
50. F. A. ENGEL, "La Gorge de Huarangal: Ebauche d'une Monographie de Geographie Humaine Prehistorique, *Inst. Fr. Et. And.* 2, no. 2 (1973).
51. T. F. LYNCH and K. A. R. KENNEDY, "Early Human Cultural and Skeletal Remains from Guitarrero Cave, Northern Peru," *Science* 169 (1970).
52. F. ENGEL, "La Grotte du Megatherium a Chilca et les Ecologies du Haut-Holocene Peruvien," in L. J. Pouillon and P. Maranda, eds., *Echange et Communication* (Paris: Mouton, 1972).
53. PIRES-FERREIRA, PIRES-FERREIRA, and KAULICKE, "Preceramic Animal Utilization."
54. MACNEISH, PATTERSON, and BROWMAN, *Central Peruvian Prehistoric Interaction Sphere.*
55. C. VITA-FINZI and E. S. HIGGS, "Prehistoric Economy in the Mount Carmel Area of Palestine: Site Catchment Analysis," *Proceedings of the Prehistoric Society for 1970* 36 (1970).
56. OFER BAR-YOSEF, *The Epipaleolithic in Palestine and Sinai* (Ph.D. diss., Hebrew University, 1970).
57. J. L. PHILLIPS, *Development of Agriculture in Israel* (in press).
58. C. S. COON, *Seven Caves* (London: Jonathan Cape, 1957).
59. THOMAS W. JACOBSEN, "17,000 Years of Greek Prehistory," *Scientific American* (June 1976).
60. JAMES MELLAART, *The Neolithic of the Near East* (New York: Charles Scribner's Sons, 1975).
61. HOLE, FLANNERY, and NEELY, *Prehistory and Human Ecology.*
62. WILLEN VAN ZEIST, "The Oriental Institute Excavations at Mureybit, Syria: Preliminary Report on the 1965 Campaign. Part III: The Paleobotany," *Journal of Near Eastern Studies* 29, no. 3 (1970).

63. HOLE, FLANNERY, and NEELY, *Prehistory and Human Ecology*.
64. H. E. WRIGHT, JR., "The Environmental Setting for Plant Domestication in the Near East," *Science* 194, no. 4263 (1976).
65. ARLETTE LEROI-GOURHAN, "Pollen Grains of Gramineae and Cerealia from Shanidar and Zawi Chemi," in P. J. Ucko and G. W. Dimbleby, eds., *The Domestication and Exploitation of Plants and Animals* (Chicago: Aldine Publishing Co., 1969).
66. RALPH S. SOLECKI, "Shanidar Cave: A Late Pleistocene Site in Northern Iraq," *Report of the VIth International Congress on Quaternary Warsaw*, vol. 4 (Lodz, 1964).
67. RALPH S. SOLECKI, "Zawi Chemi Shanidar: A Post-Pleistocene Village Site in Northern Iraq," in *Report of the VIth International Congress*.
68. R. BRAIDWOOD, "Prehistoric Investigations in Southwestern Asia," *Proceedings of the American Philosophical Society*, 116, no. 4 (August 1972).
69. P. F. TURNBULL and C. A. REED, "The Fauna from the Terminal Pleistocene of Palegawra Cave: A Zarzian Occupation Site in Northeastern Iraq," *Fieldiana Anthropology* 63, no. 3 (1973).
70. R. J. BRAIDWOOD and BRUCE HOWE, *Prehistoric Investigations in Iraqui Kurdistan*, The Oriental Institute of the University of Chicago, Studies in Ancient Oriental Civilization, no. 31 (Chicago: University of Chicago Press, 1960).
71. PHILIP E. L. SMITH, "Ganj Dareh Tepe," *Iran* 13 (1975).
72. BRAIDWOOD and HOWE, *Prehistoric Investigations*.
73. P. C. MANGELSDORF, R. S. MACNEISH, and G. R. WILLEY, "Origins of Agriculture in Middle America," in R. C. West, ed., *Handbook of Middle American Indians*, vol. 1: *Natural Environment and Early Cultures* (Austin: University of Texas Press, 1964).
74. MARGARET A. TOWLE, *The Ethnobotany of Pre-Columbian Peru* (Chicago: Aldine Publishing Co., 1961).
75. JANE RENFREW, *Paleoethnobotany: The Prehistoric Food Plants of the Near East and Europe* (New York: Columbia University Press, 1973).
76. K. C. CHANG, *Rethinking Archaeology* (New York: Random House, 1967).
77. LEWIS R. BINFORD, *New Perspective in Archaeology* (Chicago: Aldine Press, 1968).
78. WALTER W. TAYLOR, *A Study of Archaeology*, American Anthropological Association Memoirs, no. 69 (Washington, D.C., 1948).
79. JOHN E. YELLEN, *Archaeological Approaches to the Present* (New York: Academic Press, 1977).
80. JAMES DEETZ, *Invitation to Archaeology* (New York: Doubleday, 1967).

MY CAST
OF CHARACTERS

"Doc" J. ADAMS (1900–   ). Another rare great teacher at Colgate who made me cognizant of logic and the scientific method. (p. 46)

RALPH BEALS (1900–   Ph.D., California, 1930). The creator of the department of Anthropology at UCLA who taught me that archaeology was closely linked to anthropology. (p. 6)

ROBERT BELL (1918–   Ph.D., Univ. of Chicago, 1947). Archaeologist who got to finish up the dendrochronological studies at Kincaid. (p. 32)

JOHN BENNETT (1914–   Ph.D., University of Chicago, 1946). One of the enthusiastic young men of the thirties at the University of Chicago who disappeared into social anthropology.

LEWIS BINFORD (1930–   Ph.D., Michigan, 1964). The messiah of the New Archaeology who is always stimulating to talk with. (p. 52)

GLEN BLACK (1900–1964). He was the father of Indiana archaeology and his digs in the Angel Mounds, near the mouth of the Wabash, were models for those of us digging in the twin Kincaid Mounds. (p. 9)

GEORGE BRAINERD (1909–1956, Ph.D., University of California, Los Angeles, 1937). One of those unsung heroes of archaeology who did great work in the Near East, Yucatán, and on ceramics, and who first opened the door for me on the world of archaeological field techniques. (p. 6)

JOSEPH CALDWELL (1916–1973, Ph.D., University of Chicago, 1957). He was, for awhile, my roommate as well as digging companion in the last days at Kincaid. His monograph, "Trends and Traditions in the Prehistory of the United States," has left an indelible mark on studies of that area. (p. 9)

ERIC O. CALLEN (1912–1971, Ph.D., McGill, 1950). A botanist who, through working with us, developed a whole new set of techniques and methods for the study of human coprolites and ancient diets. We will sorely miss him. (p. 27)

241

JOE CHAMBERLAIN (1912–   ). Some of my first archaeology was done with Joe in central Illinois and he, too, disappeared from archaeology during World War II.

JOFFRE COE (1916–   Ph.D., Michigan, 1958). One of my night-stalking companions at the University of Michigan who is one of the most beautiful excavators I know.

FAY-COOPER COLE (1881–1961, Ph.D., Columbia, 1914). He was the founder of the University of Chicago's anthropology department with its great school for training archaeologists. A fine administrator, inspirational teacher, and truly a father to many of us. It is impossible to tell how much I owe to him. He was a great man. (p. 8)

ANGEL GARCIA COOK (1938–   Ph.D., University of Mexico, 1966). I "fathered" Angel's first archaeology in El Riego Cave, Tehuacan, where he took the techniques I taught him and improved on them. Now, like a father, I am proud of all he has accomplished for Mexican archaeology. (p. 12)

JOHN COTTER (1912–   Ph.D., Columbia, 1940). John is another archaeologist who got his start with WPA and went on to make U.S. Park Service Archaeology what it is today. (p. 9)

FRED EGGAN (1906–   Ph.D., Chicago, 1933). An ethnologist and social anthropologist at Chicago who had some sympathy for us archaeologists.

GORDON EKHOLM (1909–   Ph.D., Harvard, 1942). He was the archaeologist of the American Museum of Natural History who really introduced me to Meso-American archaeology and encouraged me to dig at his Panuco site. (p. 10)

NORMAN EMERSON (1918–   Ph.D., University of Chicago, 1954). My drinking and digging buddy at Kincaid who not only taught me archaeological techniques but also taught these skills to a number of generations of young Canadians at the University of Toronto and inspired even more to be cognizant of archaeology. (p. 8)

GLEN EVANS (1911–   ). A geologist and paleontologist, who on that brief but uncomfortable trip into the Canyon Diablo, taught me much about the kind of evidence necessary to prove early man was, in fact, early.

KENT FLANNERY (1936–   Ph.D., University of Chicago, 1964). Another young archaeologist who in his student days worked with me in Tehuacan and who also has gone on to greater accomplishments in the New (Ecological) Archaeology. We learned much from each other in our many discussions. (p. 12)

JAMES FORD (1911–1968, Ph.D., Columbia, 1949). In my estimation one of the great archaeologists of the twentieth century who never got the recognition he deserved. While a superb archaeologist, fine archaeological surveyor, who always faithfully wrote up what he dug up, he also could brilliantly discuss theory (preferably with friends over a bottle of bourbon). There were giants in those days and he was one of them. (p. 9)

MELVIN (MIKE) FOWLER (1928–   Ph.D., University of Chicago, 1959). My partner in the excavation of the famous Coxcatlan Cave of Mexico where we both learned much and thoroughly enjoyed ourselves doing so. (p. 12)

WALTON GALINAT (1923–   Ph.D., University of Wisconsin, 1953). The former assistant of Paul Mangelsdorf in the corn studies who, of late, has joined the opposition—those who believe corn came from teosinte. (p. 22)

LOUIS GIDDINGS (1909–1964, Ph.D., University of Pennsylvania, 1951). One of the great archaeological explorers of Alaska whose promising career was cut short by a tragic automobile accident.

PETER GRANT (1880–1955). An enthusiastic amateur archaeologist from Manitoba who not only was a delightful bush companion in Canada but, also, in Tamaulipas. (p. 83)

JAMES BENNETT GRIFFIN (1905–   Ph.D., University of Michigan, 1936). The benevolent despot of archaeology of the Eastern United States. Jimmy and Ruby not only shaped my career, but I love them both dearly. (p. 31)

WILLIAM HAAG (1910–   Ph.D., Michigan, 1948). Another crackerjack archaeologist of WPA and TVA who made Colonel Webb's Kentucky salvage program work. He is still doing good archaeology in the southeast. (p. 9)

FLORENCE HAWLEY (1906–   Ph.D., Chicago, 1936). Veteran ethnologist and archaeologist who tried to teach me about dendrochronology in the Midwest. (p. 32)

JUNE HELM (1924–   Ph.D., University of Chicago, 1958). My friend and ex-wife, a fine Northwest ethnologist, sociologist, and anthropologist, who also shaped my career and, as the Griffins, I love dearly. (p. 16)

MORTIMER HOWE (1916–1945). An aspirant archaeologist who took me under his wing in my first year at Colgate but who unfortunately never did do archaeology for he fell on one of those Pacific Island beaches in World War II. (p. 3)

H. HYLANDER (1900–   ). One of those rare great teachers at Colgate who really made me become interested in nature and ecology. (p. 46)

WILLIAM IRVING (1928–   Ph.D., Wisconsin, 1964). Another arctic explorer cum archaeologist whose career continues to have many successes and whom I have known and enjoyed for a quarter of a century.

DIAMOND JENNESS (1886–1969, M.A., Cambridge, 1912). The greatest Canadian archaeologist and anthropologist who I had the privilege to know. (p. 51)

JESSE JENNINGS (1909–   Ph.D., University of Chicago, 1943). He is another of the Chicago "Kincaid Boys" who got his start on WPA archaeology and who has gone on to fame (desert-like) and fortune (?) in American archaeology. (p. 9)

FREDERICK JOHNSON (1904–   D.Sc., Tufts, 1966). A longtime archaeological colleague in the Yukon, Mexico, and New England, as well as my friend who first initiated me into the mysteries of the interdisciplinary method. (p. 12)

IRMGARD JOHNSON (1918–   Escuela de Anthropologia, Mexico). The expert on Mexican textiles who did a fine job for us in both Tamaulipas and Tehuacan. (p. 24)

DAVID KELLEY (1925–   Ph.D., Harvard, 1957). Another delightful colleague of southwest Tamaulipas who is full of stimulating speculations about archaeological matters. (p. 83)

J. CHARLES KELLEY (1911–   Ph.D., Harvard, 1948). An "old China hand" working in northern Mexico who was a stimulating colleague when I worked in Tamaulipas.

ALFRED VINCENT KIDDER (1885–1963, Ph.D., Harvard, 1914). From many standpoints "Doc" was the father of modern archaeological techniques and methods. His work in northeastern Arizona, the famous Pecos investigations, and his later endeavors in Yucatán for the Carnegie Foundation resulted in publications that are landmarks for twentieth century archaeology. From the beginning he was "my ideal." (p. 3)

MADELINE KNEBERG (1912–   Ph.D., University of Chicago, 1939). The organizer of WPA archaeology for the state of Tennessee. Our one liberated female TVA archaeologist. (p. 9)

ALEX KRIEGER (1911–   Ph.D., Mexico, 1954). In those early hardship days in Tamaulipas he was my friend and my colleague in Texas who taught me much about Texas archaeology, typology, and early man. (p. 37)

TOM LEWIS (1896–   ). Madeline's partner in Tennessee investigations. (p. 9)

WILLARD LIBBY (1907–   Ph.D., Chicago, 1938). Another great scientist—this time in atomic physics and carbon 14—whom I had the privilege to know. (p. 21)

URVE LINNAMAE (1943–   Ph.D., Calgary, 1969). Another of our Ayacucho supervisors who will leave her mark on Canadian archaeology.

JOSÉ LUIS LORENZE (1918–   ). A Spanish-Mexican archaeologist who is interested in early-man studies and who was of assistance early in my career in Mexico. (p. 21)

LUCHO LUMBRERAS (1936–   Ph.D., University of San Marcos, 1960). The best Peruvian archaeologist with whom it was a privilege to work in Ayacucho.

JOHN MACGREGOR (1905–   Ph.D., University of Chicago, 1946). A fine Southwestern archaeologist who introduced me to the mysterious techniques of ceramic analysis. (p. 34)

PAUL C. MANGELSDORF (1899–   D.Sc. Harvard, 1925). My famous botanical partner in the "great corn hunt." It was a privilege as well as an education to work with a truly great scientist. I owe him and his wife, Peggy, much! (p. 21)

PABLO MARTINEZ DEL RIO (1892–1963, National University of Mexico, 1944). Don Pablo was one of the gentlemen of Mexican archaeology who really started the study of early man in Mexico and who gave me encouragement with my preceramic remains when no one else paid any attention to them.

PAUL MAYNARD (1915–   ). One of the fine young archaeologists at the University of Chicago in the thirties who disappeared into the U.S. Navy in World War II.

JAMES V. O. MILLAR (1919–   Ph.D., Calgary, 1970). One of my over-age Calgary students whom I took from a remunerative career in mining and made into a northern Canada archaeologist. Students like him make teaching worthwhile.

ANTOINETTE NELKEN-TERNER (1931–   M.A., Mexico, 1962; Sorbonne, 1958). My laboratory assistant and partner in both the Tehuacan and Ayacucho investigations whose hard work was in part responsible for their successes. (p. 12)

SAM OTTO (1902–   ). A barrenland trapper from Yellowknife, NWT, Canada, who not only baptized me into "bush" exploration but showed me my first northern archaeological sites on a hair-raising ten-day barrenland canoe and airplane trip.

TOM PATTERSON (1932–   Ph.D., University of California, 1964). My stimulating companion when I entered Peruvian archaeology who taught me much about the subject.

FREDRICH PETERSON (1928–   ). One of those G.I.'s who went to Mexico to study, fell in love with the country and archaeology and stayed to become an "old China hand"—the perfect administrator for the Tehuacan expedition. (p. 87)

ROBERT REDFIELD (1897–1958, Ph.D., Chicago, 1928). A brilliant social anthropologist whose inquisition-like classes made me cognizant of anthropological theory and its application to archaeological fact. (p. 76)

WILLIAM A. RITCHIE (1903–   Ph.D., Columbia, 1940). The pioneer in the archaeology of New York State and in the Northeast and as well a delightful colleague during my late-1940 days of working on the Iroquois.

DOUGLAS SCHWARTZ (1929–   Ph.D., Yale University, 1955). Another young archaeologist who I initiated into the mysteries of archaeological field techniques and who has gone places.

C. EARLE SMITH (1920–   Ph.D., Harvard, 1953). Smitty has been the archaeologist's botanist since his student days when he worked in Bat Cave. Since then he has worked with a variety of archaeologists in Tehuacan, Oaxaca, Peru, the Valley of Mexico, to name a few. (p. 27)

WATSON SMITH (1897–   Ph.D., Brown University, 1932). "Wat" who showed me in my first years in Arizona "how beautiful it is" to dig skillfully. (p. 6)

ALBERT SPAULDING (1914–   Ph.D., Columbia, 1946). The real father, or at least, godfather of the New Archaeology who started it all in the 1940s. (p. 52)

WALTER W. TAYLOR (1914–   Ph.D., Harvard, 1943). One of the few archaeologists who really took a hard look at our methods, theories, and techniques and who aggravated some of us, like me, to think more clearly about what we were doing and where we hoped to go. (p. 41)

WILLIAM E. TAYLOR (1928–   Ph.D., Michigan, 1965). Bill was my colleague and administrator in those Ottawa days, who not only went on to become an Eskimo expert, but also is the leader in Canadian archaeology.

HÉLMUT DE TERRA (1900–   ). German nobleman, Burmese explorer, early-man archaeologist in Mexico—a character out of a Kipling novel—with whom I spent an adventurous week in the Canyon Diablo, Tamaulipas, looking at my caves that had early geology and archaeology. (p. 21)

ROBERT VIERRA (1936–   Ph.D., University of New Mexico, 1975). Another of our Ayacucho supervisors whom I introduced to field archaeology while he introduced me to the "wonders" of statistics and computers. (p. 121)

DR. JOHN WHITNAH (1878–1942). One of the grand old men of Colgate University in geology and archaeology who early gave me encouragement. (p. 6)

WAYNE WIERSUM (1944–   ). One of the fine young student archaeological supervisors in Ayacucho who has a bright future.

CHARLES WILDER (1906–   ). One of those great supervisors of WPA (Work Progress Administration—Relief) archaeology associated with the "great leap forward" of American archaeology in connection with salvage in TVA (Tennessee Valley Authority). (p. 9)

GORDON WILLEY (1911–   Ph.D., Columbia, 1942). One of the leaders of American archaeology in the twentieth century whom I have known since WPA days and with whom I have always had stimulating discussions. (p. 18)

ROGER WILLIS (1912–   ). In my mind the finest archaeological technician we had at the University of Chicago. He and his wife, Blackie, nursed me through my days at Kincaid. Roger disappeared from archaeology into a defense plant during World War II. (p. 7)

JOHN WITTHOFT (1920–   M.A., University of Pennsylvania, 1946). "Mr. Pennsylvania Archaeology" who did his first formal digging with me at the Diehl and Overpeck sites along the Delaware River.

DONALD WRAY (1918–1960, Ph.D., University of Chicago, 1946). A professional sociologist and fine amateur archaeologist who worked with me at "his" Weaver site when we first established Illinois Hopewell chronology.

INDEX